Best Wines!
The Gold Medal Winners

by Gail Bradney

A Print Project Book

Copyright © 1997 by Lowell Miller and Gail Bradney
All rights reserved. Second edition, 1998
First edition copyrighted in 1996

ISSN 1088-8608
ISBN 0-9651750-1-4

Published by:
The Print Project
P.O. Box 703
Bearsville, NY 12409

Distributed to the book trade by:
Independent Publishers Group
814 North Franklin Street
Chicago, IL 60610
(312) 337-0747

Printed and bound by:
McNaughton and Gunn, Inc., Saline, MI

Cover design by:
Howard Blume

BEST WINES! can be purchased for educational, business, or sales promotional use. For information please write to The Print Project.

CONTENTS

ACKNOWLEDGMENTS

There are many people I'd like to thank who helped me in numerous ways with the book.

Michael Beames, my research assistant, is responsible for this edition's quantum leap in scope and quality. His competence, intelligence, and uncomplaining nature helped me immeasurably.

I'm grateful to Yvette Peters, my office helper, and to Howard Blume, graphic artist extraordinaire.

Thanks to all of the wineries who responded to countless calls and faxes, in particular the good people at Geyser Peak, Kendall-Jackson, and Beringer, who were exceptionally generous in sharing their time and business know-how.

I'd like to especially acknowledge Ken Onish, world's smartest guy when it comes to South African wines; Jan Stuebing of AUSTRADE, who has an encyclopedic brain; Jane Cunliffe, at the New Zealand Trade Commission, for all her help; and Guillermo Esteves, at the Argentine Embassy, who tried his very hardest to get me in touch with those elusive Argentine wineries.

I'm grateful to all of the competition directors, who in some cases got me results when they were still confidential, particularly to "Pooch" Pucilowski at California State Fair; to Rob Schwartz, of the very fine San Francisco Fair International, for his support and brilliant ideas; and to Rick Cooper and Jon Winsell of Beverage Testing Institute, for their enthusiasm and confidence in the book.

Thanks to Carol and Bob Matthews, who have the best wine shop in Woodstock, for their time, support, and advice.

Susan Sewall deserves a place in heaven for her patience and all she's done to mentor and inspire me, and to promote *Best Wines!*

Harriet Bradney is the best sales rep (and mother) an author could ever hope for.

What I owe to Lowell Miller cannot be put into words. He's a gold medal man.

And to my son, Finn, for being so patient with his mommy.

INTRODUCTION

I'd had it with *chewy mouth feels, long lingering finishes, grassy thistle on the nose,* and *cigarbox aromas.* As a freelance proofreader and copyeditor in my early thirties, I'd picked apart, corrected, reread, and reworded close to ten thousand pages of wine listings and tasting notes for five encyclopedic tomes by Robert Parker, perhaps America's most renowned wine writer, and pioneer of the now-familiar point system for rating wines. Well, at least I was fabulously knowledgeable about wine, right? Not right.

The truth is, except for occasionally jotting down Parker's 90+ and under $15 recommendations, I can't say that as a wine enthusiast I benefitted much from the books. As I once told a friend who thought I had the world's best job, "You'd *have* to pay me to read this stuff."

This is not to slight Robert Parker. He is, by all accounts, one of the most ethical and accomplished wine writers around. But like most wine experts, he's part of the wine snob culture that assumes if you really love wine, you'll want to become an expert yourself. And that means poring through monthly wine magazines, yammering in winespeak with the corner wine merchant, and becoming a devotee of one or more of the acclaimed wine critics who want you to believe they have the inside scoop on what's best out there.

But these experts don't speak to the typical wine drinker. In my case, at least, I didn't *want* to become an authority. I just wanted to find a good bottle of wine at a reasonable price! Yet I couldn't just rely on someone else's opinion, since Parker himself warns that "Best Buys" lists in wine magazines are often inextricably linked to advertising dollars, and wine columnists can be swayed by a winery's savvy PR. Wine retailers have other reasons for promoting certain labels, frequently a function of what's crowding their back rooms.

Feeling left out by the wine snob culture, and slightly anxious about my lack of confidence when shopping, I found one or two labels I liked, and stuck with them. If I found myself in an unfamiliar wine shop, I'd go blank. I'd wander around the store looking for old reliable, and when it wasn't there, I'd choose the same varietal from a different producer from the same region, usually based on price and label design. I'm not embarrassed to admit this, because it's a common practice among the wine drinkers I talk to.

This behavior is symptomatic of what I call "wine anxiety." You, too, are susceptible to this common malady if:

- You buy the same wine over and over again.
- You secretly panic when your companions hand you the restaurant wine list.
- Your eyes glaze over when you enter an unfamiliar wine shop.
- You only know two brands of champagne, and one of them you can't afford.
- You believe the subtleties of a $50 bottle would be wasted on you.
- Between a top-flight Oregonian Pinot Noir and an unknown French burgundy, you'd choose the French bottle.
- You'd be insecure about serving a sweet wine to your dinner guests.

I could go on, but you get the picture. *Wine anxiety is nothing more than a lack of confidence.* Happily, I've found a cure for wine anxiety, and it involves no work. I've found a way to buy a great bottle of wine every time, a way to be both self-assured and adventuresome when I shop. I've become knowledgeable almost in spite of myself! *Best of all, I'll never waste money on a bad bottle again!*

Here's the secret: *I only choose wines that panels of the world's most renowned experts have named "best" in prestigious wine competitions held around the world each year.*

What's remarkable about this method is that it really works. Gold medal winners are always great, and often they're downright ethereal. One reason you're unlikely to be disappointed by gold medal wines is that they're judged "blind," which means the judges don't know the identity of the wines they're evaluating until the medals have been awarded. *It's entirely objective*—no media bias, no insidious claw of advertising money, no recommendations from an individual who may not share your taste.

I look at it this way. If you could only see three or four movies each year, wouldn't you want to see the top award winners from, say, Cannes, the Academy Awards, Sundance, and others of similar repute? I know I would. And the same holds true for wine. In the case of wine competitions, there are about two dozen leading judgings held regionally, nationally, and internationally each year that winemakers vie to compete in. These competitions are prestigious because their judges' standards are highest, and their judging procedures are beyond reproach.

Every wine in this book received one or more gold medals from these top national and international competitions. They're all "New World" wines, which is winebiz lingo for "non-European" wines. My reason for focusing on New World wines is twofold: (1) People who drink *only* French or Italian wines are close-minded wine snobs who aren't hip to the trends (and won't use this book anyway!); and (2) The selection of wines in this book accurately reflects a typical American wine shop or grocery store—that is, mostly American wines, with a respectable representation from the other popular New World winemaking regions including Australia, Chile, and South Africa. You'll also find gold medal wines from Canada, Argentina, New Zealand, and more.

It's to the New World that wine aficionados are turning. Open up any well-regarded, upscale wine publication and you'll see that the majority of top picks or cellar selections are non-European. A recent *New York Times* article reported that European wine production and profits are plummeting, while those in the New World are on the rise.

Here you'll discover those "well-kept-secret" wines—the California Bordeaux-style red that beat one of the oldest and most famous French labels in a blind tasting conducted in France; the Chilean wine made by one of France's top winemakers that sells for under $10; the Australian Shiraz that's won multiple golds for the last eight vintages; the rare Canadian icewines considered peerless in the wine world—and the list goes on and on.

Part I of *Best Wines!* is a collection of short chapters that range in subject from the ins-and-outs of wine competitions, to the latest findings on wine's health benefits, to brief primers on tasting wine, storing wine, and pairing wine with food.

You need to learn very little about wine from books. Most of your learning should happen inside your mouth. And since the world's leading experts have done the work for you by eliminating all but the very best wines, your only homework is to try different types, from different winemaking regions, in the price range you prefer. *You have nothing to lose but your wine anxiety!*

Part II comprises the "Best Lists" so you can see at a glance which gold medal wines stand out among their peers by virtue of winning the most golds or by being the best bargains. *These are the wines you'll want to stock up on.*

Part III lists the gold medal winners in a format that's easy to use while shopping or dining out. The gold medal wines are organized in the same broad categories you'll find in wine shops: Red, White, Blush, Sparkling, and Dessert. Each of these broad categories is broken down into different types or varietals (in Red Wines you'd find, for example, Cabernet Sauvignon, Merlot, Zinfandel, and so on). The full names of the wines are listed alphabetically within each section.

Each wine entry also includes its winemaking region (e.g., California or Australia) and suggested retail price. Wines that are $15 and under have a dollar symbol ($) in front of the name so you can quickly find bargains while shopping, and non-American wines are marked with a small flag icon (🏳). Every wine in this book is available in the United States and/or Canada. Finally, all gold medals and other special awards bestowed on each wine are listed at the end of each entry. (See page xii for a key to the wine competition abbreviations.)

Once you have the hang of it, you'll get hooked on the *Best Wines!* method of wine shopping. Readers report that it's really changed the way they choose and appreciate wine. Rather than feeling like an outsider, they're confident participants in the wine culture now.

Cure your wine anxiety once and for all, and discover the wines the world's experts love best.

Cheers!

Gail Bradney, Woodstock, New York

KEY TO SYMBOLS AND ABBREVIATIONS

℗   A non-American wine. All non-American wines I included in the book can be purchased in the U.S., except for a handful of Canadian wines that aren't exported to the U.S. yet. You'll know which these are because I've indicated the suggested retail price in Canadian dollars: (Can $).

$ A wine that's $15 or less.

THE TOP 24 WINE COMPETITIONS

By researching the field, polling wineries, and interviewing competition directors, I've found the best two dozen wine competitions in the world. To qualify for inclusion in *Best Wines!* a competition must have impeccable standards, extremely knowledgeable and experienced judges, and ethical solicitation procedures and entry requirements. Further, all judging must be done blind, where the judges don't know the wines' identities at the time of judging.

There are many fine wine competitions in the world, a few of which I could not include. Some happened too early or too late in relation to my publication schedule; others are excellent, but too small in scope. For example, smaller counties in California hold well-regarded wine competitions, but only include wineries of their region. Australia has a few worthy candidates other than Sydney International, but again their scope is of more relevance to Australians, who can easily obtain these wines.

Below are the competitions from which I compiled the gold medal winners, along with their corresponding abbreviations.

AT   1996 Atlanta Wine Summit
AW   1996 American Wine Society Commercial Wine Competition
BR   1997 Concours Mondial, Brussels

CA	1997 California State Fair Commercial Wine Competition
DA	1997 Dallas Morning News Wine Competition
FF	1997 Farmer's Fair Riverside County International Wine Competition
IV	1997 Intervin International
IW	1996 International WINE Challenge, London
LA	1997 Los Angeles County Wine Competition
NE	1997 Enological Society of the Pacific Northwest Wine Competition
NW	1997 New World International Wine Competition
OC	1997 Orange County Fair Wine Competition
OR	1997 Oregon State Fair Wine Competition
PR	1997 Pacific Rim International Wine Competition
SD	1997 San Diego National Wine Competition
SF	1997 San Francisco Fair International Wine Competition
SY	1997 Sydney International Wine Competition
TG	1997 Taster's Guild Wine Competition*
VL	1997 Vino Ljubljana, Slovenia
VN	1997 Vinalies Internationales, Paris
WC	1997 West Coast Wine Competition
WS	1996 International Wine and Spirits Competition, London
WWC	The World Wine Championships, Beverage Testing Institute**

* Taster's Guild, an excellent competition, gave out too many gold medals this year, in my opinion. From a consumer's point of view, the stingier the judges, the better. Therefore, I've only included their Double Gold medal winners, which means that *all four judges* gave these their highest marks.

** See Appendix 1.

PART I

Essays to Sip and Swirl

1

WINE TASTING

Do I Detect Cigarbox Aromas?

I've opened up a random page of a well-known wine monthly to get a sampling of how perky and precocious taste buds might experience the latest Oregonean Pinot Noirs. In one, a gamey edge rallies in on the fine finish. In another, a mouthful of plum notes features silkiness lurking beneath slightly tannic scratchiness. Yipes!

Let's be honest. When wine flavors come in "hints," "suggestions," "touches," and "subtle notes," there's a good chance that most of us will miss out. But must we? Can *we* learn to detect black currant flavors wrapped in an ethereal layer of sophisticated new oak? Can *our glass* conjure up cigarbox aromas?

Determined to find out how mere mortals might invite an expansive, sensory experience like the ones the famous wine writers seemed to be having, I researched the subject. It turns out that to properly taste wine, you have to understand two basic concepts. The first is that most of what we perceive as taste is actually more closely related to smell. And the second is that to fully appreciate a glass of wine, you have to consciously use your brain; i.e., think, consider, analyze, and then put it all together into language.

To prove the first point, all you have to do is think of that repulsive medicine your mother used to administer. If you pinched your nose (and made a horrible face) while drinking it down, there was virtually no flavor. It's also why we have little appetite when our nose is congested with a cold. What's the point of eating when you can't taste?

The sorry news is that a hound dog is much better equipped than we are to pick up all the subtleties in a glass of wine, since dogs and other animals have more acute olfactory sensors than humans. Still, our olfactory receptors allow us to experience around ten thousand different aromas, which is nothing to snort at. These receptors are found in the nose but also in the retronasal passage, at the back of the mouth.

Our mouth, on the other hand, can pitifully distinguish but four kinds of taste: sweetness, on the tip of the tongue; saltiness, a little further back on the sides; sourness, on the sides even further back; and bitterness, near the back center of the tongue.

So what does this anatomy lesson have to do with fine wine enjoyment? A lot. To fully experience the magic of what a great glass of wine can offer, you want to liberate as many aroma molecules as you can to maximize your senses of taste and smell. First, swirl the wine in the glass (didn't you always wonder why the heck you were doing this?) directly under your nose so you can sniff in the bouquet.

Next, take a small sip and "whistle in" some air along with it to direct the vapors to that waiting retronasal passage. My late-forty-something companion, a child of the sixties, likes to call this "bonging his wine." (Introducing the concept as such lets you know which of your dinner guests inhaled during their college days.) Don't worry about the noise. The slurpier it sounds, the better you'll taste the wine.

While the wine's in your mouth, you can "chew" it, as some tasters do. Literally move your teeth and tongue around as though the wine were solid. The key here is to make sure that it touches every part of your mouth and tongue before you let it slide down your throat. (If you were at a real wine tasting, you'd spit it out to avoid the goofy effects such multiple samplings would soon have on your judgment.)

Using all of the information you've just collected, you can now embark on the second part of the tasting equation—the thinking part. Unlike canines, whose brains might engage in a thought process something like this—stinking garbage . . . behind Biff's trailer? . . . must dig under fence now!—we humans have the ability to analyze the whole experience and put it into language that transcends and elevates the thing itself.

It's not that hard. Think about the initial associations that came to mind when you first sniffed and swirled. These are the famous bouquets and aromas you'll find in professional tasting notes. Don't limit yourself to grapes. Complex wine may emit aromas as varied as flowers, weeds, fruits, vegetables, candy—even meat and tobacco. Your ability to describe what you perceive will improve with experience.

As for what happened "on the palate," as wine writers like to call the sensations inside the mouth, here's where the more cerebral stuff enters in. Saltiness isn't really a factor with wine. Sourness is experienced as acidity—a measure of how "zingy" the wine is. Sweetness is self-explanatory. And bitterness is something you shouldn't taste at all if you're drinking good wine.

But besides these, there are other qualities to consider. One respected authority calls the mouth more of a "measurer," which is an apt description. You can evaluate what the wine feels like inside the mouth: how "heavy" it feels (weight/body); how astringent or puckery it makes your mouth (from the tannins); how long the flavor and aroma components linger after you've swallowed (length). You might also consider such things as how much punch the alcohol delivers, and in the case of sparkling wines, how the mousse, or bubbles, feel on your tongue.

Most important is the *balance* of all these elements. When you consider all of the above qualities, are any overwhelming? A really fabulous wine will have balance as well as complexity—which means the same thing whether describing wine or one's lover.

You might want to take notes just for the fun of it, especially when trying a new wine with a group of friends. After going through this process once or twice, you'll become more confident. And you'll never drink or think about wine quite the same way again. But don't forget the single most important factor about the wine you're tasting: you should *like* it.

2

WINE STORING

Medieval Catacombs versus My Pantry

If "a man's home is his castle" were literally true, none of us would have a wine-storing problem, as all castles come with underground catacombs that are vibration-free, dark, damp, and kept at a steady 55 degrees F. Ignore the muffled screams coming from the torture cell one level down and you've got yourself one heck of a great place to show off, following a hearty repast with guests.

However, most of us have to make do with the Clorox-scented pantry, the old-shoe-leather closet, or the moldy basement in our home. If you're a rare-wine collector/investor, go get yourself a free-standing, obscenely expensive, custom-made wine cellar that regulates temperature and humidity, or have one built. But if you're like most of us who wish to *drink* and *enjoy* the wine in the foreseeable future, you probably have a perfectly adequate "cellar" in your home already.

Wine is a living substance. Inside a wine bottle the water, acids, alcohol, and tannins interact in an exquisite dance. Hopefully, this performance will cause the maximum flavor, aroma, and body to emerge from the fruit in perfect balance. Your job is to not hinder this process.

Following are four main rules that will protect your wine from unnecessary ruin, whether you're storing it for next week or next year.

1. Keep wines at a constant temperature not exceeding 70 degrees F. More important than the wine's temperature is the *constancy* of that temperature. Temperature changes should occur slowly; wild swings are undesirable. I cringe with embarrassment when I remember the once-iced champagne that sat outside in blistering 85-degree heat for two days after my wedding under the rental canopy. I actually returned cases to the wine shop for a refund! I hope they're not reading this.

Tip: Common and seemingly appropriate wine-storing places in your home may be really bad in terms of temperature variation. A kitchen cabinet or shelf above your refrigerator is a poor choice since the refrigerator generates a lot of heat. Likewise, the furnace room in your basement, as well as the wall shared by the furnace room, isn't ideal. If you live in a northern climate, a closet or pantry that has an outside wall may experience significant variations in temperature.

2. Keep wines in the dark. Light—especially direct sunlight—isn't good for wine. Ignore the appeal of those sunny kitchen counters you see in stylish living magazines, the ones with bowls of fruit, bouquets of flowers, and three or four wines artfully arranged in a wicker rack beneath the skylight. You can be sure that the critters inside those wine bottles are squirming from light exposure, and the owner of those bottles may end up with something undrinkable.

3. Keep wines in a humid place. Don't let those corks dry out. If they do, oxygen will get inside the bottle and turn your wine into vinegar. This is the same rationale behind storing bottles on their sides; contact with the wine keeps the corks moist and expanded. Humidity at about 50 percent is essential, and 70 to 75 percent is ideal.

4. Keep wines in a vibration-free place. Particularly true of Old World–style, more expensive wines, there will be sediments in the wine. If these get all stirred up, it upsets the delicate balancing act occurring inside the bottle.

Tip: Don't put your wine rack above a washing machine or in an insulated garage that doubles as a wood shop (where big power tools will be in frequent use). Wines also hate to travel. If your wine has just been shipped to you or jostled around on a car trip, let it settle down for a day or two before opening.

❧ 3 ❧
WINE COMPETITIONS

What They Are and How They Work

Last edition I got into some hot water back home, or rather my folks did, when I used the example of Morgan County Illinois's annual Pork Queen Contest to illustrate how *not* to run a competition. The hairdresser, with my father tipped back in the sink, her glinting clippers nearby in blue liquid vials, twanged that *she* had been a Pork Queen contestant years back, and that winners were *not chosen* on the basis of the pork-belly poundage their dads had contributed to the local economy. What could he say?

My apologies to every last Pork Queen. (Cut the local gal-gone-good some literary slack, will ya?) However, I stand by my original premise: competitions aren't reliable gauges of merit unless there's some way to ensure that the judging is completely objective. In the case of the wine competitions in this book, all judgings were conducted "blind." (No such luck for the judges presiding over that dusty, manure-smelly event at the local fairgrounds each year.)

What makes wine competitions different from such awards as the Pulitzer, the Oscar, the Grammy, and the Pork Queen is that there's no possibility of bias. No politics, no personal egos, no predisposition based on the influences of slick advertising or industry gratitude. (How often has some aged geezer on his last legs hobbled off with his first Oscar for his final, but mediocre, role?)

HOW THEY WORK

For wine judgings, imagine a row of identical wine glasses, each containing an inch or so of wine, each ID'ed with a small number. Expert tasters, including wine writers, winemakers, Masters of Wine, scholars of oenology, and the like, in panels of usually four or five, sit behind tables and taste each one, deliberately and repeatedly. They make notes, take their time, and then rate each wine with a final score, zero to ten or twenty, typically, depending on the competition.

In all professional wine judgings, competing wines are grouped into types and classes so that each wine can be fairly evaluated alongside its peers. Some, but not all judgings, group wines in price categories as well. Thus, the panels will taste, say, Zinfandels between the prices of $12 and $16. Since a sweet Riesling shouldn't be judged against a dry one, wines are also grouped according to residual sugar levels. In any given class, the judges might taste a dozen wines or more than a hundred, depending on the size and scope of the competition. *The judges won't know who made the wine and where it's from.*

I WAS THERE

Since the premise of this book is that gold medal winning wines are superior to most others, I knew I'd have to check out a wine competition firsthand to make sure my claims were true. While on a media tour for the first edition, I went behind the scenes at the 1996 Atlanta Wine Summit, an international wine competition, to do some old-fashioned investigative journalism. It was a real eye-opener.

I was immediately impressed by the diligence, earnestness, and serious demeanor of the judges. Different panels were sequestered in separate rooms. In back was harried director Bruce Galphin amidst hundreds of bottles labeled and lined up. The staff was bustling about, setting up trays of glasses, washing glasses, labeling glasses, marking off lists. Chief of judges Parks Redwine (no, I didn't make it up), red-faced and serious, was fussing in and out of the back room while I interviewed Bruce.

It's a stressful and difficult thing to pull off. In the case of Atlanta, they received over two thousand entries from eleven countries. The wines have to be sorted through, classes and codes assigned. Judges have to be solicited. The Atlanta Wine Summit is unusual in that it takes place over two weeks to prevent "judge burnout," according to

Galphin. (Most professional judgings are intense two- or three-day events.)

HOW THEY DIFFER

Every wine competition has its differences. Orange County Fair, for example, is the only wine competition I know of to purchase and enter the wines itself. Every California wine available for sale in Orange County is judged. This is a great way to run a competition, in my opinion, since many small wineries don't enter competitions because of the cost. Yes, there is usually an entry fee for the wine producers; wine competitions have to pay their staff. In some cases, they get huge sponsors to fund the event so they can turn a nice profit. The California State Fair claims to be the oldest in America; they've been around since 1854. The International Wine Challenge appears to be the biggest; over 6,500 wines from around the world scrambled to compete in their most recent one. Sydney's Top 100 competition serves food alongside the wines, which is unique. The International Wine & Spirits Competition does a chemical analysis of each wine, the results of which are factored into the judges' scores at the end.

Standing apart from the rest is The World Wine Championships, run by the renowned Beverage Testing Institute. The ratings comprise numerical scores and reviews of hundreds of wines evaluated by BTI's highly trained professional staff over the course of a year. Again, all wines are tasted blind to avoid any possibility of bias. The World Wine Championships merits special mention since they're similar to but not exactly a wine competition. See Appendix 1 for more about this revered mother of all wine judgings.

DO COMPETITIONS HAVE MERIT?

After observing the Atlanta Wine Summit judges, I'd have absolutely no hesitation in buying any one of their gold medal picks. Watching these wine pros at work was astonishing.

The kind of trained palate and levels of concentration required to judge wines professionally is not something I possess—or even care to develop.

The judges in Atlanta would sniff a single wine sample, swirl, and sniff again. They'd take notes. Another swirl, another sniff. Next, they'd eye that wine against the white tablecloth and take more notes. A sip, a slurping sound, then a spit. A thoughtful look. More notes. Another sniff and sip and spit. Even more notes. A piece of bread and they'd be on to the next glass. Wow!

When a gold-medal-caliber wine was tasted, the excitement in the room was palpable. The judges' marks for these wines almost always agreed. *A truly superior wine stands out from the crowd, regardless of one's personal preferences.*

Some wine writers challenge the merits of wine competitions (interestingly, these critics often have a stake in readers' relying on *their* wine picks). If a *panel* of experts who've spent their lives studying, tasting, writing about, and talking about wine can agree, in a blind tasting, that a wine is far and above its peers, how can one argue? One person can be wrong, but can all five experts on a panel be mistaken?

What's even more compelling is that many wines in this book received golds from more than one competition. This means that against different competitors, from different judges, in a different time and place, an entirely new panel of eminently qualified wine experts *also* felt so strongly about the wine that they gave it their top award. Those that won three or more golds (see Chapter 7, Best of BEST WINES!) are unquestionably among the best wines you can find anywhere in the world. Many are not too pricy. *These multiple gold medalists are the bottles I stock in my cellar.*

Not surprisingly, such double and triple gold medal winners are the same ones the wine writers praise, and the gold medal wines under $15 are the same ones that make up the well-known "best buys" lists in wine magazines. (See Chapter 8 for the Best Bargain Wines.) So while they may disparage wine competitions, critics often end up wildly endorsing and endlessly raving about the gold medal winners anyway. Go figure.

I can promise you from my own wine-tasting experience that wine competitions have loads of merit. The gold medal winners really are outstanding. But what's best is that this compilation of top winners means less work for the wine lover. *Let the experts do all the hard work.* You can skip the reading and studying and checking best buys lists and schmoozing with the local wine seller. Pick only top-rated wines. That's all the work that's necessary. Wine competitions exist for a number of good reasons, and helping consumers overcome the intimidation factor when choosing wine is certainly one of them.

ARE ALL COMPETITIONS OF EQUAL MERIT?

No! No! No! And that's why for this book I've screened out only the top two dozen competitions in the world—the ones whose standards are beyond reproach, the ones whose judges are among the most qualified and respected wine authorities on the globe. These are the "Oscars" of the wine world, the competitions from which all winemakers want to win medals. To win a gold medal from one or more of these top twenty-four wine competitions is truly an honor. Some of the competitions I used for this edition are so stingy with their medals that a silver or even bronze medal from them is coveted by the leading wine producers.

For a complete list of the competitions I selected for this book, see page xii.

❦ 4 ❦

WINE AND HEALTH

What You Love Is Great for You

If you haven't heard the good news about the benefits of moderate wine consumption to your health, you probably live in a cave. There are many benefits to having one to three glasses per day, particularly when consumed with your dinner. Isn't it good to know that, for once, what you love is actually good for you?

The following information was researched and compiled from a number of sources, including leading medical journals, major wine references, mainstream newsmagazines, wine trade monthlies, and Internet sites of top university oenology departments and leading wine organizations. The studies from which the data were collected go back as far as 1947 and are as recent as 1997, from respected medical researchers around the world.

WINE AND THE HEART

Read the most recent U.S. Government Dietary Guidelines for Americans and you'll get the mainstream view on wine and health. Surprisingly, it states that *moderate drinking is associated with a lower risk for coronary heart disease*. If Uncle Sam approves, you've got to believe that rigorous testing and analysis is behind that statement.

Thousands of people from all over the world— including Japanese men living in Hawaii; Chicago General Electric workers; the good folks of Framingham, Massachusetts; Aussies in Busselton, Western Australia; elderly villagers in rural Greece; Californians in Alameda County; thousands of doctors and nurses; and of course the famous 13,000 French people of "French Paradox" fame—have been poked, prodded, monitored, and questioned in studies related to alcohol consumption and the heart. The results are consistent and positive:

moderate drinking is good for your heart in a number of ways.

Lowers risk for angina. New data from Harvard's ongoing Health Study reveals that among 22,000 male physicians participating in the study, those who drank two drinks per day had a 56 percent lower risk for angina pectoris (chest pain). Angina, caused by a lack of blood to the heart, is considered a warning sign for heart attack risk.

Prevents arterial clotting. Wine, especially red wine, contains *phenolic compounds,* which are effective antioxidants. These are the compounds that impart bitterness and astringency to wine, and allow for long aging (which makes sense, since the antioxidants counteract the oxygen that ruins wine over time). In our bodies, these phenolic compounds, particularly *resveratrol and the flavonoids* (sounds like a futuristic rock band) inhibit clotting of the arteries and other internal blood clots, such as those that cause strokes. Wine's ability to inhibit the clotting activity of platelets, a condition known as thrombosis, substantially reduces the risk of heart attack.

Improves cholesterol levels. Having wine with your meal can counter the adverse effects of fat in your bloodstream by positively affecting your cholesterol levels. Along with the alcohol, phenolics found in wine alter blood lipid (fat) levels by lowering your LDL levels, the "bad" cholesterol that is implicated in arterial clogging, and by raising your HDL, the so-called good cholesterol. What's more, one study discovered that those who drank wine with their dinner, as opposed to those who drank mineral water, not only experienced improved cholesterol numbers, but the effects were still detectable early the next morning.

Lowers blood pressure. Experts agree that high blood pressure contributes to coronary heart disease and overall mortality. New evidence points to another aspect of wine's cardioprotective benefits: its ability to positively affect systolic and diasystolic blood pressure. The lowest blood pressure levels in subjects of a recent Harvard study were found in those who consumed one to three drinks per day (wine or alcoholic spirits), even factoring in such things as smoking, a family history of hypertension, adjustments for pulse rate, and medication use.

WINE AND STROKES

Just as moderate wine drinking benefits the heart by helping to prevent the formation of arterial plaque, which can clog arteries and blood vessels, it also aids in preventing cerebrovascular disease caused by internal blood clotting. Several renowned researchers have determined, in a number of different studies, that wine drinkers enjoy a dramatically reduced risk of the most common type of stroke.

WINE AND AGING/MORTALITY

Mortality studies have always mystified me. I guess what it comes down to is this: given that 100 percent of the population die 100 percent of the time, what's the percentage who die from X disease and why?

Mortality researchers have launched a number of studies to determine wine's role in mortality. The 12-Year Copenhagen Study, perhaps the most famous of wine-and-health studies, found a 49 percent reduction in mortality among the study's participants who drank three to five glasses of wine per day (not exactly moderate, in my opinion). It was those flavonoids again, with their antioxidant properties, that were found to have a significant preventive effect on diseases of the heart as well as some forms of cancer.

Another recent study monitored 8,000 people for ten years and found that people who drink one or two glasses of wine per day live longer and are less likely to die from all causes than either abstainers or heavy drinkers.

Yet another study focused on factors important in predicting healthy aging, defined as living independently at a high level of physical and mental function, without requiring outside aid. Except for being a nonsmoker, the most important factor predicting healthy aging was being a moderate drinker.

Finally, the lifestyles and diets of elderly inhabitants of three rural Greek villages were studied by a team of Greek researchers to see if they could find the secret to these old folks' "fountain of youth." It turned out that these elderly people ate a healthy Mediterranean diet consisting of legumes, fruits, vegetables, grains, monounsaturated fats (mostly olive oil), small amounts of meat and dairy, and a daily moderate amount of wine with meals. The researchers concluded that wine, an integral part of their diet, was an essential element in helping these elderly villagers avoid disease and illness and live to such ripe old ages.

By the way, wine drinkers have much lower mortality rates than either beer or spirits drinkers.

WINE AND ALZHEIMER'S

A ten-year-old study from France has just concluded that elderly persons who were also moderate drinkers showed a 75 percent decrease in Alzheimer's disease. Additionally, these elderly folks had an 80 percent decrease in the rate of dementia compared with nondrinkers.

WINE AND CANCER

Oversimplified, antioxidants are substances that are thought to prevent cancer. There are compounds in the body known as free radicals, which are highly reactive forms of molecules that can weaken cell walls, thus allowing those cells to oxidize. When cells are oxidized, they die or are subject to mutation, which can result in cancer. Phenolics, found in red wine, block free radicals, thus preventing harmful oxidation. Researchers emphasize the importance of polyphenols as anticancer agents, and wine is rich in both the quality and quantity of polyphenols.

In one University of Davis study, specially bred mice were fed dealcoholized wine solids and were found to be free of tumors 40 percent longer than their siblings with no wine in their diets.

The Harvard University Nurses' Health Study found that while excessive alcohol consumption increases the risk of developing many cancers, light to moderate wine drinking significantly decreased cancer risk in the subjects. Another important study found women who drank moderate amounts of wine daily were at a 7 percent decreased risk of breast cancer.

WINE AND BACTERIAL DISEASES

An exciting recent study done at West Virginia University found that wine can protect you from the kinds of bacterial diseases one can get from tainted shellfish, bad water, and spoiled meat or poultry. The three culprits studied were E. coli, salmonella, and shigella. The researchers found that wine kills these bacteria.

Wine was tested alongside pure alcohol, tequila, and bismuth salicytate (the active ingredient in Pepto Bismol) to see what effect each had on 10 million colony-forming units of shigella, salmonella, and E. coli. Wine was the most effective in destroying these critters, with good old Pepto Bismol coming in a distant second, and alcohol and tequila bringing up the rear. In other words, it's something specific in wine, not just the alcohol, that has this beneficial effect.

WINE'S OTHER BENEFITS

There's a long list of other maladies that may be prevented or beneficially affected by moderate wine drinking, and the list will get longer, since money is being funneled into these studies by governments, drug companies, and large university medical departments. Here's a short list:

Treats iron-deficient anemia. Wine has long been prescribed to treat anemia. It helps vegetarians and others by stimulating the body's ability to absorb minerals and other nutrients.

Lowers the risk for bone/joint diseases. More studies continue to suggest that moderate wine consumption by postmenopausal women may help prevent osteoporosis, since these women have higher levels of estrogen-related hormones. (Estrogen deficiency is a key factor in the development of osteoporosis.) Further, moderate amounts of wine in the diet may also increase bone density.

Reduces the likelihood of diabetes. Two recent reports have confirmed earlier ones that conclude moderate drinkers (in this case, wine *or* spirits) experience a 40 percent decrease in the likelihood that they will develop adult onset diabetes.

Reduces the risk of gallbladder disease. It's been shown that red- and white-wine drinkers benefit from a one-third reduced risk of developing gallstones and the subsequent complications of gallbladder disease.

Reduces the formation of kidney stones. A recent study compared wine with twenty-one other beverages to determine which were most strongly associated with decreased risk for the formation of painful kidney stones. Wine came out ahead, reducing the risk of stone formation by 39 percent. Another study found that alcohol in general was associated with a lower incidence of kidney stones.

🍷 5 🍷

WINE BUYING

Perils and Pleasures of Gold Medal Wine Shopping

Once I realized that buying gold medal wines was a surefire way to avoid a disappointing bottle every time (without having to become an expert), I decided to write this book for others like myself who are tired of being pushed around by the wine bully culture.

But as I became the user of my own book I uncovered some of the pitfalls of gold medal wine shopping. Here are some tried and true shopping tips to help avoid frustration.

RIGHT BRAND AND TYPE, WRONG VINTAGE

Not an uncommon problem. Let's say the wine you want is a 1995. But your wine shop is still carrying 1994. It's because that's the vintage his or her distributor stocks. Until the distributor sells out of 1994s, you may be out of luck, at least at that wine shop. I've found that wine retailers in smaller towns and particularly East Coast towns carry earlier vintages. West Coast and large-city wine retailers sell out the fastest and have the most current vintages.

Before trying one of the other options below, ask the owners if they can order that particular vintage. Depending on how sophisticated their connections are, they may be able to call any one of several distributors to track down that vintage for you. And wine shop owners are happy to do it. It never occurred to me before I began this project that I could get absolutely any wine I wanted most of the time. *All I had to do was ask.*

You can also try another area wine shop. Many times wine stores in a single town will have different distributors, which means they may have in stock different vintages than their competitors.

Another option is to contact the winery directly. Most wineries have toll-free 800 numbers, so calling information is free (800-555-1212). Many wineries also have websites. Either way, getting in touch with the winery directly can be lots of fun. The majority of wineries have free newletters that keep you informed about great deals, fun events, and other wine news. And most of them aren't snobbish in the least. In fact, they'll usually treat you like gold, and they may be able to ship you bottles at a price that might top what you'd find at the wine shop.

Yet another way is to hook up with a mail-order or Internet wine retailer (see Appendix 3 for a selective listing) and they might stock the gold medal wine you seek. Most of them will get it for you even if they don't normally stock it. This has become one of my favorite ways to shop. My wine of choice is delivered right to my door!

Last, but not necessarily as a last resort, you can buy the vintage your winemonger stocks even though it's not listed in this edition. Since 1995, when I started the *Best Wines!* project, I've researched hundreds of gold medal wines. Not surprisingly, it's really the wineries, not the wines, that are winning the golds. Every year there are surprises, but generally speaking the very best wineries produce gold medal winning wines year after year. If the 1995 Chardonnay won two gold medals, you can be confident that the 1996 will be delicious. And it may end up winning one or more golds as well. See Appendix 4 for a complete listing of the Gold Medal Wineries.

A winemaker who knows how to produce a stunning Chardonnay one year will most assuredly be able to do it again the next year too. If that weren't true, wineries would go out of business.

"TINYTOWN WINES" DOESN'T CARRY IT

My folks live in a fairly small town in central Illinois. Jug wines often occupy more shelf space than fine wines in rural areas and smaller towns. The solution to this problem is basically the same as above. First talk to the wine merchant. Next, try outside sources.

THE PRICE LISTED IN BOOK ISN'T RIGHT

Shame on you. Would an Episcopalian-raised former Midwesterner lie to her readers? Well, sure. All writers are liars. But I wouldn't lie about the wine prices. The prices listed in this book reflect *suggested retail prices* and were provided by the wineries themselves, or in some cases by the competitions, who themselves obtained the price from the winery. But buyers beware. Even in little Woodstock, New York, the same wine can vary as much as three dollars from wine shop to wine shop.

Furthermore, there's a built-in dilemma I face as author. Namely, once a wine wins a gold medal, and especially if it wins two or three, the media buzz goes way up, and so, often, does the price. In other words, I'm part of the problem. Giving these wines publicity, albeit well-deserved, gives them more value. And the consumer suffers.

One solution is to do some competitive shopping if you can. Try different shops; try some alternatives to wine shops mentioned above. Another solution is to buy up a gold medal winner when you see it, especially if the price is what you're expecting. The combination of increasing media exposure and decreasing availability won't move the price in your favor.

NOW, ON TO THE PLEASURES

The real fun of writing this book for me has been the freedom I now feel to experiment with new wines. If the merchant doesn't carry the brand you want, look in the book for alternatives. In other words, don't get hung up on the same label, region, or type of wine to which you're accustomed.

Since every wine in this book won the highest award against dozens, sometimes hundreds, of competitors, you can be confident that you won't be disappointed. Want an inexpensive Cabernet? Try one from Chile or Washington instead of California. Want a zingy Chardonnay? Look to Canada or Australia. Love red wine? Try a Bordeaux-style blend or an Italian-American varietal. Try serving a sparkling wine before dinner to your guests. Have a chilled ice wine rather than parfaits for dessert.

I recently went to a celebration for a friend's MBA party. My companion and I were asked to bring red wine for twenty people. Book in hand, we strolled down the aisles of a large wine retailer and picked out six gold medal winners, ranging from a bargain $6 Chilean Merlot to a moderate $10 California Petite Sirah to an extravagant $24 Oregonean Pinot Noir. We also chose a Zinfandel, a Cabernet, and an Australian Shiraz, each around $15. Wonderfully, although we hadn't tried any of these wines, we knew they'd be a smash—and they were.

If I want to buy an inexpensive wine, I scan down the lists for the "under $15" symbol ($). See also Chapter 8, Best Bargain Wines. When I want a wine that will dazzle even the most biased wine drinker, I buy a BBW (see Chapter 7), a wine that's won three or more gold medals.

Another pleasure associated with using this book is the gratifying feeling of being a smart shopper. For instance, there are a lots of wineries in the book that picked up numerous golds. Because they're listed alphabetically by type, you can compare a "regular" Pinot Noir, say, with a Reserve Pinot Noir. Often, the less expensive one may have more golds and more special awards. By all means, buy the cheaper one!

I got out of my wine-buying rut by exploring gold medal wines instead. You can too!

🍷 6 🍷

WINE AND FOOD

A Marriage Made in Heaven

I love red wine. I so prefer it to white that I usually drink it with anything I'm serving for dinner. However, I'm always inspired when a thoughtful hostess has put together an interesting wine-and-food combo that releases me from my red-wine routine. On more than one occasion I've found myself pleasantly surprised. Recently I had an elegant, spicy Thai meal where the host poured me a glass of Gewurztraminer, a varietal I never buy for myself. I was mesmerized by its beautiful duet with the exotic food flavors.

The old (incorrect, unimaginative) rules of white wine with seafood and poultry, red wine with red meats, no longer apply. Naturally, there are some classic couples that aren't likely to break up, such as a blockbuster Cabernet Sauvignon with a killer steak, but in general there are no limits to wine-and-food combining beyond that of your imagination.

There are, however, some helpful general guidelines that great chefs and humble cooks alike follow when they want to get the most out of both their wine and their food.

MATCHING WEIGHT AND FLAVOR INTENSITY

Pay attention that your wine and your food are of equal weight. This way, the food doesn't overpower the wine, and vice versa. Following this one rule makes it possible to find the right wine match for any food, no matter your expertise.

I was recently in a dilemma, although it was of the culinary, not life-or-death, variety. My five-year-old son and I were celebrating the end of the week together at a local, very nice restaurant in Woodstock. The waitress read off the specials, which included ostrich. "Ostrich, Mommy. I want ostrich," came the predictable words out of my son. Okay,

I'd try it for him. But for me, I wanted the right wine to wash it down (all twenty-two dollars of it, without the feather boa). I ordered a medium-bodied Pinot Noir.

That story had a happy ending—at least until the bill came. The ostrich was superb, my son ate all of his vegetables, we both had a tale of dubious adventure to relate to our friends, and the wine I chose was perfect, since ostrich tastes a lot like filet mignon, but even lighter and less gamy. My Pinot Noir was medium bodied, smooth, and sexy. Its intense fruit and moderate tannins went well with the delicate but flavorful red-tasting meat.

Hearty, robust dishes match up well with equally full-bodied wines, which is why young, tannic reds go well with grilled game and red meat, or why fruity, round, soft, uncomplicated wines should be consumed with equally simple foods, such as nonspicy vegetarian dishes or picnic fare.

But don't make blanket generalizations about foods. For example, *stir-fry* chicken doesn't have the heft of *roast* chicken served in a dark wild mushroom sauce. Always consider the way the food is prepared when determining how to find its perfect wine mate.

Similarly, every food and wine has an intensity or density of flavor, and this is important to keep in mind. A food that's sweet, for example, needs a wine that's at least as sweet. A lemony seafood dish would call for a zesty, lively wine with a lot of acidity, but medium-bodied with not so much oakiness, such as Sauvignon Blanc. Salty foods go nicely with sparkling wines and, traditionally, aperitifs such as sherry. Very spicy foods may be light, yet intensely flavored. Therefore, choose a wine that is also light-bodied but intense, such as a semisweet Riesling.

FOODS THAT MAKE WINE TASTE WEIRD

It's long been known that artichokes and asparagus are wine-unfriendly. In the case of the former, artichokes contain a substance called cynarin that makes water taste sweet and wine, metallic. Some people report that asparagus does the same.

Chocolate is the subject of great debate. Slick ads for "An Evening of Wine and Chocolate" occasionally land in my post office box, and are worded as if the event organizers are meeting in a speakeasy and plotting the overthrow of the government. I mean, is it seditious to consider such a pairing? Apparently so. For one, it's hard to find a wine that's sweeter than chocolate. Also, chocolate coats the mouth, which is deadly for wine tasting.

Cheeses are also a problem for wine lovers, specifically because they're often salty, strong-flavored, high in fat, and because they coat the mouth. Many experts agree that sweet wines are generally the best wines to drink with cheeses, and white wines fare better than do reds. But of course the variety of cheeses makes it impossible to make sweeping recommendations. So either steer clear or be willing to experiment.

Having said all this, when it comes to supposedly poor food-and-wine pairings, you can pretty much ignore the above, unless you're having a wine expert for dinner. You'll no doubt notice that many of the tasting notes in Part II that came from the winemakers themselves often recommend both chocolate and cheese to complement their wine. It's a matter of personal taste. Be adventuresome.

PART II

Best Lists

7

BEST OF **BEST WINES!**

Triple-Plus Gold Medal Winners

I have a confession to make: I've become obsessed with gold medal wines. When my companion chooses a bottle at the wine shop, I check the book to see if it's a gold medal winner. If not, I shrug my shoulders and tell him he'll have to take the blame if it's no good. Truth is, he's become a convert too. (Does he really have a choice, girls?)

A wine that's won one gold medal will rarely disappoint. But when I want *a stupendous wine,* a wine I know will be fantastic even if it's a varietal I don't normally drink, I seek out a BBW—Best of BEST WINES!

You can't possibly go wrong with a BBW, a wine that's walked away with at least three gold medals from three different top competitions. If you think about it, it means that no less than fifteen renowned wine authorities gave it their highest mark. Each wine here was chosen best out of a combined field of anywhere from, say, 60 to 300 competing wines of the same type.

And you'll be pleasantly surprised to see how many of these sure bets are $15 and under, as indicated by a dollar symbol ($).

It's easy to get caught up in gold medal counting. Last year I discovered Jordan J, for example, a California sparkling wine with *seven* gold medals. To say that each perfect tiny bubble exploded ecstatically on my tongue and tingled every sense from my nose to my toes would be an understatement. It was simply divine. (Not too surprisingly, Jordan J is a BBW *again* this year.)

These BBW's are the crème de la crème, the killer wines, the ivy leaguers, *the bottles to stock.*

The basic wine descriptions, or tasting notes as they're called, come either from the winemakers or the competition judges, and then are edited by me. If the tasting notes seem daunting, refer to Appendix 2, a glossary to untangle winespeak.

$Adler Fels 1996 Gewurztraminer

Region: California, Sonoma County

Golds/Awards: Gold (SD, NW, WWC-90 pts, CA); Best New World Gewurztraminer (NW); Best of Class (CA)

If you're a Gewurz fan, run out for this one. Not only is it a bargain, but it would be difficult to find a wine with more experts agreeing on its virtues. The wine has a full golden sheen, is moderately full bodied and extracted, with balanced acidity. Its flavors are reminiscent of tropical fruits, subtle spices, and minerals, with mineral aromas that reveal a rich palate with a sweet entry through a juicy finish. This is distinguished by a sumptuous, glycerous mouth feel. **$11**

Alderbrook 1995 Kunde Vineyard Merlot

Region: California, Sonoma Valley

Golds/Awards: Gold (PR, LA, NW, SF, Taster's Guild, Citrus Fair, Tenn. Intern'l); Best of Class (PR, NW)

The nose is expansive and exhibits essence of cherries, cedar, rose petal, and vanillin. The rich, full mouth feel exudes flavors of chocolate, black cherry, tea leaves, spicy/smoky oak, and cola. Dark and dense in color, this wine has great structure, complexity, and a long finish. **$22**

Alderbrook 1995 Late Harvest Kunde Vineyard Muscat de Frontignan

Region: California, Sonoma Valley

Golds/Awards: Gold (AT, FF, NW, six other '96 golds); Double Gold (TG, SF); Best of Class (FF)

This wine's been collecting golds since 1996. If you're not a dessert-wine lover, do yourself a favor and try this one. You'll find aromas of honey, pear, orange blossom, sweet toffee, vanilla, and ripe pineapple, as well as rich, sensual textures. The wonderful acid/sugar balance releases a burst of flavors that coat your palate with a finish that's crisp and refreshing. **$20**

$Alderbrook 1996 Saralee's Vineyard Gewurztraminer

Region: California, Russian River Valley

Golds/Awards: Gold (SD, OC, NW, SF, Citrus Fair)

The winemaker says this is his winery's finest Gewurz ever. This "rich and vibrant wine" conjures up scents of spicy carnations, sweet vanilla, apricots, and honeysuckle. Flavors of grapefruit and pears complement the perfect sugar and acid balance, which creates the impression of appealing dryness. Check out that price! **$10**

$Anapamu 1995 Barrel Fermented Chardonnay
Region: California, Central Coast
Golds/Awards: Gold (DA, AT, OC)

Look for a spicy tropical nose followed by a rich and generous mouth feel. This wine's palate is complex and layered. (Unbeatable price too.) **$12**

$Armida 1995 Chardonnay
Region: California, Russian River Valley
Golds/Awards: Gold (WC, NW, CA); Best of Class (NW)

The 1995 growing season was rather long and cool, providing ample time for the Chardonnay fruit to reach full maturity. This BBW exhibits aromas of pear and green apple with scents of toasty oak. The finish is clean and crisp with a hint of vanilla. **$15**

$Barefoot Cellars NV White Zinfandel
Region: California
Golds/Awards: Gold (SD, FF, CA, Taster's Guild); Chairman's Award (FF)

Look for the tropical flavor of pineapples, ripe peaches, and juicy strawberries. The zesty finish is clean and apple-crisp. According to the winemaker, this wine goes well with sweet or spicy foods, veggies, pasta, ham, poultry, lamb, or seafood. Or try it as an aperitif. (And it's a real deal to boot.) **$4.99**

$Baron Herzog 1995 Late Harvest Johannisberg Riesling
Region: California, Monterey County
Golds/Awards: Gold (SY, FF, CA); Best of California, Best of Class, Best of Region (CA)

This wine exhibits intense notes of pineapple, dried apricot, and ripe apple. It's a wine that should accompany your favorite dessert and, for fun, can be enjoyed with sliced apples and cheese, fresh strawberries, or with strudel. It's also a wine that you can cellar for many years. **$14**

Bartholomew Park Winery 1994 Desnudos Vineyard Cabernet Sauvignon

Region: California, Sonoma Valley
Golds/Awards: Gold (SD, FF, PR, OC)

Not three but *four* gold medals! The wine-maker, waxing poetic, says as the liquid garnet pours into your glass, the dark fruit esters foretell of rich raspberry, spicy flavors. Ring in the next millennium over a bottle of this Cabernet—or just pop the cork tomorrow. (Translation: this wine will improve with age, but is drinkable now.) The rich oak and spiciness make this a terrific match for steak au poivre or a cassoulet. And try it with black forest cake, truffles, or an English stilton. By the way, only 592 cases of this beauty were produced, so if you see a bottle in your wine shop or restaurant, better snatch it up. **$20**

Beaulieu 1993 Georges de Latour Private Reserve Cabernet Sauvignon

Region: California, Napa Valley
Golds/Awards: Gold (DA, AT, NW)

This Cab showcases its dark ruby color as a preview of its depth and concentration. Rich oak aromas are wrapped around smells of ripe cherry, black currant, and blackberry. Intense full flavors of cherry, cassis, and berry are balanced with crisp acids and firm yet subtle tannins. The complexity of this wine is evident in the lingering finish that echoes the layers of flavors on the palate. A great vintage, this wine will age beautifully and improve well into the next century. **$40**

Benziger 1993 Tribute Red Estate

Region: California, Dry Creek Valley
Golds/Awards: Gold (LA, FF, NW); Chairman's Award (FF)

Benziger actually produces over twenty different wines in making this blend, extracting the finest flavors from the grapes grown in each block before deciding on the final combination. In this case, it's 55% Cabernet Sauvignon, 27% Cabernet Franc, 9% Merlot, and 9% Petit Verdot—a classic red Bordeaux-style blend. Look for intense smoke and black fruit aromas and lively fruit character with plenty of concentration and backbone. Will age wonderfully for 5 to 8 years. Try it with lamb or beef stew. **$23**

$Benziger 1994 Cabernet Sauvignon

Region: California, Sonoma County
Golds/Awards: Gold (FF, NW, WWC-91 pts); Chairman's Award (FF); Best of Class (NW)

Look for a rich purple color, medium body, full acidity, and lots of fruit extract. The wine is oaky and dry, with flavors of chocolate, cherry cordial, and blackberries. It's delightfully ripe and fruity, with a juicy mouth feel and a classy, persistent finsih. The fruit is tangy and appealing. Sure to improve in the near term, this wine drinks well now. (And it's a bargain besides.) **$15**

Benziger 1994 Imagery Series Larga Vista Vineyards Sangiovese

Region: California, Dry Creek Valley
Golds/Awards: Gold (PR, LA, NW, WWC-92 pts); Best of Class (PR)

Say it slowly—*Sahn-Gee-oh-VAY-Say*—and feel how it rolls luxuriously off your tongue. Italian-American red wines like this one are made for romantic nights. The judges describe it as mildly tannic, reminiscent of chocolate, brown spice, red berries, and dill. Attractive chocolate aromas show oak influences. It has a sweet berry fruit entry with some toasty aromas and is quite fleshy and generous in a reasonably open-knit style. Very accessible now. **$17.99**

Beringer 1994 Knights Valley Cabernet Sauvignon

Region: California, Knights Valley
Golds/Awards: Gold (WC, SF); Four-Star Gold (OC)

The flavors of this wine are predominantly wild berries—particularly boysenberry and blackberry—with a slight herbal aroma. It has toasty vanilla tones that match well with the intense berriness in the fruit. Nice dry tannins in the finish top it off. Although the wine is approachable now, with time the tannins will soften and the wine will be even better. **$17.50**

$Bonterra 1994 Organically Grown Grapes Cabernet Sauvignon

Region: California, North Coast
Golds/Awards: Gold (SD, LA, CA); Best of Class (LA, CA)

I buy organic meats and vegetables, so why not wine too? The difference here is that this product is *less* expensive than many of its nonorganic counterparts. In this wine, pure varietal aromas and flavors of ripe cherry and blackberry are complemented by an intriguing pepper spice, captivating smoky complexities, and by a fine toasty vanilla spiciness from oak aging. **$12**

Chateau St. Jean 1991 Reserve Cabernet Sauvignon

Region: California, Sonoma County
Golds/Awards: Gold (AT, SD, WC, WWC-93 pts, NW); Double Gold (TG); Cellar Selection (WWC)

Like most great Cabernet Sauvignons, this one is blended with other varieties for perfect balance, in this case Merlot, Cabernet Franc, Malbec, and Petit Verdot. It has a complex nose redolent of black cherries, mint, and cedar, highlighted by French oak. Concentrated plum and currant, cassis and chocolate flavors are followed by a long, rich, smooth finish. A wine with this many golds around its neck has to be unbelievable. **$38**

Chateau Ste. Michelle 1994 Cold Creek Vineyard Merlot

Region: Washington, Columbia Valley
Golds/Awards: Gold (FF, NW, WWC-92 pts); Chairman's Award (FF); Cellar Selection (WWC)

Wonderful, incredible, stupendous Merlots are coming out of Washington State. This beauty is intense, dark red with purple highlights, full bodied, highly extracted, heavily oaked, and moderately tannic. Flavors conjure up cedar, pine, black fruits, and tea. The aromas are of deep dark fruit with oak accents. It has a solid and dense palate with fruity depth and a firm but lengthy finish. Although highly structured, it may need some cellaring for maximum enjoyment. **$28**

Chateau Ste. Michelle 1994 Indian Wells Vineyard Merlot

Region: Washington, Columbia Valley
Golds/Awards: Gold (FF, NW, WWC-90 pts); Best of Class (NW); Cellar Selection (WWC)

It may be impossible to go wrong with a Merlot from this winery. The color of this one is deep crimson; it has medium to full body, lots of extract, and moderate oak. With flavors and aromas of black fruits, tea, and chocolate, it has a silky entry with deep fruity flavors that give way to textured tannins through a lengthy, toasty, but firm finish. Elegant and generously proportioned with enough structure to cellar well. **$30**

Chateau Ste. Michelle 1995 Cold Creek Vineyard Chardonnay

Region: Washington, Columbia Valley
Golds/Awards: Gold (PR, NW); Double Gold (SF); Best of Class (NW); Best Chardonnay (SF)

This winery has consistently produced award-winning Chardonnays for more than a decade. Aromas of toast and ripe pear are followed by classic flavors of pear, apple, and creamy spice. Ten months of oak aging gave this wine a rich mouth feel and a long, lingering finish. **$26**

Chateau Souverain 1993 Winemaker's Reserve Cabernet Sauvignon

Region: California, Alexander Valley
Golds/Awards: Gold (PR, FF, SF)

Look for a black ruby color, full body, and highly extracted fruit. This dry beauty is reminiscent of dried plums, herbs, and earth. It has a rich, deep style with some bold fruit character on the palate balanced with good tannins. Drinkable now, this wine will be even better in a year or two. **$30**

Clos du Bois 1993 Briarcrest Cabernet Sauvignon

Region: California, Alexander Valley
Golds/Awards: Gold (PR, IV, CA)

Blackberry and cassis flavors from the grape harmonize with oak smokiness, cedar, tobacco, and chocolate. Unfined and unfiltered, this Cabernet is an excellent example of balance and elegance. Enjoy it with grilled meats, pasta with tomato-based sauces, or firm, dry cheeses. **$22**

Clos du Bois 1995 Calcaire Chardonnay

Region: California

Golds/Awards: Gold (IV, LA, FF)

This wine is medium bodied with lush, tropical fruit flavors and balanced, creamy oak notes. If you keep it in your cellar for the next several years it will develop further. **$18**

$Concannon 1994 Petite Sirah

Region: California, Central Coast

Golds/Awards: Gold (AW, IW, SY)

This red competed against world-famous wines in two prestigious international competitions, in Sydney and in London, and walked away with a gold at each! Fresh raspberry flavors and spicy black pepper complement the richness of plums found in the fruit. A year's aging in predominantly French oak barrels further softens this delicious, medium-bodied red wine. This accessible style pairs well with a wide range of foods, from wild game to chocolate. By the way, with several Petite Sirahs in this book, it's clear that Concannon's winemaker has mastered this varietal. Almost any one by this producer is likely to be great. **$9.95**

$Cypress 1994 Cabernet Sauvignon

Region: California

Golds/Awards: Gold (PR, OC, NW); Best of Class (NW)

The wine has a medium garnet color and aromas of black cherry, black olive, and chocolate with a bouquet of cedary oak. On the pallet the lively, intense berry fruit melds with the toasty oak flavor creating a "user-friendly" Cab of exceptional quality and value. **$8.75**

David Bruce 1994 Chalone Pinot Noir

Region: California

Golds/Awards: Gold (DA, NW, WWC-92 pts); Double Gold (TG)

You can't go wrong with a David Bruce Pinot Noir. This one is deep reddish-purple, medium bodied, highly extracted, and has moderate oak and mild tannins. The flavors and aromas are reminiscent of ripe raspberries and exotic spices. The wine has a deep, rich nose and a full, layered, fruity palate intermingled with generous oaky flavors. A well-concentrated mouth feel and some tannic structure indicate that this should cellar well in the short term. **$30**

David Bruce 1994 Pinot Noir
Region: California, Russian River Valley
Golds/Awards: Gold (LA, NW, WWC-92 pts); Best of Class (LA); Cellar Selection (WWC)

Wow! It's not easy to rate a 92 from The World Wine Championships. Look for a wine that's dark red with medium body and fruit extract, that's moderately oaky and mildly tannic. Aromas of blackberries, brown spice, vanilla, and smoke will greet your nose, accompanied by youthful, concentrated flavors. Quite drinkable now, this one will also improve with short-term cellaring. **$25**

$David Bruce 1995 Petite Syrah
Region: California, San Luis Obispo
Golds/Awards: Gold (LA, OC, WWC-90 pts); Cellar Selection (WWC)

Whether at a book signing or a business meeting, I often bring this wine to impress upon people that fabulous gold medal wines don't have to be expensive. I haven't met a single soul who didn't fall in love with this one. It's dark ruby/blue-purple, medium bodied, with balanced acidity, nice extract, and lots of tannins. The flavors and bouquet bring up blueberries, violets, flowers, and marmalade. It has a compact texture and a youthful feel, with a grapy, layering sensation A nice touch of floral fragrance and a curious, citruslike sweet/tart note pervades on the finish. **$14**

David Bruce 1995 Shell Creek Vineyard Reserve Petite Syrah
Region: California, Paso Robles
Golds/Awards: Gold (DA, OC, WWC-95 pts); Cellar Selection and Best Buy (WWC)

Only one point shy of getting a coveted Platinum from The World Wine Championships, this is definitely a wine to put in your cellar. The moderate price-to-quality ratio can't be beat anywhere. Of inky purple color, it's full bodied with balanced acidity and loads of extract and tannins. Look for black plum, sandalwood, toffee, and violets in the flavors and aromas. The texture is lush and jammy, with a huge extract of chewy fruit. It's richer as the intensity builds with sweet fragrance and plush creamy spice. This beauty is just starting to show its lovely character. **$18**

De Loach 1994 O.F.S. Estate Bottled Cabernet Sauvignon

Region: California, Russian River Valley
Golds/Awards: Gold (PR, LA, FF); Double Gold (CA); Chairman's Award (FF); Best of Class (CA)

The 1994 "Our Finest Selection" (O.F.S.) Cab is a well-balanced wine with smooth texture, medium body, and a deep, rich garnet color. It has an intensely varietal nose with pleasant cedar tones. Flavors of black cherry and rich cassis mingle as this complex wine shows beautiful light notes of dill and green olive complemented by cedar and toasty oak components. **$16**

De Loach 1995 O.F.S. Estate Bottled Chardonnay

Region: California, Russian River Valley
Golds/Awards: Gold (PR, OC, WWC-91 pts); Double Gold (CA); Best of Class (CA)

Medium straw with a pale gold cast, this dry wine is medium bodied, has balanced acidity, moderate extract, and mild oakiness. With a flavor and aroma profile reminiscent of ripe citrus, toasted oak, and minerals, it possesses a ripe fruity style and a textured lengthy mouth feel that lingers through the flavorsome finish. Well-concentrated flavors and fine length are classy pointers. **$27.50**

De Loach 1995 O.F.S. Estate Bottled Zinfandel

Region: California, Russian River Valley
Golds/Awards: Gold (DA, PR, WWC-92 pts); Best of Class (PR)

Expect a deep inky, reddish purple color; medium to full body, lots of extract, and moderate tannins. It has black cherries, raspberries, cocoa, black tea, and floral, berrylike aromas; a rich, textured palate with good concentration of flavors; and some firm tannins on the spicy finish. Sound structure means this wine could improve with some cellaring. **$25**

Dr. Konstantin Frank 1995 Riesling Icewine
Region: New York
Golds/Awards: Double Gold (TG); Gold (NW, WWC-90 pts); Best New World Riesling (NW)

If you've never tried icewine, now's your chance. It lasts for a long time, and a tiny glassful is all you and your guests will need of this sumptuous dessert wine. Full golden yellow, this wine is moderately full bodied, with balanced acidity and truckloads of extract. In the nose one finds hints of pineapple, sweet peach, and dried herbs. Lively juicy fruit flavors are cleanly expressed with a subtle herbaceous hint through the finish. Complex flavors emerge through the sweetness. **$29.95**

Dry Creek Vineyard 1994 Reserve Cabernet Sauvignon
Region: California, Dry Creek Valley
Golds/Awards: Gold (AT, SD, WWC-91 pts); Cellar Selection (WWC)

Deep ruby with a purple cast, this one's medium bodied, moderately extracted, and dry. Scents of berries, plums, and flowers greet the nose. Extremely decadent and fresh tasting, it has a nicely integrated touch of wood and a rather astringent finish. Well structured and quite backward now relative to its potential, it may need some time in your cellar. **$25**

Dry Creek Vineyard 1995 Reserve Fumé Blanc
Region: California, Dry Creek Valley
Golds/Awards: Gold (PR, LA, AT)

Fumé Blanc is a highfalutin name for the white wine better known as Sauvignon Blanc. In this wine, exotic citrus notes interplay with grassy, herbal aromas. Lime and pear flavors are punctuated by crisp lemon. A touch of hazelnut cascades through creamy, buttery layers of toasty oak. Firm acidity and the long, rich finish create a wine of exceptional balance and grace. This one will age gracefully for the next four to eight years. **$15.75**

$Eberle 1995 Côtes-du-Robles
Region: California, Paso Robles
Golds/Awards: Gold (PR, SD, FF); Best of Class (PR)

If you love French Rhône wines, you'll love wines like this being produced by America's

"Rhône Rangers." This one's a blend of Syrah, which contributes blueberry and darker fruits, as well as weight; Mourvèdre, for structure, tannins, and color; Counoise, which adds strawberry, melon, and spice; Grenache, with its raspberry fruit; and Viognier, for perfume and roundness. Expect rich, intense fruit not hidden in a sea of oak. This wine is complex but quite drinkable now. The winemaker calls this a "bistro-style" wine. You can even chill it if you like. **$13**

Edmeades 1995 Zinfandel
Region: California, Mendocino County
Golds/Awards: Gold (PR, IV, LA)

The winemaker says, "I strongly believe in showing what a vineyard site distinctly offers. We are very meticulous in our selection of grape sources and very hands off in our winemaking process." Since Zinfandel is also his "favorite wine," you can be sure that this one won't disappoint. It's smooth, ripe, and spicy with a pretty core of plum, cherry, and wild berry flavors, and becomes supple and elegant on the finish. **$19**

$Fetzer 1996 Gamay Beaujolais
Region: California
Golds/Awards: Gold (LA, OC, CA); Best of Class (CA)

Fresh aromas of strawberry jam are followed by lightly sweet cherry and berry fruit flavors. This tangy red is a cool companion for any occasion, especialy picnic or light barbecue fare such as glazed ham, grilled chicken wings, and sausages. It's ready to drink now and should be enjoyed slightly chilled. **$6.99**

$Fetzer 1996 Gewurztraminer
Region: California
Golds/Awards: Gold (SD, LA); Double Gold (CA);
Best of Class (SD, CA)

Soft aromas of honeysuckle and citrus are accented with floral notes of gardenia and jasmine. The mouth feel is delicate and elegant, layered with pineapple and ginger-spice flavors and a long, clean finish. **$6**

Ficklin Vineyards NV Aged 10 Years Estate Bottled Tawny Port
Region: California, Madera
Golds/Awards: Gold (DA, WWC-90 pts); Double Gold (CA); Best of Class (CA)

It's pale brick with a mahogany rim, medium bodied, has balanced acidity, good extract, and medium sweetness. The flavors and aromas are reminiscent of nuts, raisins, and dried apricots. Warming and elegant, with rich nutty character throughout and a smoothly textured, decadently sweet finish, this is a classic tawny port from traditional Portuguese grape varieties. **$22**

Firestone 1993 Red Reserve
Region: California, Santa Ynez
Golds/Awards: Gold (AT, OC, NW); Best U.S. Red (AT); Best of Show (AT)

A blend of 35% Cabernet Sauvignon, 31% Cabernet Franc, 27% Merlot, and 7% Malbec. It's an excellent ambassador for the Santa Ynez Valley appellations with its soil-inflected flavors of mineral, chocolate, ginger, currants, and spice. Full-bodied with excellent structure, this Bordeaux-style blend will repay careful cellaring and can improve for 10 to 15 years. Serve it with leg of lamb, grilled meats, and osso bucco. **$30**

$Galleano 1996 Carignane
Region: California, Cucamonga Valley
Golds/Awards: Gold (PR, FF, NW); Best of Class (NW)

Carignane is known as Carignano in Italy and Cariñena in Spain. It is France's most planted variety, five times more common than Chardonnay, for example. This delicious, full-bodied red has great complexity of fruit. **$8**

Gallo Sonoma 1992 Estate Cabernet Sauvignon
Region: California, Northern Sonoma
Golds/Awards: Gold (AT, SD, WWC-91 pts); Double Gold (TG)

This special-occasion wine is deep ruby with a purple cast, is moderately full bodied, has loads of extract, and is quite tannic. The aromas conjure up black fruits and leather. The wine is deep, weighty, and firm with a succulent entry and lush palate presence. It has a long solid finish with well-integrated oak accents. **$45**

Gallo Sonoma 1993 Frei Ranch Vineyard Cabernet Sauvignon

Region: California, Dry Creek Valley
Golds/Awards: Gold (DA, LA, FF, NW, CA)

I've said it before and I'll say it again: take another really good look at Gallo's wines if you haven't done so lately, especially the Gallo Sonoma offerings. They're amazing! The unique combination of climate and soil at Frei Ranch yields red wine grapes with firm tannins, dense colors, and aromas and flavors of concentrated cherry, berry, plum, and spice. This one is also a very good value for a five-gold Cabernet. **$18**

Gallo Sonoma 1994 Estate Chardonnay

Region: California, Northern Sonoma
Golds/Awards: Gold (AT, AW, WWC-91 pts)

Another super winner from Gallo. A light-golden-colored Chard, this one's dry and moderately full bodied, has good acid balance, and medium extract and oak. Look for brown spice, cream, tropical fruit, and oaky aromas, with big citrus, extracted flavors that carry through to the brown spice finish. Creamy and layered, this one's a powerful and structured wine with fine acidity and some youthful edges. **$30**

Gary Farrell 1995 Zinfandel

Region: California, Russian River Valley
Golds/Awards: Gold (DA, SD, WC, LA, OC, NW, WWC-91 pts, CA, Citrus Fair); Best of Class (NW, CA); Best New World Zinfandel (NW); Sweepstakes Red (NW, CA)

Gary Farrell makes knock-out Zinfandels that shake up the wine world. His 1994 Zin received eight golds from major national and international competitions, and this 1995 version has done the same. In fact, since 1990 his Zinfandels have been winning top awards every year. In other words, you can't go wrong with a Gary Farrell Zinfandel, especially this reasonably priced beauty. This is a visually breathtaking wine, with its youthful deep purple hue. Its intense, deeply filled aromas of raspberries, blackberries, and creamy oak lead to attention-getting flavors that are insatiably long and wonderfully proportioned. **$20**

Geyser Peak 1994 Reserve Shiraz
Region: California, Sonoma County
Golds/Awards: Gold (FF, NW, WWC-90 pts); Best of Class (NW); Cellar Selection (WWC)

The color is black cherry, blackish ruby with a purple cast. It is full bodied, has full acidity, is loaded with extract, and is quite dry and tannic. Scents of walnuts, mocha, black plum, and sandalwood greet the nose. Possessing a bold, deep texture, this wine is pungent on the palate, displaying force and rich woody tones with plenty of stuffing, ample fruit, and fragrance. It will harmonize with some more time in the bottle. **$32**

Geyser Peak 1994 Trione Cellars Reserve Alexandre Red Meritage
Region: California, Alexander Valley
Golds/Awards: Gold (DA, PR, AW, IV, FF, Grand Harvest Awards, Citrus Fair); Best of Class (PR); Double Gold (TG); Chairman's Award (FF)

Wow! Look at those golds and other awards! This blend of Cabernet Sauvignon, Merlot, Petit Verdot, Malbec, and Cabernet Franc is elegant, full-bodied, and extremely complex. Ripe cherry-berry aromas enhanced by vanillan oak lead to lush flavors of raspberry fruit, spice, and cigarbox herbaceousness, with delicious, medium tannins and a long, spicy finish. Approachable now, yet will further improve with age because of its superior structure and flavor profile. **$28**

$Geyser Peak 1995 Shiraz
Region: California, Sonoma County
Golds/Awards: Gold (PR, WC, NW, SF); Best of Class (PR, WC); Grand Champion (PR); Best Pacific Rim Red Wine (PR)

Peak's Australian winemaker calls this Shiraz "truly seductive." The nose displays a mixture of fruit characters including blackberries, anise, and black pepper. Maturation in small oak has enhanced the nose with subtle vanillin characters. The palate is soft and silky on the finish with a full-bodied richness indicative of this variety. **$15**

Geyser Peak 1995 Winemaker's Selection Petite Verdot

Region: California, Alexander Valley
Golds/Awards: Gold (WC, NW, CA); Best New World Petite Verdot (NW); Best of Class (NW)

Petite Verdot is one of the less known varieties of Bordeaux. It's generally blended with Merlot and Cabernet Sauvignon and adds color and structure to blends. A rich and powerful wine, this one is black and dense in color, and shows spicy fruit enhanced by cedary oak character. Although it has a big flavorsome palate with evident tannin, this wine nevertheless is incredibly soft for all of its intensity. **$20**

Geyser Peak 1995 Winemaker's Selection Cabernet Franc

Region: California, Alexander Valley
Golds/Awards: Gold (PR, NW, CA); Best of Class (PR, NW)

Since last edition I've seen a lot more gold-medal-caliber Cabernet Francs. Maybe it's time to get out of the Cabernet Sauvignon rut and try this varietal. This herbaceous medium-bodied wine is full flavored with berry fruit characters and some rich spice. Hints of cedar round out the relatively soft palate. **$20**

$Geyser Peak 1996 Sauvignon Blanc

Region: California, Sonoma County
Golds/Awards: Gold (SD, WC, VL, OC); Double Gold (TG)

Here's an elegant but full-flavored Sauvignon Blanc showing distinct varietal fruit character. The nose displays the typical asparagus, grassy green olive, apple characters. The palate is crisp and balanced. At this price, with all of these golds, one should buy a whole case! **$8.50**

$Gloria Ferrer 1988 Royal Cuvée Brut

Region: California, Carneros
Golds/Awards: Gold (AT, WC, LA, NW, WWC-90 pts); Best of Class (LA); Grand Champion (NW); Best New World Sparkling Wine (NW)

Looking for a superior bubbly that won't break your wallet? This dazzler has a light, golden-straw color enhanced by tiny persistent bubbles that rise to form a crown of foam at the edge of the glass. Aromas of strawberry, cherry, ripe apple, lime, and spice combine with bottle bouquets of toasted yeasty bread and toasted almonds. The creamy smooth mousse explodes into bright fruity citrus flavors. Firm acidity balances the full rich body leading to a long, crisp finish. **$14**

$Gloria Ferrer Champagne Caves NV Blanc de Noirs

Region: California, Carneros
Golds/Awards: Double Gold (TG); Gold (FF, OC); Best of Category (FF)

Full of bright strawberry, raspberry, and black cherry fruit with a nice touch of spice and a warm, mouth-filling finish. Excellent as an aperitif or try it with fresh seafood, sushi, or chocolate dessert. Another reasonably priced sparkler from this winning winery. **$15**

Greenwood Ridge Scherrer Vineyard 1995 Zinfandel

Region: California, Sonoma County
Golds/Awards: Gold (DA, NW, CA); Best of Class (NW, CA)

These Zinfandel grapes come from a 75-year-old vineyard. This is a hand-crafted wine with a supple texture and jammy maple, raspberry, cherry flavors. It's beautifully balanced, and will go well with a variety of dishes, from pizza and hamburger to pasta and roast duck. **$16**

Grgich Hills 1993 Cabernet Sauvignon

Region: California, Napa Valley
Golds/Awards: Gold (DA, WWC-91 pts); Double Gold (TG)

The color of this Cabernet is deep purple with a saturated ruby rim. Expect moderately full body, balanced acidity, and lots of extract and oakiness. This dry beauty will conjure up flavors of ripe cherries, currants, and green pepper. It exhibits lush varietal aromas and a gorgeously extracted palate of ripe fruit. Finishing firmly with a perfectly proportioned acidic element, this is an infant with years of development in front of it. **$28**

$Guenoc 1994 Red Meritage

Region: California, Lake County
Golds/Awards: Gold (SD, FF); Double Gold (CA);
Best of Class (CA)

This excellently priced red Bordeaux-style blend combines 51% Cabernet Franc, 28% Merlot, 12% Cabernet Sauvignon, and 9% Petit Verdot. Look for touches of cloves and cinnamon; cassis and cherries; and round flavors of mint and coffee. It has a well-balanced structure auguring further complexity and depth in the years to come. **$15**

Guenoc 1994 Vintage Port

Region: California
Golds/Awards: Gold (DA, OC); Double Gold (TG);
Four-Star Gold (OC)

Aromas of rich black fruits, toffee, and vanilla combine with flavors that are deep, long, and full with ripe blackberry, blueberry, and plum fruits, moderate sweetness, and balanced acidity. The finish is smooth and warm with soft tannins and excellent structure. Try serving this port with walnuts, pistachios, mild creamy cheeses, mincemeat pie, crème brûlée, berry tarts, custard, or bittersweet chocolate. **$25**

Guenoc 1995 Genevieve Magoon Reserve Chardonnay

Region: California, Guenoc Valley
Golds/Awards: Gold (AT, AW, IV, WWC-90 pts);
Cellar Selection (WWC)

With this unbelievable list of golds, could this wine be anything but brilliant? The winemaker describes his Chardonnay as having decadently rich varietal aromas of apple, pear, honey, and citrus laced with spicy, buttery notes. The full flavors are intense and exotic, while the finish is opulent, silky, and long. A Chardonnay that goes well with lobster, wild mushrooms, or poultry with fresh herbs. **$25**

$Hart Winery 1996 Grenache Rosé

Region: California, Cucamonga Valley
Golds/Awards: Gold (SD, FF, NW); Chairman's
Award (FF); Best of Class (NW); Best New World
Rosé (NW)

Made in a dry style, this rosé has intense
strawberry and cranberry scents with flavors that
linger on and on. A wonderful wine at a moderate
price! **$7.50**

Hartford Court 1995 Hartford Vineyard Zinfandel

Region: California, Russian River Valley
Golds/Awards: Gold (OC, NW); Double Gold (SF);
Best Zinfandel (SF)

A small block of 80-year-old vines provided
the grapes for this wine. Planted on gravelly loam
benchlands near the Russian River, this dry-
farmed vineyard is pruned for low yield and consistently produces Zinfandel with concentrated,
powerful flavors. This Zin is tremendously dense
with remarkably supple tannins. The rich aroma
combines dense raspberry and sweet caramel.
Mouth-filling black cherry and blackberry fruit are
accented by cinnamon and classic peppery Zinfandel character. **$40**

Jordan J 1993 Brut

Region: California, Russian River Valley
Golds/Awards: Double Gold (TG, CA); Gold (OC);
Four-Star Gold (OC); Best of Class (CA)

I'm not a champagne person. Or rather, I
didn't used to be until I tried the 1990 J from last
year's book that won seven gold medals. Now I tell
all of my friends to buy a bottle for their birthday,
anniversary, graduation—you name it—party. I fell
in love with the 1990. I flipped over the 1991. And
now I can't wait to try the 1993. The winemaker
says the 1993 J displays layers of fresh berry, Asian
pear, apple, and fig aromas interlaced with a hint
of vanilla and light toasty notes. The midpalate is
broad and fresh with a mix of fresh fruit flavors
leading to a long finish marked by soft acids and a
slight roasted almond flavor. It should continue to
develop and improve with bottle time, acquiring
more depth yet keeping its elegant structure. **$25**

Kendall-Jackson 1994 Grand Reserve Unfiltered Cabernet Franc

Region: California

Golds/Awards: Gold (SD, IV, FF); Chairman's Award (FF)

Look for blueberry, blackberry, and white pepper backed by nuances of smoky oak in this wine. It has a full and supple mouth feel with vanilla oak and berry notes. **$18**

Kendall-Jackson 1994 Grand Reserve Zinfandel

Region: California

Golds/Awards: Gold (IV, FF, OC); Chairman's Award (FF)

The opululent nose of blackberry, strawberry, and boysenberry leads to rich, jammy flavors that are enhanced by a hint of black pepper. This is a mouth-filling wine that is soft and supple right through the lingering finish. This Zin is full-bodied yet youthful and enjoyable. **$25**

Kendall-Jackson 1995 Grand Reserve White Meritage

Region: California

Golds/Awards: Gold (PR, FF, NW); Best of Class (NW); Best New World Meritage-Type White (NW)

Displaying complex combinations of floral and fruit aromas, with background notes of smoky oak, this is a rich, mouth-filling wine with big melon and fig flavors accented by a creamy finish. A blend of 74% Sauvignon Blanc and 26% Semillon. **$25**

$Korbel 1991 Master's Reserve Blanc de Noirs

Region: California

Golds/Awards: Gold (LA, NW, CA); Best of Class (CA)

I continue to be surprised by American sparkling wines that are of such high quality yet have low price tags, as does this one. The color is pale straw with a green gold cast. It's medium to light bodied, and offers up aromas and flavors of citrus and minerals. **$13.99**

⌖Lawson's 1991 Shiraz

Region: Australia, Padthaway
Golds/Awards: Gold (IW, WS); Best Rhône-Style
Wine (IW, SY)

Here's a mishmosh of excerpts from the Sydney judges: "deep red cerise color with hints of purple; spicy, with eucalyptus and mint on the nose; black cherry fruit and high-toned vanilla oak; mouth filling; sweet finish; a complex and striking wine." By the way, the wine was evaluated alongside grilled beef scotch fillet served with pan-fried chopped baby button mushrooms, all in a cream reduction sauce. Yum! **$25**

$Maddalena 1995 Johannisberg Riesling

Region: California, Monterey/Santa Barbara
Golds/Awards: Gold (SD, WC, LA); Best of
Class (SD, LA)

A blend of grapes from the two best regions in California for growing Johannisberg Riesling, the wine shows opulent peach nectar and honey characters. Its crisp acidity is carefully balanced with residual sugar, yielding an elegant wine that's wonderful to drink. **$7**

⌖Magnotta 1991 Limited Edition Merlot

Region: Canada
Golds/Awards: Gold (VL, IV, WWC-91 pts); Best
Buy (WWC)

Berry red with a brick cast, this Merlot is medium bodied with flavors and aromas reminiscent of earth, dried herbs, and black fruits. It has an elegant rounded palate with an earthy backnote that carries through to a lengthy, subtle finish. A very French-styled wine showing real class. **$18**

$Meridian 1994 Cabernet Sauvignon

Region: California
Golds/Awards: Gold (PR, SD, OC)

It's quite rare to find a Cabernet this inexpensive, especially one with intense, concentrated flavors. Check it out. **$11**

Meridian 1995 Reserve Pinot Noir

Golds/Awards: Gold (NW, WC, OC); Best of
Class (WC)
Region: California, San Luis Obispo/Santa Barbara

Look for concentrated flavors in this wine, with
a good balance of tannin and structure. The winery
says only the best barrels are given the "reserve"
designation. **$17**

$Mirassou 1996 "White Burgundy" Pinot Blanc

Region: California, Monterey County
Golds/Awards: Gold (AT, WC, LA); Best of Class (WC)

A dry, medium-bodied wine, this one has an
exceptionally creamy texture; ripe tropical fruit
aromas of pineapple, banana, and pear; and hints
of vanilla, butter, and smoky French oak. It has
fresh pear flavors that evolve into pineapple, a very
creamy texture with vanilla undertones, and a refreshing finish with a touch of spicy oak. It pairs
well with a wide variety of foods including chicken,
pork, ham, veal, seafood, and cream-sauced pastas.
The winemaker suggests this as an excellent alternative to Chardonnay. **$10.95**

$Perry Creek 1995 Wenzell Vineyards Mourvèdre

Region: California, Sierra Foothills
Golds/Awards: Gold (DA, FF, NW); Chairman's
Award (FF); Best of Class (NW)

Bright currant and wild berry aromas blend
nicely with a touch of French oak. Smooth and
supple in the mouth, the fruit flavors hold together
nicely in the finish. **$12.50**

Plam 1993 Cabernet Sauvignon

Region: California, Napa Valley
Golds/Awards: Gold (PR, FF, WWC-92 pts);
Chairman's Award (FF); Cellar Selection (WWC)

Just beginning to come into its own, this
wine will develop even more over time. Deep red
in color, it offers up fruity, berry aromas. The palate encounters layers of black fruit, currants, and
spice, balanced with suitable tannins for structure
and undertones of toasty oak. Though it will
benefit from cellaring, this very promising wine is
definitely drinkable now. **$35**

$Quady 1990 Vintage Starboard
Region: California
Golds/Awards: Double Gold (TG, CA); Gold (OC);
Best of Class (CA)

Following the Portuguese tradition, Quady declares a Vintage Port only in years where the quality of the wine—ripeness, concentration, and flavor—is superb. The 1990, characterized by intense, perfectly ripened Tinta Cao and Tinta Amarela fruit, and a perfect balance of sweetness, body, acidity, and soft tannins, can be enjoyed now but would benefit from an additional 5 to 10 years of bottle aging. **$14**

$Quady 1995 Essensia
Region: California
Golds/Awards: Gold (OC, WWC-90 pts); Double
Gold (TG)

Quady wins gold medals year after year for their various Muscats, and they usually sell out quickly. From 100% Orange Muscat, the Essensia has an aroma reminiscent of orange blossom and apricot, and a lingering, refreshing aftertaste. Dessert in a glass. **$13.50**

$Quady 1996 Electra
Region: California
Golds/Awards: Gold (PR, NW); Double Gold (CA);
Best of Class (NW)

This is a new type of dessert/picnic wine—light, delicate, and refreshing, like a breath of springtime, a bouquet of flowers, and the taste of peach and melon—with only 4% alcohol. This wine goes well with spicy picnic fare, salads, pasta, and dessert. **$7.50**

$Quady 1996 Elysium
Region: California
Golds/Awards: Gold (SD, LA, FF); Double Gold
(CA); Best of Class (CA)

Quady, a specialist in Muscat, made this one from 100% Black Muscat. The wine has an aroma of roses and a complex lycheelike flavor. It's great with vanilla-flavored desserts, dark chocolate, blue cheese, and candlelight. **$13.50**

Richardson 1995 Horne Vineyard Cabernet Sauvignon

Region: California, Sonoma Valley
Golds/Awards: Gold (SD, OC, SF); Four-Star Gold (OC)

I caught the winemaker off-guard when I called, but he nevertheless rattled off quite an elaborate and detailed description of this gold medal winner. The vineyard is in one of the cooler parts of Sonoma, and it was the kind of vintage that allowed the grapes to get fully ripe. This rich wine is medium to full bodied, has fruity, berry flavors with a hint of cassis, and a modest level of toastiness that brings roundness to the wine, adding just a hint of chocolate-vanilla smoothness to enhance the berry tones. **$18**

℞ Rosemount 1994 Mountain Blue Shiraz Cabernet Sauvignon

Region: Australia, Mudgee
Golds/Awards: Gold (SY, NW, WWC-90 pts); Best of Class (NW); Cellar Selection (WWC-90 pts)

This beauty has a deep ruby color with a violet rim. It is full bodied, has balanced acidity, is highly extracted, and heavily oaked. Look for mild sweetness and flavors/aromas reminiscent of blackberries, coconut, and ripe plums. The wine offers lush aromas and gorgeous, superripe fruit in a heavily extracted format. Tannins are ample and well integrated, allowing creamy wood elements full play. A firm finish suggests long-term potential. **$25**

Santa Barbara Winery 1995 Syrah

Region: California, Santa Barbara County
Golds/Awards: Gold (PR, NW, WWC-90 pts); Best of Class (NW); Best New World Shiraz/Syrah (NW); Cellar Selection and Best Buy (WWC)

The colors are inky blackish ruby-purple. The body is medium to full. This dry, tannic wine has balanced acidity, is highly extracted, and offers up scents of violets and herbs. The texture is rich, the palate compact yet robust. It's quite jammy, as rich fruit plays with heady fragrance and light spice.

Showing well now, this one will continue to improve with age. **$16**

Sebastiani 1994 Sonoma Cask Barbera
Region: California, Sonoma County
Golds/Awards: Gold (LA, OC, NW); Best of Class (NW); Best New World Barbera (NW)

This Italian red has about 16% Rhône varietals blended with it to create an interesting hint of spiciness. It's medium to dark crimson in color. Cherries and berries are its main features, with generous vanilla oak flavors on the palate. The wine has plummy Barbera varietal characteristics and the aforementioned slight spiciness from the Rhône varietal blenders. The finish is soft, tangy, and nicely oaked. Perfect with tomato dishes and sauces, duck, pork, or ham. **$20**

$Sierra Vista 1996 Fleur de Montagne
Region: California, El Dorado
Golds/Awards: Gold (SD, LA, OC)

Literally "flower of the mountain," this wine is a harmonious blend of mountain-grown Rhône varieties—Syrah, Grenache, Mourvèdre, and Cinsault. The wine is medium bodied with multidimensional fruit flavors, finesse, balance, and spice. Very drinkable now, with its fine, soft tannins and good acid it will age well for 4 to 5 years. Try it with grilled fish or lighter pasta dishes, herb chicken, and poultry as well as red meats. It's also rich enough to stand up to tomato-based sauces or spicy cuisine such as Cajun. Blackened salmon and barbecued pork tenderloin are two of the winemaker's favorite pairings. **$13.50**

$Silvan Ridge 1995 Semi-Sparkling Early Muscat
Region: Oregon
Golds/Awards: Gold (FF, WWC-90 pts); Double Gold (SF); Best of Category (FF)

Here's a nice change-of-pace wine. In appearance, it's very pale straw with a silver cast. Moderately light bodied, the wine features balanced acidity and medium extract. Aromas of tangerine, orange blossom, and fresh lilac greet the nose. It has a lively, spritzy mouth feel with crisp acids and wonderfully focused fruit flavors that linger on the mouth-watering finish. **$12**

Stonestreet 1994 Pinot Noir
Region: California, Russian River Valley
Golds/Awards: Gold (AT, WC, NW, Taster's Guild)

Stonestreet is truly a gold medal winery, winning golds every year. But getting four for a single wine is amazing. This rich, complex, balanced wine has aromas of oaky spice, raspberry, and black cherry; flavors of ripe plums and cherries; full, lush texture; and a tannic finish. It's capable of aging through the beginning of the next century and beyond. **$30**

$Swedish Hill 1995 Late Harvest Vignoles
Region: New York, Cayuga Lake
Golds/Awards: Double Gold (TG, SF); Gold (NW)

This dessert in a glass will bring up honey, apricot, and melon flavors and scents. Rich and full bodied, it's a perfect cheesecake wine. **$11.99**

Venezia 1994 Meola Vineyards Cab. Sauvignon
Region: California, Alexander Valley
Golds/Awards: Gold (PR, WC, FF); Best of Class (PR)

Part of the Geyser Peak family of wineries, Venezia is making oodles of incredible wines, many of which are in this book by virtue of winning golds (three or more each, in the case of this one and the ones below). This wine is a rich, deeply colored, minty Cabernet with spicy oak. On the nose the characters of dark berries and cassis dominate with a background element of cedary oak. **$20**

Venezia 1995 Bianca Nuovo Mondo
Region: California; Northern Sonoma
Golds/Awards: Gold (AT, FF, SF)

If you'd like to be a white wine drinker, but you seem to always gravitate toward reds, grow a little and pick up a bottle of this one or the one below. Learning from the French, who've been in the wine biz longer than we New Worlders, Venezia and other wineries are producing delicious blends of Bordeaux and other white grape varieties that transcend the ordinary. A blend of 56% Sauvignon Blanc and 44% Semillon, this wine is imbued with dominant citrus characters of lemon and lime with sweet melons, an underlying note of toasty oak, and a long, flavorsome palate. The wine finishes with crisply balanced natural acidity. **$20**

Venezia 1995 Stella Bianca White Table Wine
Region: California; Sonoma County
Golds/Awards: Gold (PR, AT, AW, NW,); Best New World Semillon-Chardonnay (NW); Best of Class (PR, NW)

A blend of 50% Chardonnay, 49% Semillon, and 1% Sauvignon Blanc, this beauty displays distinct vanilla and tropical fruit aromas enhanced by smoky barrel-fermented characters. The palate is rich with a creamy roundness from *sur lie* aging and balanced acidity. **$20**

Venezia 1995 Nuovo Mondo Sangiovese
Region: California
Golds/Awards: Double Gold (TG); Gold (SD, CA); Best of Class (SD, CA)

This wine is truly a unique blend combining the elegance of Sangiovese (79%) with the richness of Shiraz (21%). It flaunts an array of characters combining raspberry and cherry with pepper and spice from the Shiraz. Spicy elements roll onto a palate that's soft and round. **$24**

Windsor Vineyards 1993 Cabernet Sauvignon
Region: California, Sonoma County
Golds/Awards: Gold (NW, WWC-90 pts, CA)

This winery wins buckets of golds every year, and makes lots of different varietals. But you won't find Windsor wines in stores or restaurants because they only sell directly to consumers, which is how they're able to sell such top-class wines at such reasonable prices. A rich ruby color, this rich, dry wine is medium bodied, with balanced acidity and plentiful extract and oak. The bouquet offers up hints of cherries, vanilla, and coconuts. It's highly drinkable thanks to forward fruit and a smooth, balanced structure. By mail-order only, (800) 333-9987. **$20**

Windsor 1994 Shelton Signature Series Pinot Noir

Region: California, Russian River Valley
Golds/Awards: Gold (WC, NW, CA); Best of California and Best of Class (CA)

Windsor has loads of wines in this book, and did last year too, which goes to show that it's the winery, not the wine, that's the real gold medal winner. This Pinot Noir is reasonably priced, especially when one considers that at least a dozen experts awarded it their top marks. It's a nicely aged Pinot that does a balancing act between pepper, black cherry fruit, and oak, allowing all three to coexist fairly evenly. It has softened since its release, and will continue to do so for another few years. Windsor wines are available by mail-order only, (800) 333-9987. **$16**

8

BEST BARGAIN WINES

It seems too good to be true: gold medal winning wines that are kind to the wallet. But it *is* true, and there are lots of 'em in this book. All of the wines in Part III with a dollar symbol ($) are $15 and under. However, some of these wines are better bargains than others. For example, a $14 Pinot Noir would be a great find, since that varietal tends to be quite pricy. On the other hand, a $14 Gamay Beaujolais wouldn't be a stunning deal at all (this varietal usually runs under $8) unless it was a flawless, absolutely spectacular example of the varietal.

White wines are generally less expensive than reds, so if you're a white-wine lover, you're in luck. And there are certain varietals that are almost always bargains, Chenin Blanc, for example, or White Zinfandel (technically rosé), to name two.

I like to buy under-$15 bottles for my own personal consumption, but to splurge on more expensive wines for special occasions with friends. (Contrary to those TV commercials in which the woman gushes, "After all, *I'm* worth it.") But the way I see it, there's nothing wrong with seeking bargain wines for myself, as long as they're gold medal winners.

While some of these wines competed against wines in their same price range, others were up against—but still unseated—bottles twice their price.

There are a number of bargain wines in this chapter that are also BBW's (Best of BEST WINES!, or triple-plus gold medal winners). Talk about getting the most bang for your buck!

I've included tasting notes for some of my personal favorites, and brief commentary on others. But every wine in this chapter is an undisputable "best buy" and worthy of seeking out next time you're wine shopping.

Here are some highlights.

CABERNET SAUVIGNON

It's not uncommon to find $50-and-up Cabs in your wine shop. In fact, the second priciest wine in this book is a Cabernet Sauvignon ($120, Ridge). Cabernet Sauvignon is a world-class varietal that commands center stage of the market. If you find a Cab under $15 you're doing well. But to find a *gold medal winning* Cab under $15 is magnificent fortune. One tip is to look to other countries, particularly Chile, which can't ask for the kind of prices, say, the Aussies can. At least not yet. Here are several of my favorite bargain Cabs, as well as a complete listing of those **$15 and under.**

Audubon Collection 1993 Graeser Vineyards Cabernet Sauvignon
Region: California, Napa Valley
Golds/Awards: Gold (IW); James Rogers Trophy (IW)

This inexpensive wine grabbed my attention because of where it won the gold. The International Wine Challenge draws wines from the oldest, most prestigious wineries in Europe. This $15 bottle was up against some of the greatest French Cabs on the globe, many, no doubt, three and four times its price. Impressive! And it also took the trophy there too! The winemaker describes it as having intense black currant, cherry, and raspberry flavors combined with hints of herb and eucalyptus. This is a complex Cabernet with layers of aromas and flavors. Drinkable now for its bright, youthful character, this wine will also improve with further bottle age. **$15**

Cathedral Cellar 1994 Cabernet Sauvignon
Region: South Africa
Golds/Awards: Gold (VL); Champion Wine (VL)

Try a South African wine, if you haven't already. Cabs from South Africa are still great bargains. This full red wine has nuttiness and black pepper on the nose, balanced with vanilla flavors from the small oak maturation. The tannins harmonize with the full and fruity flavors. **$12**

Vina Gracia 1994 Premium Cabernet Sauvignon
Region: Chile, Cachapoal Valley
Golds/Awards: Gold (VN, BR)

One of the perks of writing a wine book is learning about and trying new wines. This one turned out to be a delightful surprise. With golds from Brussels *and* Paris, this little upstart is trying to break into the American market with a kicky, mod label design and a very competitive price. The winemaker calls it harmonious and spirited, and I'd agree. **$12.99**

Beaulieu 1994 Cabernet Sauvignon, CA, $15
Belvedere 1994 Cabernet Sauvignon, CA, $13.50
Benziger 1994 Cabernet Sauvignon, CA, $15—*A BBW: See write-up, Chapter 7.*
Beringer 1993 Cabernet Sauvignon, CA, $15—*This winner of two golds is a* wonderful *dinner party wine, for people who appreciate a really delicious red—and want lots of it. One of my favorites.*
꒰**Boland 1994 Cabernet Sauvignon,** SAFR, $10.99
Bonterra 1994 Organically Grown Grapes Cabernet Sauvignon, CA, $12—*A BBW: See write-up, Chapter 7.*
Canyon Road 1995 Cabernet Sauvignon, CA, $8
꒰**Carmen 1995 Reserve Grande Vidure Cabernet,** CHI, $9.99
Cedar Brook 1994 Cabernet Sauvignon, CA, $8.99
Charles Krug 1993 Cabernet Sauvignon, CA, $14
꒰**Chateau La Joya 1996 Cabernet Sauvignon,** CHI, $10.99
Chateau Souverain 1994 Barrel Aged Cabernet Sauvignon, CA, $15—*Winner of two golds.*
Cloninger 1992 Cabernet Sauvignon, CA, $15
Clos du Bois 1994 Cabernet Sauvignon, CA, $15—*Beat out many higher-priced Cabs at Intervin, one of the stingiest competitions when it comes to handing out golds.*
꒰**Clos Malverne 1994 Cabernet Sauvignon,** SAFR, $12.99
Columbia Crest 1994 Cabernet Sauvignon, WA, $10.99
Cypress Winery 1994 Cabernet Sauvignon, CA, $8.75—*A BBW: See write-up, Chapter 7.*
Domaine Michel 1994 Cabernet Sauvignon, CA, $12
꒰**Etchart 1995 Cabernet Sauvignon,** ARG, $6.99
Famille Bonverre 1995 Cabernet Sauvignon, CA, $9

Fetzer 1993 Barrel Select Cabernet Sauvignon, $12.99

Forest Glen 1993 Cabernet Sauvignon, CA, $12

Forest Glen 1994 Cabernet Sauvignon, CA, $9.99—*Winner of two golds.*

Gallo Sonoma 1994 Frei Ranch Vineyard Cabernet Sauvignon, CA, $14—*This isn't your father's Gallo! Gallo has transformed itself into a world-class winery worth looking into again. They have six gold medal Cabs in this book, but this one won a double gold and was named best Cabernet Sauvignon at San Francisco Fair International. No easy task, especially at this bargain price.*

Geyser Peak 1995 Cabernet Sauvignon, CA, $15

Glen Ellen Expressions 1994 Cabernet Sauvignon, CA, $11

Gordon Brothers 1992 Cabernet Sauvignon, WA, $14.49

Haywood 1995 Vintner's Select Cabernet Sauvignon, CA, $8

J. Lohr 1994 Seven Oaks Cabernet Sauvignon, CA, $14

ⓟ**Jacob's Creek 1994 Cabernet Sauvignon,** AUS, $7.99

Jodar Wine Company 1992 Cabernet Sauvignon, CA, $10.99

Kiona 1995 Cabernet Sauvignon, WA, $14.99

Lake Sonoma 1993 Cabernet Sauvignon, CA, $15

Lava Cap 1995 Cabernet Sauvignon, CA, $15

ⓟ**Manso de Velasco 1995 Cabernet Sauvignon,** CHI, $14

Meeker 1993 Dry Creek Valley Gold Leaf Cuvée (Cabernet Sauvignon), CA, $15

Meridian 1994 Cabernet Sauvignon, $11—*A BBW: See write-up Chapter 7.*

Napa Ridge 1992 Reserve Cabernet Sauvignon, CA, $15—*A BBW: See write-up, Chapter 7.*

Napa Ridge 1993 Reserve Cabernet Sauvignon, CA, $15

Napa Ridge 1995 Reserve Cabernet Sauvignon, CA, $9—*Three different Napa Ridge Cabs, all great prices, all gold medal winners. You definitely can't go wrong with any of Napa Ridge's $15-and-under Cabernets.*

Nevada City 1994 Sierra Foothills Cabernet Sauvignon, CA, $13

Pedroncelli 1994 Three Vineyard Cabernet Sauvignon, CA, $12.50

Pedroncelli 1995 Vintage Selection Cabernet Sauvignon, CA, $10

Robert Mondavi 1994 Coastal Winery Cabernet Sauvignon, CA, $11

☙**Santa Digna 1995 Cabernet Sauvignon,** CHI, $6.99

Sebastiani 1994 Cabernet Sauvignon, CA, $12.99—*Winner of two golds.*

Silver Ridge 1993 Cabernet Sauvignon, CA, $9.99

Staton Hills 1992 Cabernet Sauvignon, WA, $14.95

Stone Creek 1994 Special Selection Cabernet Sauvignon, CA, $6.89

Sutter Home 1992 Reserve Cabernet Sauvignon, CA, $11.95

☙**Swartland 1994 Cabernet Sauvignon,** SAFR, $9.99—*A World Wine Championship "Best Buy."*

Taft Street 1995 Cabernet Sauvignon, CA, $12

Tessera 1995 Cabernet Sauvignon, CA, $9.99

Trellis Vineyards 1995 Cabernet Sauvignon, CA, $13.99—*Winner of two golds.*

Troon Vineyards 1995 Cabernet Sauvignon, OR, $13.50

Turning Leaf 1993 Sonoma Reserve Winemaker's Choice Barrel Aged Cabernet Sauvignon, CA, $10

Twin Hills 1992 Cabernet Sauvignon, CA, $15

Venezio Vineyard 1994 Cabernet Sauvignon, CA, $10.50

☙**Vina Tarapaca 1992 Gran Reserva Cabernet Sauvignon,** CHI, $15—*This winery is producing wonderful wines at wonderful prices. Keep a watch out for this label!*

W.B. Bridgman 1993 Cabernet Sauvignon, WA, $11.99—*A World Wine Championships "Best Buy."*

Weinstock 1995 Cabernet Sauvignon, CA, $10.99

Wellington 1993 Cabernet Sauvignon, CA, $14

Wellington 1993 Random Ridge Cabernet Sauvignon, CA, $15

Windsor 1994 Cabernet Sauvignon, CA, $11—*Order by mail only, (800) 333-9987.*

Zabaco 1993 Cabernet Sauvignon, CA, $9

CHARDONNAY

There was a time when this varietal was inexpensive nearly across the board. Now it's not uncommon to find many $20-plus bottles on the shelves of a large wine shop. With Chardonnay, don't forget to check out the excellent ones from Australia, Canada, Oregon, and Washington. The real bargains for me are gold medal Chardonnays **$10 and under.** Here are some favorites:

Callaway 1995 Calla-Lees Chardonnay
Region: California, Temecula
Golds/Awards: Gold (NW); Best of Class (NW)

Every year this winery wins golds for their inexpensive but delicious Calla-Lees. It's elegant and fruity and has lively, fresh green apples, lemons and toasty vanilla flavors. Balanced by a creamy finish, this Chardonnay will go well with broiled chicken, chowders, veal, or grilled fish. **$10**

Fetzer 1996 Sundial Chardonnay
Region: California
Golds/Awards: Gold (SD, WC)

Here's another one that brings home gold medals year after year (this year it won two!) and appears on everyone's "Best Buy" list. It has fresh tropical citrus and apple aromas and flavors with hints of butter and oak-spice. Ripe fruit flavors are delightful and appealing with roasted chicken, pasta, and appetizers. It's a great price too. **$6.99**

℞ Hardy's 1995 Chardonnay
Region: Australia, Padthaway
Golds/Awards: Gold (AT)

Not all of their Chardonnays are this reasonably priced, but this Australian winery consistently manages to produce spectacular bargains that still bring home the gold. This yellow-straw-colored wine is light bodied, subtly extracted, has mild oak, and is dry. The aroma/flavor profile is reminiscent of vanilla, honey, and citrus. **$7**

Hogue Cellars 1995 Chardonnay
Region: Washington, Columbia Valley
Golds/Awards: Gold (PR, AW)

Chardonnay grown in Columbia Valley has a high level of natural acidity well balanced by vivid varietal flavor. This one has aromas of vanilla, pineapple, and Golden Delicious apples. On the palate, these notes are reiterated, with the addition of toasty oak, peach/pear, coconut, mango, and citrus. The mouth feel of this wine is especially rich and soft. Well-structured, this Chardonnay matches exceptionally with fresh and full-flavored dishes such as grilled chicken with citrus salsa. **$10**

Seaview 1994 Chardonnay
Region: Australia
Golds/Awards: Double Gold (TG)

This Australian bargain has a light straw-yellow color with vibrant green hues, indicative of its youth. The fresh and lifted aroma shows peachy varietal characters with a hint of passionfruit, intensified by subtle, integrated vanillin oak that doesn't dominate the wine. Full flavored and complex, the wine features melon and tropical fruit with well-integrated, soft oak. The palate is well balanced and finishes clean and dry, with a lingering, soft butterscotch flavor. **$8.99**

Blossom Hill 1995 Chardonnay, CA, $5
Bridgeview 1995 Blue Moon Chardonnay, OR, $7.99
Callaway 1994 Calla Lees Chardonnay, CA, $10
Canyon Road 1996 Chardonnay, CA, $7.99—*Winner of two golds.*
Concannon 1995 Select Vineyard Chardonnay, CA, $9.95
℘**Concha y Toro 1995 Trio Chardonnay**, CHI, $9.60
Duck Pond 1996 Barrel Fermented Chardonnay, OR, $8—*Winner of two golds.*
Fallbrook 1995 Chardonnay, CA, $6.99

Ferrante 1996 Barrel Fermented Chardonnay, OH, $9.99

Hahn 1995 Chardonnay, CA, $10

♫**Hardys Nottage Hill 1996 Chardonnay,** AUS, $7

Indigo Hills 1995 Chardonnay, CA, $10

♫**Lindemans 1996 Bin 65 Chardonnay,** AUS, $7.

Louis M. Martini 1995 Chardonnay, CA, $10.50

Michael Pozzan 1995 Special Reserve Chardonnay, CA, $10

Rutherford Vintners 1996 Chardonnay, CA, $8.99

Taft Street 1995 Chardonnay, CA, $10

Tessera 1995 Chardonnay, CA, $9.99

Villa Mt. Eden 1994 Chardonnay, CA, $9.50

DESSERT WINES

In my view, all dessert wines are bargains, since a little nip is all you need. Also, sweet wines are generally inexpensive because they come in smaller bottles, .375 ml as opposed to the usual .75 ml of a normal-size wine bottle.

GEWURZTRAMINER

You'll find lots of inexpensive Gewurztraminers in this book, and many in a typical wine shop. That's because it's just not a varietal that commands high price tags. However, I consider gold medal bottles **$8 and under** a really *really* good deal.

Beringer 1996 Gewurztraminer, CA, $8—*Winner of two golds.*

Concannon 1995 Arroyo Seco Gewurztraminer, CA, $7.95

Fetzer 1996 Gewurztraminer, CA, $6—*A BBW: See write-up, Chapter 7.*

Geyser Peak 1996 Gewurztraminer, CA, $7.50— *Winner of two golds.*

M.G. Vallejo 1995 Gewurztraminer, CA, $7

Sutter Home 1996 Gewurztraminer, CA, $5.95— *Winner of two golds.*

ITALIAN-VARIETAL REDS

Often now when I shop for red wines I'll walk straight past the Cabernet Sauvignons over to the more unconventional reds, such as Italian reds produced in California. They're not usually the least expensive of the reds, but the gold medal winners are always very good since they have to compete with the varietals most Americans know and buy. Any Italian red priced **$15 or under** is a great deal. Here are some best bargains:

Abundance 1994 Vintner's Preferred Sangiovese, CA, $9.99
Bargetto 1996 Dolcetto, CA, $15
Boeger 1994 Vineyard Select Barbera, CA, $15
Chameleon Cellars 1995 Sangiovese, CA, $15— *Winner of two golds.*
Folie à Deux 1995 Sangiovese, CA, $15
Temecula Crest 1995 Nebbiolo, CA, $15
Vino Noceto 1995 Sangiovese, CA, $12

MERLOT

Merlots are gaining in popularity—and going up in price. Finding a gold medal Merlot that's **$15 or under** is a real catch. If you love Merlot, the Chilean section in your wine shop is a great place to look. That country is coming out with some very respectable Merlots that are easy on the pocketbook. Some of my favorite Merlot deals:

☞ Casa LaPostolle 1995 Cuvée Alexandre Estate Merlot
Region: Chile, Rapel Valley
Golds/Awards: Gold (SF)

Here's a Chilean winery to watch. France's Marnier family, of Grand Marnier fame, has pumped millions of dollars into this winery, hired Michel Rolland (of Chateau Le Bon Pasteur fame) to be the winemaker, and is now producing French-style fine wines at Chilean prices. I served this wine last year at some book signings, and it was a hit. (The 1994 version of this wine won golds last year too.) It's deeply colored, rich, round, and supple. Approachable now, this one can also be cellared for several years. **$15**

Charles Krug 1995 Merlot
Region: California, Napa Valley
Golds/Awards: Gold (LA)

Here's a classy winery. If you don't know about them, you should. This Merlot is a brilliant ruby color with a nose of fresh black cherry aromas and a hint of cinnamon. The wine is soft and rich in the mouth, with bright fruit flavors, good structure, and an elegant, complex finish. The winemaker suggests garlic-stuffed leg of lamb, rich seafood such as roast monkfish, or hearty stews as ideal food accompaniments. **$15**

M.G. Vallejo 1995 Merlot
Region: California
Golds/Awards: Double Gold (TG)

This wine has gained a reputation as "an insider's Merlot" because of its low profile, high quality, and good value. Look for aromas of dark black cherry, menthol, mint, eucalyptus, and blackberry. Hints of ripe black olive and maple emerge from oak aging. The flavor profile is rich black cherry, smooth silky blackberry, menthol, mint, and vanilla. The wine is very complex, rich in the mouth, and finishes silky soft. The winemaker suggests trying this one with grilled meats, hearty pasta dishes, and game. **$6.99**

ꚃ**Vina Tarapaca 1995 Reserve Merlot**
Region: Chile
Golds/Awards: Double Gold (TG)

One of Chile's most prestigious labels is now available to U.S. wine lovers thanks to California's famous winery, Beringer, who believe in this label so much that they're importing it and marketing it in the States. All of Tarapaca's wines represent great value, and this one's no exception. Check it out. **$9**

Bel Arbor 1996 Vintner's Selection Merlot, CA, $6.99—*A California wine made with Chilean grapes.*
Cedar Brook Winery 1995 Merlot, CA, $8.99
ꚃ**Chateau La Joya 1996 Merlot**, CHI, $9.99
Chateau Souverain 1994 Merlot, CA, $13.50
Columbia Crest 1994 Merlot, WA, $11—*Washington State is producing some of America's best Merlots nowadays. This is a remarkable deal, as are many of this winery's offerings.*
Forest Glen 1995 Merlot, CA, $9.99
Fox Hollow 1996 Merlot, CA, $8.99—*Winner of two golds.*

Domaine St. George 1994 Premier Cuvée Merlot, CA, $11.99—*Picked up a gold at Intervin, one of the toughest judgings, competing against higher-priced Merlots.*

Grand Cru 1996 Merlot, CA, $7.99

🏠 **Eikendal 1996 Merlot,** SAFR, $13.99

🏠 **Fairview 1994 Merlot,** SAFR, $14.99

Gold Hill 1994 Estate Bottled Merlot, CA, $15

🏠 **Hawthorne Mountain Vineyard Merlot,** CAN, $13.49

Lorval Wines 1995 Merlot, TX, $8.99

Nevada City 1994 Sierra Foothills Merlot, CA, $14

Page Mill 1994 O'Shaughnessy Vineyard Merlot, CA, $15

Patrick M. Paul Vineyards 1993 Conner Lee Vineyards Merlot, WA, $12—*A World Wine Championships "Cellar Selection" and "Best Buy." Great deal for a Washington State Merlot.*

Plum Creek Cellars 1994 Merlot, CO, $12.99

Rutherford Ranch 1995 Merlot, CA, $11

🏠 **Santa Carolina 1995 Reserve Merlot,** CHI, $8.99

Sebastiani 1994 Sonoma Cask Merlot, CA, $14.99—*Winner of two golds.*

Taft Street 1994 Merlot, CA, $14

Wildhurst 1995 Merlot, CA, $12—*A World Wine Championships "Best Buy."*

York Mountain 1994 Merlot, CA, $14

Yorkville Cellars 1995 Organically Grown Merlot, CA, $15

PETITE SIRAH

I *love* Petite Sirah. If you're looking for a fruity, sassy red with plenty of character friendly enough for a crowd, pick up a bottle of **$15-or-under** Petite Sirah, of which there are quite a few in this book.

Bogle 1995 Petite Sirah

Region: California

Golds/Awards: Gold (NW); Best of Class (NW)

Imagine your boyfriend's ex-girlfriend and her adult children—the ones he helped raise years ago—all at his house for a Fourth of July nonfamily reunion. I was in charge of the wine. I started the crew off with *several* bottles of Bogle (they're elbow-benders), then we graduated to the more expensive stuff later on. Take it from me: this wine takes the edge off any occasion, and you don't have to feel bad about buying lots of it. Blackberry and orange peel aromas come forward in the bouquet. Lush tannins surround the big jammy flavors—a potpourri of berries, spice, and hints of oak. **$8**

Granite Springs 1995 Petite Sirah
Region: California, El Dorado
Golds/Awards: Gold (SF, Amador County Fair); Double Gold (CA); Best of Class (CA)

San Francisco is a tough competition. The fact that this wine won a gold there (against higher-priced wines) as well as a double gold from California State Fair and even a third gold from another competition made me want to know more. It has intense aromas of black pepper; rich, delicious, spicy, jammy fruit; and a lingering black pepper finish. **$13**

Concannon 1994 Petite Sirah, CA, $9.95—*A BBW: See write-up, Chapter 7.*
Concannon 1995 Select Vineyard Petite Sirah, CA, $9.95—*Winner of two golds.*
David Bruce 1995 Petite Sirah—*A BBW: See write-up, Chapter 7.*
Guenoc 1994 Petite Sirah, CA, $14.50—*One of my favorite gold medal wineries.*
Parducci 1994 Petite Sirah, CA, $9.99
Windsor 1994 Petite Sirah, CA, $11—*Order by mail only, (800) 333-9987.*

PINOT BLANC

It's not as easy to find inexpensive Pinot Blancs as, say, Chenin Blanc or some of the other white varietals. But bottles **$15 and under** are worthy of snatching up, particularly when they're gold medal winners like the ones below:

Chateau St. Jean 1993 Robert Young Vineyards Pinot Blanc, CA, $12
Lockwood 1994 Pinot Blanc, CA, $9—*The judges at World Wine Championships loved this*

wine. Not only did it rate 91 points, but it tied for "National Champion Pinot Blanc" against more expensive bottles, and was named a WWC "Best Buy." This one's an unbeatable bargain.

Mirassou 1996 White Burgundy Pinot Blanc,
    CA, $10.95—*A BBW: See write-up, Chapter 7.*

🏵**Sumac Ridge 1995 Private Reserve Pinot Blanc,**
    CAN, $10.95

PINOT NOIR

Pinot Noir, the grape from which burgundy is made, is one of the most difficult—and prized—wines to produce. California and now Oregon, which has a climate similar to that of Burgundy, France, are the New World leaders making this varietal. It's generally expensive, so if you find one that's **$15 or under,** as are all of the gold medal wines below, snatch it up. Keep in mind that Oregonean Pinots are generally much harder to find since they are produced in smaller quantities.

Tualatin 1995 Pinot Noir
Region: Oregon, Willamette Valley
Golds/Awards: Gold (WC)

One of Oregon's outstanding wineries, Tualatin makes consistently delicious Pinots year after year. This one's a wine of medium color and body with intense aromas of cherries and a hint of mint. Ready to drink now but will continue to age. **$12.50**

Bridgeview 1996 Pinot Noir, OR, $10.99
Firesteed 1996 Pinot Noir, OR, $9.99
Foris 1995 Pinot Noir, OR, $11
Indian Creek Winery 1994 Pinot Noir, ID,
    $14.95—*Don't be surprised that this wine comes from Idaho. Idaho is to the wine world right now what Oregon was a few years ago—relatively unknown but up-and-coming.*
McHenry 1993 Massaro Vineyard Pinot Noir,
    CA, $15—*A World Wine Championships "Best Buy."*

Meridian 1995 Pinot Noir, CA, $14—*A consistently fine winery. This Pinot won three golds, two of them from top competitions, in addition to special awards such as "Sweepstakes Red" from the Monterey Wine Fest.*

Napa Ridge 1995 Pinot Noir, CA, $10—*Winner of two golds.*

Talus 1995 Pinot Noir, CA, $7.99

Windsor 1995 Private Reserve Pinot Noir, CA, $13—*Order by mail only, (800) 333-9987.*

RED BLENDS

Depending on the constituent varieties used, red blended wines can be quite pricy, as in the Bordeaux-style California wines that knock out their French competitors in international tastings. You're apt to find some very good Australian deals, however, since their wines are still priced below comparable California bottles. I find many of the wines below endlessly enjoyable and fascinating. They're all **$15 or under,** which is a deal and a half. This is my personal favorite wine category.

Ca' del Solo 1994 Big House Red
Region: California
Golds/Awards: Gold (IW)

At a recent family get-together on the Connecticut shore, I brought out four bottles of red wine (all gold medal winners, of course), this being the cheapest by far (in that state it was only $7!). Guess what? This was everyone's favorite. The kooky but famous winemaker at Bonny Doon, who produces this label, combined the following grapes: Mourvèdre, Carignane, Barbera, Charbono, Souzão, Grenache, Syrah, Nebbiolo, and Cinsault. In other words, everything but the kitchen sink. It's fun, it's delicious, and your guests will love it! Guaranteed. **$8.50**

⚲Jacob's Creek 1995 Shiraz Cabernet
Region: Australia
Golds/Awards: Gold (VL)

This deep crimson red wine displays intense, fresh plum and berry fruit aromas balanced with spicy oak highlights. It's medium bodied with ripe plum and berry fruit flavors supported by soft grape and oak tannins. A long, lingering finish tops it off. **$6.99**

Jory 1996 Purple Gang
Region: California
Golds/Awards: Gold (LA, CA)

Jory's winemaker says this wine is an organization of various criminal elements: chiefly Cabernet Franc, Cabernet Pfeffer, and Carignane, with smaller amounts of Syrah, Gamay, and Merlot. Jory's red blends are winning golds left and right. This one won two. Worth a try at this price. **$15**

⌂Lindemans 1994 Padthaway Cabernet-Merlot
Region: Australia, South Australia
Golds/Awards: Gold (AT, Hobart)

Here's a velvety smooth, full-flavored wine and a good example of the modern Australian Cabernet-blended style. The wine is vibrant crimson in color with good depth. The bouquet is dominated by lifted plum fruit with overtones of mint, berry, and chocolatelike complexity against a background of vanillin oak. The palate has soft raspberry and plum fruit flavors with a silky long finish. The wine is medium bodied with an abundance of rich, ripe berry fruit complemented by sweet vanillin oak. **$14.99**

Beringer 1992 Meritage, CA, $14
Boeger 1994 Majeure Reserve (Rhône-style blend), CA, $9
Concannon 1994 Raboli Field Blend (Rhône-style blend), CA, $12.95
Eberle 1995 Côtes du Robles, CA, $13—*A BBW: See write-up, Chapter 7.*
⌂**Eikendal 1996 Classique** (Cabernet Sauvignon/Merlot), SAFR, $13.99
Granite Springs 1994 Carousel Series (Bordeaux-style blend), CA, $12
Guenoc 1994 Red Meritage, CA, $15—*A BBW: See write-up, Chapter 7.*
Horton 1993 Montdomaine Heritage (Bordeaux-style blend), VA, $15
Jekel 1990 Red Meritage—*A World Wine Championships "Best Buy."*

Jekel 1991 Sanctuary Estate Red Meritage, CA, $10.

Jory 1995 Black Hand (Mano Nera) (Rhône/Italian blend), CA, $15

Madrona 1995 Estate Bottled Shiraz/Cabernet, CA, $10

Paul Thomas 1995 Cabernet-Merlot, WA, $11— *One of my favorite Washington labels, and always a good value.*

Quivera 1995 Dry Creek Cuvée, CA, $13— *Winner of two golds.*

River Run 1995 Cote d'Aromas (Rhône-style blend), CA, $15

Rosemount Estates 1996 Grenache Shiraz, AUS, $8.95—*Winner of two golds.*

Sierra Vista 1996 Fleur de Montagne (Rhône-style blend), CA, $13.50—*A BBW: See write-up Chapter 7.*

Vigil Vineyard 1995 Terra Vin (Rhône-style blend), CA, $12

Worden 1994 Cabernet/Merlot, WA, $15

RIESLING

If you're a Riesling fan, you're in luck. Lots of gold medal wineries produce inexpensive Rieslings. You'll find lots under $15 in Part III, but below I'm featuring only those that are **$8 and under**. When shopping for this varietal, don't forget the Northwestern wineries—Oregon and Washington—who are turning out some of the best and most interesting.

Hogue Cellars 1996 Johannisberg Riesling

Region: Washington, Columbia Valley
Golds/Awards: Gold (FF)

Lively and medium dry, this wine has ripe and fruity aromas and flavors, including tangerine and jasmine, with pear and citrus notes. The palate offers an attractive interplay of sugar and acid. It matches well with highly seasoned foods, poultry, and salads. It also makes a fine aperitif. **$6.50**

Willamette Valley Vineyards 1996 Riesling
Region: Oregon
Golds/Awards: Double Gold (TG); Gold (Newport
Wine Festival and McMinnville Wine Classic)

This lovely wine has aromas of honeysuckle
flowers, citrus, peaches, and cream. The fresh and
lively flavors are of peaches, honey, and rind
steeliness. The sweetness is well balanced by fresh,
bright acidity and a hint of effervescence inviting
another sip. **$7.75**

Beringer 1996 Johannisberg Riesling, CA, $8
**Cedar Creek 1996 Waterfall Mist Dry White
    Riesling**, WI, $8
**Concannon 1995 Select Vineyard Limited
    Bottling Johannisberg Riesling**, CA, $7.95
Concannon 1996 Johannisberg Riesling, CA,
    $7.95—*Winner of two golds.*
Fetzer 1996 Johannisberg Riesling, CA, $6.99—
    Winner of two golds.
**Geyser Peak 1996 Trione Cellars Johannisberg
    Riesling**, CA, $7.50—*Winner of two golds.*
Hogue Cellars 1995 Johannisberg Riesling,
    WA, $6
Hoodsport 1995 Riesling, WA, $7.99
J. Lohr 1996 Bay Mist Riesling, CA, $7.50
**Maddalena Vineyard 1995 Johannisberg
    Riesling**, CA, $7—*A BBW: See write-up,
    Chapter 7.*
Maurice Car'rie 1996 Johannisberg Riesling,
    CA, $4.99
**Mirassou 1996 Fifth Generation Family
    Selection Johannisberg Riesling**, CA,
    $7.50—*A World Wine Championships "Best
    Buy."*
Secret House 1996 White Riesling, OR, $8
Springhill Cellars 1996 White Riesling, OR,
    $7.50

SAUVIGNON BLANC

It's probably more unusual to find a bottle of Sauvignon Blanc over $15 than to spot one under $15.
That's why the wines listed below are Fumé and
Sauvignon Blancs **$8 and under,** which makes
them an extra bargain. If you're tired of heavily

oaked (and more pricy) Chardonnays and want something refreshing and different, pick out a bottle of Sauvignon Blanc for a change.

Clos Du Bois 1996 Sauvignon Blanc
Region: California, Sonoma County
Golds/Awards: Gold (FF, CA); Chairman's Award (FF); Best of Class (CA)

This winery consistently produces quite a number of gold medal wines each year. The melon, citrus, and oak-spice flavors of the subtly herbaceous Sauvignon Blanc make it compatible with fresh oysters, and many seafood and vegetarian dishes. Try it with fresh grilled fish and pasta with vegetables. **$8**

Vichon 1995 Sauvignon Blanc
Region: California, Mediterranean grapes
Golds/Awards: Gold (LA)

In order to make tasty wine at a competitive price, many wineries are looking to places other than California to buy their grapes. The Mondavi family, who owns Vichon, decided to go to the Languedoc-Roussillon, the oldest vineyard land in France, for the grapes that went into making this wine. The wine has expressive fruit and meadow flower aromas, and flavors ranging from melon and tropical fruit to stony, mineral qualities, to delicate herbs, grasses, and flowers. This wine is perfect with fresh, simply prepared seafood, chicken, and fresh vegetable dishes. Enjoy it with cracked crab or a Mediterranean fish soup. **$7.99**

Arbor Crest 1996 Sauvignon Blanc, WA, $6.50
Canyon Road 1996 Sauvignon Blanc, CA, $6.99
Concannon 1995 Sauvignon Blanc, CA, $7.95
Corbett Canyon 1995 Coastal Classic Sauvignon Blanc, CA, $4.99
Maurice Car'rie 1994 Sauvignon Blanc, CA, $4.99
Montevina 1996 Fumé Blanc, CA, $7
Napa Ridge 1995 Sauvignon Blanc, CA, $6
Oxford Landing 1994 Sauvignon Blanc, AUS, $7—*A World Wine Championships "Best Buy."*
Ste. Genevieve NV Sauvignon Blanc, TX, $7.99
Sterling 1995 Sauvignon Blanc, CA, $8

SEMILLON

Like most other white wines, Semillon isn't terribly pricy as a rule. The ones listed below, however, were rated "best" in major wine competitions, yet they're **$10 or under**. A great buy if you're a Semillon lover, or just looking to get out of the Chardonnay doldrums.

♺**Basedow 1996 Semillon (White Burgundy),** AUS, $10

Hogue Cellars 1996 Semillon, WA, $8.99

SPARKLING WINES

Are you one of those who believes that really good sparkling wine has to cost, say, $50? It's not true. Below are some phenomenal sparklers, all **$15 or under.** When you want to celebrate with more than one "toast" per guest, these are the ones to buy. They're such great deals, you won't even have to wait for a special occasion to serve up the bubbly. Don't turn up your nose at the nonchampagne-style sparklers until you've tried them. They will surprise you, as they no doubt surprised the judges who gave them golds.

Ballatore NV Gran Spumante
Region: California
Golds/Awards: Gold (DA, NW)

Sometimes wine choice should be made more on the basis of the occasion (and company) than on what food is being served. Spumante? Never, said I. But then I tried this one and now understand why it won not one but two gold medals from leading expert judges. It's fun, and was actually perfect for the crowd I was in—very occasional drinkers, inexperienced with wine, who nevertheless wanted something festive and light for the celebration. The winemaker describes it as a delicate, aromatic Muscat-type flavor and nose. It has a sweet mouth feel, yet it doesn't leave a lingering sweet sensation. Take it from me: it wasn't cloying in the least. **$6.49**

Glenora 1992 Brut

Region: New York

Golds/Awards: (WWC-90 pts); Best Buy (WWC)

New York used to be more famous for its sparkling wines than California. Many New York wineries are making a strong comeback, including this one. The judges at World Wine Championships describe it as straw-colored, moderately full bodied, with flavors and aromas reminiscent of stone fruits, smoke, and yeast. There is some yeast complexity in this generous, full-flavored style with good balancing acidity. Rather champagnelike. **$12.99**

Korbel NV Sparkling Champagne Chardonnay

Region: California

Golds/Awards: Gold (LA)

This sparkling wine made by the *méthode champenoise* is primarily from Chardonnay grapes, and offers ripe pear and apple flavors and a creamy mouth feel. It's well suited to a variety of appetizers, but it's also extremely flexible with pasta, seafood, and poultry main courses, as well as lighter veal dishes. **$12.99**

Wente NV Reserve Brut

Region: California, Arroyo Seco/Monterey

Golds/Awards: Gold (FF, WWC-91 pts)

This sparkling beauty is pale straw with green-gold highlights, moderately full bodied, with balanced acidity, and has an impressive concentration of flavors and aromas of stone fruits and flowers. **$12**

Windsor 1994 Blanc De Noirs

Region: California, Sonoma County

Golds/Awards: Gold (FF, CA)

This winery wins a stunning number of golds every year. Here's the catch: they only sell through the mail. They say they can mail to anywhere in the continental U.S., so what are you waiting for? This double-gold recipient is refined and elegant, made primarily with Pinot Noir grapes, with a hint of rose and a whisper of fruit. They'll even customize the label for a wedding or other special occasion. (800) 333-9987 **$14**

Buena Vista Carneros 1990 Blanc de Blanc, CA, $14

Chandon NV Cuvée 391 Blanc de Noirs, CA, $12—*A World Wine Championships "Best Buy."*

Cook's Wine Cellars NV Sweet Spumante, CA, $3.99

Culbertson NV Brut, CA, $10

Firelands Winery NV Sparkling Riesling, OH, $9.95

Gloria Ferrer Champagne Caves NV Blanc de Noirs, CA, $15—*A BBW: See write-up, Chapter 7.*

Gloria Ferrer NV Brut, CA, $15—*Another great deal from this winery. This one won two golds.*

Gloria Ferrer 1988 Royal Cuvée Late Disgorged Brut, CA, $14—*Yet another BBW from this winery: See write-up, Chapter 7.*

Gruet NV Brut, NM, $13

Korbel 1991 Master's Reserve Blanc de Noirs, CA, $13.99—*A BBW: See write-up, Chapter 7.*

Korbel NV Rouge Champagne, CA, $11.99

Korbel NV Extra Dry Champagne, CA, $9.99

Maison Deutz NV Brut Cuvée, CA, $12.75—*This winner of two very respectable gold medals comes from a wonderful winery that wins top awards year after year for their sparklers. An excellent find.*

Meier's Wine Cellars Sparkling Pink Catawba, OH, $2.29

Silvan Ridge 1995 Semi-Sparkling Early Muscat, OR, $12—*A BBW: See write-up, Chapter 7*

Stone Hill NV Golden Spumante, MO, $8.29

Swedish Hill NV Spumante, NY, $8.99

Windsor 1994 Brut, CA, $13—*Order by mail only, (800) 333-9987.*

SYRAH/SHIRAZ

Whichever name you call it, this varietal is taking the world by storm. Australia's distinctly rich and fruity Shirazes caught on in America like wildfire. Now California Syrah (also sometimes called Shiraz) is growing in popularity. More recently,

Washington is producing some blockbuster examples. The ones below won't hurt your wallet at **$15 and under.**

♫Leasingham 1994 Classic Clare Shiraz
Region: Australia, Clare Valley
Golds/Awards: Gold (WS); Best Australian Red Wine (WS); Best Syrah/Shiraz (WS)

The International Wine & Spirits Competition is considered one of the toughest. The judges there flipped for this moderately priced Shiraz. The winemaker describes this wine as deep, intense purple with brick red hues. In the bouquet are rich, full plum and berry fruit qualities complexed by hints of herbs and mint, while further character is obtained from subtle charry American oak aromas. This wine has a refined combination of concentration, intensity, and elegance. Depth and richness are balanced by sweetness and softness. Dominating plum flavors are complemented by subtle American oak characters. It will benefit from 10 years or more of cellaring. **$11.25**

Wellington 1995 Alegria Vineyard Syrah
Region: California, Russian River Valley
Golds/Awards: Gold (SD); Best of Class (SD)

The wine has a beautiful ruby color, with aromas and flavors of raspberry and cranberry fruit, varietal Syrah smokiness, and an intriguing floral character. This is a full-bodied wine with good intensity, lively acidity, and smooth tannins that's enjoyable now yet has the capacity to age for 5 or more years. **$15**

Columbia 1995 Syrah, WA, $13—*This Washington State beauty won a Double Gold at San Francisco International, a coveted award.*

♫**Fairview Estate 1993 Shiraz Reserve**, SAFR, $14.99

Geyser Peak 1994 Shiraz, CA, $14—*This California gold medal winery has an Australian winemaker. You can be sure that the Shiraz is delicious and authentic.*

Geyser Peak 1995 Shiraz, CA, $15—*A BBW: See write-up, Chapter 7.*

Indian Springs 1995 Syrah, CA, $15

J. Lohr 1994 South Ridge Syrah, CA, $14—*Beat out many higher priced French and Australian wines at the International Wine Challenge.*

McDowell Valley Vineyards 1995 Estate Syrah, CA, $15

R.H. Phillips 1995 EXP Syrah, CA, $12

Wellington 1994 Alegria Vineyard Syrah, CA, $15—*Wow! Golds two years in a row for this winery's bargain-priced Syrah. This one's also a World Wine Championships "Best Buy."*

WHITE BLENDS

These are lovely wines as a rule. Why? Maybe it's the diplomat in me. I just like the idea of a wine-maker blending together two or three special varietals to come up with one that flaunts the best of each, while creating a new wine that's supeior to any of its component parts. The French, of course, do it all the time in their Bordeaux blends. But Americans and Australians, in particular, are now producing beautiful white blend creations too. They tend to be more expensive than other whites, so I consider the ones featured below, at **$15 and under,** to be good buys.

Beringer 1995 Alluvium Blanc
Region: California, Napa Valley
Golds/Awards: Gold (VN)

This wine is mostly Sauvignon Blanc (45%) and Semillon (44%), with 10% Chardonnay and a tiny percent Viognier to complete the magic. It has a nice mouth feel with buttery nuances added to multilayered aromas and flavors of melon, honeyed fig, pears, apples, white flowers, and spice. Yum! **$15**

Carmenet 1995 Paragon Vineyard White Meritage
Region: California
Golds/Awards: Gold (WWC-92 pts)

Getting a 92-point score from World Wine Championships is an honor any winery would die for. Here's a classic Bordeaux-style white blend made up of 75% Sauvignon Blanc and 25% Semillon. The wine is full bodied with a fine-grained texture and enticingly complex aromas of melon, citrus, and perfume. It's a versatile food wine, working well with spiced, herbed, peppered dishes, as well as classic pairings with oysters, grilled fish, and chèvre cheese. **$15**

De Lorimier 1995 Estate Bottled Spectrum
Region: California, Alexander Valley
Golds/Awards: Gold (OC, CA); Best of Class (CA)

Here's a wine that took home two golds, yet is still priced reasonably. Made from 62% Sauvignon Blanc and 38% Semillon, this Bordeaux-style white displays ripe grapefruit and pineapple from the former component, and elements of honeydew melon and pear added by the Semillon. Barrel fermentation provides a subtle toast and creamy vanilla accent. **$12**

⚘Rosemount Estates 1996 Traminer Riesling
Region: Australia, Southeast Region
Golds/Awards: Gold (PR, AT)

Here's a fun combination, Gewurztraminer and Riesling, from an excellent Australian gold medal winery. The "Traminer," as the Aussies call it, has a spicy, tropical fruit aroma reminiscent of lychees and an exotic scent, with a generous, soft palate. The Riesling adds elegance to the finish, with lifted floral flavors and a fine acidity that balances the wine to perfection. Serve this wine chilled with Cajun, Mexican, and Asian recipes, or alongside light fruit desserts. **$7.95**

Baily 1996 Montage (Bordeaux-style blend), CA, $11

Folie à Deux NV Menage à Trois (Muscat, Chardonnay, Chenin Blanc), CA, $8

⚘**Jacob's Creek 1995 Semillon-Chardonnay,** AUS, $7

⚘**Jacob's Creek 1996 Semillon-Chardonnay,** AUS, $6.99

⚘**Rosemount 1996 Semillon Chardonnay,** AUS, $7.95

⚘**Santa Ana 1996 Chardonnay-Chenin Blanc,** ARG, $3.99

Sutter Home 1996 White Soleo (Chenin Blanc/Muscat blend), CA, $4.45—*Don't be a wine snob until you've tried this light little charmer. The winery suggests serving it in a small tumbler over ice. It's packaged in a twist-top bottle. An easy-to-drink, easy-to-understand wine, especially for generation Xers who might not have a palate for serious wines just yet.*

❦**Wyndham Estate 1995 Bin TR2** (Gewurztraminer/ Riesling blend), AUS, $6.99

ZINFANDEL

I love Zinfandel, and it's lucky that one can find great Zins that are affordable. It's not as expensive a varietal as, say, Cabernet. Therefore, I consider any Zinfandel **$12 or under** to be a steal, like the ones below:

Castoro Cellars 1995 Zinfandel
Region: California, Paso Robles
Golds/Awards: Gold (SD, SF)
   This double-gold winner is described as being "exuberant." It's also jammy and fruity, round and elegant. Castoro Cellars has three gold medal Zins under $15. You probably can't go wrong with any of them. **$9.95**

Pedroncelli 1994 Pedroni-Bushnell Vineyard Zinfandel
Region: California, Dry Creek Valley
Golds/Awards: Gold (PR, NW)
   The wine shows generous fruit and subtle complexity. Rich blackberry and raspberry in the aroma and flavor are complemented by hints of mint and spice. Light on the palate, yet exceptionally mouth filling, this harmonious Zinfandel finishes long and smooth. **$11.50**

Robert Mondavi 1995 Coastal Zinfandel
Region: California, North Coast
Golds/Awards: Gold (SF)
   This one's brilliant ruby in color, conjuring up aromas and flavors of spices (cloves and black pepper), underlying cherry-berry fruit, with perhaps a hint of dark chocolate. Mild tannins and a long finish top it off. **$10**

Beringer 1993 Zinfandel, CA, $12

Castoro Cellars 1994 Zinfandel, CA, $9.95—
Winner of two golds.

Fetzer 1994 Barrel Select Zinfandel, CA, $8.99

Guenoc 1995 Zinfandel, CA, $11

Kenwood 1992 Zinfandel, CA, $12

Madrona 1995 Estate Bottled Zinfandel, CA, $10

Napa Ridge 1995 Coastal Zinfandel, CA, $9

Nevada City 1995 Sierra Foothills Zinfandel, CA,
$12

Pedroncelli 1994 Mother Clone Zinfandel, CA,
$11.50

**Sierra Vista 1995 Estate Bottled Vintner's Select
Zinfandel**, CA, $8

**Sutter Home 1990 Amador County Reserve
Zinfandel**, CA, $9.95

Talus 1995 Zinfandel, CA, $7.99

**Turning Leaf 1993 Sonoma Reserve Winemaker's
Choice Zinfandel**, CA, $10

Villa Mt. Eden 1994 Zinfandel, CA, $9.50

York Mountain 1994 Zinfandel, CA, $12

PART III

The Gold Medal Winners

9

RED WINES

Cabernet Franc
Cabernet Sauvignon
Italian Varietals
Merlot
Misc. Varietal Reds
Native & Hybrid Reds
Petite Sirah
Pinot Noir
Red Blends
Syrah/Shiraz
Zinfandel

Cabernet Franc

One of the primary blending varieties, Cabernet Franc is most often paired with Cabernet Sauvignon to add cedary, raspberry, and floral suggestions to its more assertive cousin in Bordeaux-style red blends (also known in America as red Meritage). In the New World, over the last twenty years, California and Australia in particular have upped their plantings of this variety, and are using it widely to add dimension to their Cabernet Sauvignons. In the Old World it has been used this way for many decades.

However, interest in making Cabernet Franc *as a varietal wine* has also increased in the New World, particularly in California, Long Island, Argentina, Washington State, and New Zealand.

Compared with Cabernet Sauvignon, Cabernet Franc is light to medium bodied, fruitier, lighter in color, and less tannic. At its best, it can produce a well-balanced, fruity wine that pairs well with aromatic herbs such as basil and sage, Mediterranean-style pasta dishes, baked chèvre in olive leaves, spring lamb, and game such as venison.

Cabernet Franc   RED

$Buttonwood Farm 1994 Cabernet Franc
Region: California, Santa Ynez Valley $15
Golds/Awards: Gold (LA)

**Carmenet 1993 Moon Mountain Vineyard
Cabernet Franc**
Region: California $20
Golds/Awards: Gold (WWC-92 pts); National
Champion Cabernet Franc, Cellar Selection (WWC)

**Clos du Bois 1993 Winemaker's Reserve
Cabernet Franc**
Region: California, Sonoma County $20
Golds/Awards: Gold (AT, WWC-90 pts)

Edgewood Estate 1993 Cabernet Franc
Region: California, Napa Valley $16
Golds/Awards: Gold (SD); Best of Class (SD)

**Geyser Peak 1995 Winemaker's Selection
Cabernet Franc**
Region: California, Alexander Valley $20
Golds/Awards: Gold (PR, NW, CA); Best of Class
(PR, NW)

Gold Hill Vineyard 1994 Cabernet Franc
Region: California, El Dorado $16
Golds/Awards: Gold (CA); Best of Class (CA)

**$Gundlach-Bundschu 1994 Rhinefarm Vineyard
Cabernet Franc**
Region: California, Sonoma Valley $14
Golds/Awards: Gold (PR, NW); Best of Class (NW)

Helena View 1993 Cabernet Franc
Region: California $22
Golds/Awards: Gold (WWC-90 pts)

Did You Know . . . ?
Winemaker Michael Brown from Buttonwood Farm has
an interesting food-pairing suggestion for his Cabernet
Franc. He says to serve it with grilled ostrich burger
smothered in wild mushrooms sautéed with onions and
sage. I was going to, weren't you?

Cabernet Franc   RED

Kendall-Jackson 1994 Grand Reserve Unfiltered Cabernet Franc
Region: California $18
Golds/Awards: Gold (SD, IV, FF); Chairman's Award (FF)

$Monthaven 1995 Cabernet Franc
Region: California, Napa Valley $9.99
Golds/Awards: Gold (OC)

Peju Province 1994 Cabernet Franc
Region: California, Napa Valley $25
Golds/Awards: Gold (SF)

Pride Mountain Vineyards 1994 Cabernet Franc
Region: California, Sonoma $20
Golds/Awards: Gold (SF)

$St. Julian 1995 Cabernet Franc
Region: Michigan, Lake Michigan Shore $14.95
Golds/Awards: Gold (AW)

Vigil 1995 Terra Vin Cabernet Franc
Region: California, Napa Valley $20
Golds/Awards: Gold (WC, CA); Best of Class (WC, CA)

Waterbrook 1994 Cabernet Franc
Region: Washington $19.99
Golds/Awards: Gold (WWC-91 pts)

White Hall Vineyards 1995 Cabernet Franc
Region: Virginia $17.99
Golds/Awards: Gold (DA)

Did You Know . . . ?

Cabernet Franc is a variety that flourishes in cooler climates such as Washington State and Michigan. Michigan, you say? Many people don't realize that Michigan vineyards, like those in neighboring Ohio and Ontario, benefit from the almost maritime climatic influences of the Great Lakes.

Cabernet Sauvignon

For most of the world, Cabernet Sauvignon is king of the reds. It's been widely grown in the New World for more than a century, and its popularity never seems to wane. The big, blockbuster Cabs being produced in California in particular are giving some of France's most famous wineries the jitters as they outperform their old cousins in blind tastings.

While Cabs vary from country to country and vineyard to vineyard, one can characterize them generally. They tend to be deeply colored, richly fruity, with complex structure, which means lots of acid and plenty of tannin. Some of the terms used to describe Cabernets are: black cherry, blackberry, plums, herbs, green olives, truffles, loamy earth, tobacco, leather, violet, mint, eucalyptus, tea, cedar, bell pepper, tar, and chocolate. These aren't subtle flavors and aromas!

A great Cab is capable of—indeed, requires—long aging in your cellar. Yet there are many New World examples that are complex and age worthy yet ready for early drinking. This style will generally be less expensive. The Reservas from Chile represent great value and have lots of personality, and Argentina has some wonderful and approachable Cabs too.

Because of its assertive personality, Cabernet Sauvignon is frequently blended with other varieties, most commonly Merlot, which adds subtle herbal and cherry notes, and Cabernet Franc, for its violet, spring berry, and herbal contributions. (As long as it's 75 percent Cab, the wine can be called Cabernet Sauvignon in the United States.)

It's best to drink Cabernet Sauvignon with simple, hearty foods such as roast or grilled red meat, pork, veal, and duck. With medium to lighter versions, one can be more creative. Try it with fruit-based sauces (on meat), wild mushroom dishes, garlicky Mediterranean cuisine, hard cheeses, even dark chocolate.

Cabernet Sauvignon   RED

Adelaida 1992 Cabernet Sauvignon
Region: California $19
Golds/Awards: Gold (WWC-93 pts); Cellar
Selection (WWC)

Alderbrook 1995 Cabernet Sauvignon
Region: California, Sonoma County $16
Golds/Awards: Gold (FF)

Altamura 1992 Cabernet Sauvignon
Region: California $28
Golds/Awards: Gold (WWC-92 pts); Cellar
Selection (WWC)

Atlas Peak 1994 Cabernet Sauvignon
Region: California. Napa Valley $18
Golds/Awards: Gold (SF)

**$Audubon Collection 1993 Graeser Vineyards
Cabernet Sauvignon**
Region: California, Napa Valley $15
Golds/Awards: Gold (IW); James Rogers
Trophy (IW)

**Bartholomew Park Winery 1994 Desnudos
Vineyard Cabernet Sauvignon**
Region: California, Sonoma Valley $20
Golds/Awards: Gold (SD, FF, PR, OC)

**Beaulieu 1992 Georges de Latour Private
Reserve Cabernet Sauvignon**
Region: California, Napa Valley $40
Golds/Awards: Gold (WWC-91 pts)

**Beaulieu 1993 Georges de Latour Private
Reserve Cabernet Sauvignon**
Region: California, Napa Valley $40
Golds/Awards: Gold (DA, AT, NW)

Did You Know . . . ?
Where does "French oak" of wine-barrel fame come
from? One place is Tronçais, the oldest managed forest
in France. It was established by King Louis XIV to pro-
vide straight masts for his ships.

Beaulieu 1994 Georges de Latour Private Reserve Cabernet Sauvignon
Region: California, Napa Valley $50
Golds/Awards: Gold (CA)

$Beaulieu 1994 Cabernet Sauvignon
Region: California, Rutherford $15
Golds/Awards: Gold (SD); Best of Class (SD)

$Belvedere 1994 Cabernet Sauvignon
Region: California, Dry Creek Valley $13.50
Golds/Awards: Gold (WC)

$Benziger 1994 Cabernet Sauvignon
Region: California, Sonoma County $15
Golds/Awards: Gold (FF, NW, WWC-91 pts); Chairman's Award (FF); Best of Class (NW)

Beringer 1992 Napa Valley Private Reserve Cabernet Sauvignon
Region: California, Napa Valley $60
Golds/Awards: Gold (WS); Best Cabernet Sauvignon Worldwide (WS)

$Beringer 1993 Knights Valley Cabernet Sauvignon
Region: California, Knights Valley $15
Golds/Awards: Gold (AT, SD); Best of Class (SD)

Beringer 1994 Knights Valley Cabernet Sauvignon
Region: California, Knights Valley $17.50
Golds/Awards: Gold (WC, OC, SF); Four-Star Gold (OC)

Bettinelli 1995 Cabernet Sauvignon
Region: California, Napa Valley $18
Golds/Awards: Gold (WC); Best of Class (WC)

$Bogle 1995 Cabernet Sauvignon
Region: California $7
Golds/Awards: Gold (CA)

Did You Know . . . ?
There's more Cabernet Sauvignon planted in the world than any other top-quality vine variety.

$ ♺ Boland 1994 Cabernet Sauvignon
Region: South Africa $10.99
Golds/Awards: Gold (VL)

$Bonterra 1994 Organically Grown Grapes Cabernet Sauvignon
Region: California, North Coast $12
Golds/Awards: Gold (SD, LA, CA); Best of Class (LA, CA)

Bookwalter 1994 Vintner's Select Cabernet Sauvignon
Region: Washington $38
Golds/Awards: Gold (NE)

Buena Vista 1992 Grand Reserve Cabernet Sauvignon
Region: California, Carneros $24
Golds/Awards: Gold (AT)

Byington 1993 Cabernet Sauvignon
Region: California $20
Golds/Awards: Gold (IV)

Cakebread Cellars 1993 Cabernet Sauvignon
Region: California $22
Golds/Awards: Gold (WWC-91 pts)

Canyon Road 1994 Reserve Cabernet Sauvignon
Region: California, Sonoma County $18
Golds/Awards: Gold (LA, FF)

$Canyon Road 1995 Cabernet Sauvignon
Region: California $8
Golds/Awards: Gold (SF)

$ ♺ Carmen 1995 Reserve Grande Vidure Cabernet
Region: Chile, Maipo Valley $9.99
Golds/Awards: Gold (VN)

$ ♺ Cathedral Cellar 1994 Cabernet Sauvignon
Region: South Africa $12
Golds/Awards: Gold (VL); Champion Wine (VL)

Did You Know . . . ?
Jack Cakebread, of Cakebread Cellars, gave up a career as an auto-repair-shop owner to become a world-famous vintner. Good career move, Jack.

Cabernet Sauvignon   RED

Caymus 1993 Cabernet Sauvignon
Region: California $25
Golds/Awards: Gold (WWC-91 pts)

Cecchetti-Sebastiani Cellar 1993 Cabernet Sauvignon
Region: California, Napa Valley $28
Golds/Awards: Gold (SD, OC)

$Cedar Brook 1994 Cabernet Sauvignon
Region: California $8.99
Golds/Awards: Gold (NW)

Chalk Hill 1993 Cabernet Sauvignon
Region: California $23
Golds/Awards: Gold (WWC-92 pts); Cellar Selection (WWC)

$Charles Krug 1993 Cabernet Sauvignon
Region: California $14
Golds/Awards: Double Gold (TG)

Charles Krug 1993 Vintage Selection Cabernet Sauvignon
Region: California, Napa Valley $35
Golds/Awards: Gold (FF, OC)

$ Chateau La Joya 1996 Cabernet Sauvignon
Region: Chile, Colchagua Valley $10.99
Golds/Awards: Gold (BR)

Chateau Montelena 1992 The Montelena Estate Cabernet Sauvignon
Region: California $36
Golds/Awards: Gold (WWC-90 pts); Cellar Selection (WWC)

Chateau Reynella 1994 Basket Pressed Cabernet Sauvignon
Region: Australia, McLaren Vale $22.50
Golds/Awards: Gold (SY)

Did You Know . . . ?
Chateau La Joya is the largest family winery in Chile.

Chateau St. Jean 1991 Reserve Cabernet Sauvignon
Region: California, Sonoma County $38
Golds/Awards: Gold (AT, SD, WC, NW, WWC-93 pts); Double Gold (TG); Cellar Selection (WWC)

Chateau St. Jean 1993 Cinq Cepages Cabernet Sauvignon
Region: California, Sonoma County $18
Golds/Awards: Gold (WWC-90 pts)

Chateau Ste. Michelle 1993 Cabernet Sauvignon
Region: Washington, Columbia Valley $15.99
Golds/Awards: Gold (AT)

Chateau Ste. Michelle 1993 Cold Creek Vineyard Cabernet Sauvignon
Region: Washington $26
Golds/Awards: Gold (WWC-90 pts); Cellar Selection (WWC)

Chateau Souverain 1993 Winemaker's Reserve Cabernet Sauvignon
Region: California, Alexander Valley $30
Golds/Awards: Gold (PR, FF, SF)

$Chateau Souverain 1994 Barrel Aged Cabernet Sauvignon
Region: California, Alexander Valley $15
Golds/Awards: Gold (SD); Double Gold (SF)

Cinnabar 1993 Saratoga Vineyard Cabernet Sauvignon
Region: California $25
Golds/Awards: Gold (WWC-93 pts); Cellar Selection (WWC)

$Cloninger 1992 Cabernet Sauvignon
Region: California $15
Golds/Awards: Gold (WWC-90 pts)

Did You Know . . . ?
Chateau St. Jean was Sonoma Valley's first ultramodern, multimillion-dollar winery, and the only winery to have 5 wines in *Wine Spectator*'s Top 100 Wines in 1996.

Cabernet Sauvignon   RED

Clos du Bois 1993 Briarcrest Cabernet Sauvignon
Region: California, Alexander Valley $22
Golds/Awards: Gold (PR, IV, CA)

$Clos du Bois 1994 Cabernet Sauvignon
Region: California, Alexander Valley $15
Golds/Awards: Gold (IV)

Clos Du Val 1992 Reserve Cabernet Sauvignon
Region: California $45
Golds/Awards: Gold (WWC-90 pts); Cellar Selection (WWC)

Clos LaChance 1993 Cabernet Sauvignon
Region: California $20
Golds/Awards: Gold (WWC-90 pts)

$ ⌂ Clos Malverne 1994 Cabernet Sauvignon
Region: South Africa $12.99
Golds/Awards: Gold (WWC-90 pts); Cellar Selection (WWC)

Columbia Crest 1993 Estate Series Cabernet Sauvignon
Region: Washington, Columbia Valley $16
Golds/Awards: Gold (WC)

$Columbia Crest 1994 Cabernet Sauvignon
Region: Washington, Columbia Valley $10.99
Golds/Awards: Gold (LA)

Conn Creek 1993 Limited Release Cabernet Sauvignon
Region: Napa Valley, California $18
Golds/Awards: Gold (NW)

Did You Know . . . ?

South Africa's wine industry is beginning to see a resurgence as wine lovers worldwide recognize good-quality wines coming out of that country. However, the country has to depend on exports, since its black majority remains faithful to beer. During the Apartheid years, workers were sometimes "paid" in wine, leading to rural alcoholism. Wine drinking is, therefore, now looked down upon and even discouraged by black nationalists.

Cooper-Garrod 1993 Proprietor's Reserve Cabernet Sauvignon
Region: California $35
Golds/Awards: Gold (WWC-90 pts); Cellar Selection (WWC)

Cosentino 1993 Punched Cap Fermented Reserve Cabernet Sauvignon
Region: California $34
Golds/Awards: Gold (WWC-90 pts)

Creston 1991 Winemaker's Selection Cabernet Sauvignon
Region: California $18.50
Golds/Awards: Gold (WWC-92 pts)

Curtis 1994 La Cuesta Vineyard Cabernet Sauvignon
Region: California, Santa Ynez Valley $18
Golds/Awards: Gold (FF, NW); Chairman's Award (FF); Best of Class (NW); Best New World Cabernet Sauvignon (NW)

$Cypress 1994 Cabernet Sauvignon
Region: California $8.75
Golds/Awards: Gold (PR, OC, NW); Best of Class (NW)

Dave Nichol's Cellars 1991 Personal Selection Reserve Cabernet Sauvignon
Region: California $18
Golds/Awards: Gold (WWC-90 pts)

David Bruce 1993 Reserve Cabernet Sauvignon
Region: California, Santa Clara County $18
Golds/Awards: Gold (PR)

David Bruce 1994 Reserve Cabernet Sauvignon
Region: California, Santa Cruz Mountains $18
Golds/Awards: Gold (LA); Best of Class (LA)

Did You Know . . . ?
Univeristy of Illinois scientists have found that the chemical resveratrol, found in red wine grapes, reduced the incidence of skin tumors in lab mice by up to 98%.

De Loach 1993 Estate Bottled O.F.S. Cabernet Sauvignon
Region: California, Russian River Valley $25
Golds/Awards: Gold (DA, WWC-90 pts)

De Loach 1994 O.F.S. Estate Bottled Cabernet Sauvignon
Region: California, Russian River Valley $16
Golds/Awards: Gold (PR, LA, FF); Double Gold (CA); Chairman's Award (FF); Best of Class (CA)

Dr. Konstantin Frank 1995 Cabernet Sauvignon
Region: New York $22
Golds/Awards: Double Gold (TG)

$Domaine Michel 1994 Cabernet Sauvignon
Region: California, Sonoma County $12
Golds/Awards: Gold (PR)

Dry Creek Vineyard 1994 Reserve Cabernet Sauvignon
Region: California, Dry Creek Valley $25
Golds/Awards: Gold (AT, SD, WWC-91 pts); Cellar Selection (WWC)

Eberle 1991 Estate Bottled Reserve Cabernet Sauvignon
Region: California, Paso Robles $35
Golds/Awards: Gold (LA, CA); Best of Class (CA)

Edgewood Estate 1993 Cabernet Sauvignon
Region: California, Napa Valley $18
Golds/Awards: Gold (PR)

$ ⌸ Etchart 1995 Cabernet Sauvignon
Region: Argentina, Cafayate $6.99
Golds/Awards: Gold (IV)

$Famille Bonverre 1995 Cabernet Sauvignon
Region: California $9
Golds/Awards: Gold (CA)

Did You Know . . . ?
Once the eighth richest country in the world, Argentina is working to rebuild its wine industry in the 1990s.

Farella-Park 1993 Estate Bottled Cabernet Sauvignon
Region: California $28
Golds/Awards: Gold (WWC-90 pts)

$Fetzer 1993 Barrel Select Cabernet Sauvignon
Region: California, North Coast $12.99
Golds/Awards: Gold (NW)

Flora Springs 1993 Rutherford Reserve Cabernet Sauvignon
Region: California $40
Golds/Awards: Gold (WWC-90 pts); Cellar Selection (WWC)

Folie à Deux 1995 Reserve Cabernet Sauvignon
Region: California, Napa Valley $24
Golds/Awards: Gold (LA); Double Gold (SF)

$Forest Glen 1993 Cabernet Sauvignon
Region: California $12
Golds/Awards: Gold (PR)

$Forest Glen 1994 Cabernet Sauvignon
Region: California $9.99
Golds/Awards: Gold (WC, OC)

Freemark Abbey 1992 Cabernet Sauvignon
Region: California $19
Golds/Awards: Gold (IV)

Freemark Abbey 1993 Cabernet Sauvignon
Region: California $18
Golds/Awards: Gold (IV)

Gallo Sonoma 1992 Estate Cabernet Sauvignon
Region: California, Northern Sonoma $45
Golds/Awards: Gold (AT, SD, WWC-91 pts); Double Gold (TG)

Did You Know . . . ?
The brothers Ernest and Julio Gallo started out in 1933 with a bank loan of $500 to buy winemaking equipment. Today Gallo is by far the largest wine company in the world.

Gallo Sonoma 1992 Frei Ranch Vineyard Cabernet Sauvignon
Region: California, Dry Creek Valley $18
Golds/Awards: Gold (IW)

Gallo Sonoma 1992 Library Estate Cabernet Sauvignon
Region: California, Northern Sonoma $45
Golds/Awards: Gold (SF)

Gallo Sonoma 1993 Estate Cabernet Sauvignon
Region: California, Northern Sonoma $18
Golds/Awards: Gold (LA); Best of Class (LA)

Gallo Sonoma 1993 Frei Ranch Vineyard Cabernet Sauvignon
Region: California, Dry Creek Valley $18
Golds/Awards: Gold (DA, LA, FF, NW, CA)

$Gallo Sonoma 1994 Frei Ranch Vineyard Cabernet Sauvignon
Region: Califonia, Sonoma Valley $14
Golds/Awards: Double Gold (SF); Best Cabernet Sauvignon (SF)

Geyser Peak 1993 Reserve Cabernet Sauvignon
Region: California, Alexander Valley $28
Golds/Awards: Gold (WS; WWC-90 pts)

Geyser Peak 1993 Winemaker's Selection Cabernet Sauvignon
Region: California, Alexander Valley $20
Golds/Awards: Gold (CA); Best of Class (CA)

Geyser Peak 1994 Trione Cellars Reserve Cabernet Sauvignon
Region: California, Alexander Valley $28
Golds/Awards: Gold (DA, SF)

Did You Know . . . ?
Henry T. Trione, chairman of Geyser Peak, has made it a tradition to assign dollar amounts to each award won at a major competition, and then to divide the money equally among his employees at the end of the year. Last year the lucky employees divided up $14.030!

Cabernet Sauvignon   RED

$Geyser Peak 1995 Cabernet Sauvignon
Region: California, Sonoma County $15
Golds/Awards: Double Gold (TG)

$Glen Ellen Expressions 1994 Cabernet Sauvignon
Region: California, North Coast $11
Golds/Awards: Gold (WC)

$Gordon Brothers 1992 Cabernet Sauvignon
Region: Washington, Columbia Valley $14.49
Golds/Awards: Gold (PR); Best of Class (PR)

Grgich Hills 1993 Cabernet Sauvignon
Region: California, Napa Valley $28
Golds/Awards: Gold (DA, WWC-91 pts); Double
Gold (TG)

Guenoc 1992 Beckstoffer Vineyard Cabernet Sauvignon
Region: California $40
Golds/Awards: Gold (WWC-90 pts)

Guenoc 1993 Bella Vista Cabernet Sauvignon
Region: California $25.50
Golds/Awards: Double Gold (TG)

Guenoc 1993 Beckstoffer Reserve Cabernet Sauvignon
Region: California, Napa Valley $40.50
Golds/Awards: Gold (AT)

Guenoc 1994 Bella Vista Reserve Cabernet Sauvignon
Region: California $25.50
Golds/Awards: Double Gold (TG); Gold (FF)

Guenoc 1994 Beckstoffer Reserve Cabernet Sauvignon
Region: California $40.50
Golds/Awards: Double Gold (TG); Gold (FF)

Hardys 1992 Thomas Hardy Cabernet Sauvignon
Region: Australia, Coonawarra $45
Golds/Awards: Gold (SY)

Did You Know . . . ?
The mouth and nose of Robert Parker, America's best-known wine writer, are insured for over a million dollars.

Cabernet Sauvignon   RED

Ⓟ**Hardys 1994 Cabernet Sauvignon**
Region: Australia, Coonawarra $17
Golds/Awards: Gold (BR)

$Haywood 1995 Vintner's Select Cabernet Sauvignon
Region: California $8
Golds/Awards: Gold (OC)

Hedges 1994 Cabernet Sauvignon
Region: Washington $20
Golds/Awards: Gold (SF)

Heitz 1991 Martha's Vineyard Cab. Sauvignon
Region: California, Napa Valley $65
Golds/Awards: Gold (AT, WWC-92 pts)

Heitz 1991 Trailside Vineyard Cabernet Sauvignon
Region: California, Napa Valley $45
Golds/Awards: Gold (WWC-92 pts)

Heitz 1992 Martha's Vineyard Cabernet Sauvignon
Region: California, Napa Valley $68
Golds/Awards: Gold (LA); Double Gold (SF)

Heitz 1992 Trailside Vineyard Cabernet Sauvignon
Region: California, Napa Valley $48
Golds/Awards: Double Gold (SF)

Helena View 1993 Cabernet Sauvignon
Region: California $20
Golds/Awards: Gold (WWC-93 pts)

Ⓟ**Henschke 1993 Cyril Henschke Cab. Sauvignon**
Region: Australia, Eden Valley $66
Golds/Awards: Gold (SY)

Did You Know . . . ?

You've heard of busts of Elvis, Elvis coasters, Elvis toilet paper holders . . . Now the list has expanded to wine. Graceland Cabernet is a new label, with a haunting image of Elvis's 21-year-old eyes just discernible in the background if you hold the label sideways. It retails for $22.50. (It hasn't won any gold medals yet, to my knowledge.)

⌂**Henschke 1994 Cyril Henschke Cabernet Sauvignon**
Region: Australia, Eden Valley $66
Golds/Awards: Gold (IV)

Hyatt 1992 Reserve Cabernet Sauvignon
Region: Washington, Yakima Valley $24.99
Golds/Awards: Gold (WWC-90 pts)

Hyatt 1994 Reserve Cabernet Sauvignon
Region: Washington, Yakima Valley $30
Golds/Awards: Gold (NE)

$**J. Lohr Winery 1994 Seven Oaks Cabernet Sauvignon**
Region: California, Paso Robles $14
Golds/Awards: Gold (PR)

$⌂**Jacob's Creek 1994 Cabernet Sauvignon**
Region: Australia $7.99
Golds/Awards: Gold (VL)

Jarvis 1993 Estate Grown Cave Fermented Cabernet Sauvignon
Region: California, Napa Valley $55
Golds/Awards: Gold (LA); Best of Class (LA)

$**Jodar Wine Company 1992 Cabernet Sauvignon**
Region: California, El Dorado $10.99
Golds/Awards: Gold (CA); Best of Class (CA)

Justin 1993 Cabernet Sauvignon
Region: California $18.50
Golds/Awards: Gold (WWC-90 pts)

Kathryn Kennedy 1992 Cabernet Sauvignon
Region: California $70
Golds/Awards: Gold (WWC-95 pts); National Champion Cabernet Sauvignon, Cellar Selection (WWC)

Did You Know . . . ?

In spite of, or perhaps because of, a booming U.S. wine market, France and Australia are spending ten to twenty times what American academic institutions now are willing to spend on viticultural and oenological research. Some American researchers are dismayed by this lack of U.S. foresight.

Cabernet Sauvignon   RED

Kendall-Jackson 1993 Grand Reserve Cabernet Sauvignon
Region: California $42
Golds/Awards: Great Gold Medal (BR); Gold (IV)

Kendall-Jackson 1994 Buckeye Vineyard Cabernet Sauvignon
Region: California, Alexander Valley $24
Golds/Awards: Gold (FF)

Kiona 1992 Cabernet Sauvignon
Region: Washington $20
Golds/Awards: Double Gold (TG); Gold (IV)

$Kiona 1995 Cabernet Sauvignon
*Region:*Washington $14.99
Golds/Awards: Gold (NW)

La Garza Cellars 1994 Cabernet Sauvignon
Region: Oregon, Umpqua Valley $20
Golds/Awards: Gold (PR)

$Lake Sonoma Winery 1993 Cabernet Sauvignon
Region: California, Sonoma $15
Golds/Awards: Double Gold (SF)

Lambert Bridge 1994 Cabernet Sauvignon
Region: California, Dry Creek Valley $20
Golds/Awards: Gold (SF)

Laurel Glen 1993 Cabernet Sauvignon
Region: California $40
Golds/Awards: Gold (WWC-90 pts)

$Lava Cap 1995 Cabernet Sauvignon
Region: California, El Dorado $15
Golds/Awards: Gold (CA)

Did You Know . . . ?
Ever wondered who's getting the money on a $20 bottle of California wine? Fifty percent, or $10, goes to the retailer; $2.80 is spent on marketing, administration, and distribution; $2.45 is the cost of the grapes; another $2.45 is spent on winemaking; 80 cents on interest payments; 75 cents on taxes; and the winery nets a 75-cent profit on each bottle, or 3.75 percent.

Cabernet Sauvignon   RED

Lewis Cellars 1993 Oakville Ranch Cabernet Sauvignon
Region: California $32
Golds/Awards: Gold (WWC-90 pts)

Liparita 1993 Cabernet Sauvignon
Region: California $32
Golds/Awards: Gold (WWC-92 pts)

Lockwood 1994 Estate Grown Estate Bottled Cabernet Sauvignon
Region: California, Monterey County $16
Golds/Awards: Gold (SD)

Louis M. Martini 1994 Monte Rosso Vineyard Cabernet Sauvignon
Region: California, Sonoma Valley $30
Golds/Awards: Gold (WC)

⌘**Magnotta 1991 Limited Edition Cab. Sauvignon**
Region: Canada $18
Golds/Awards: Gold (WS, IV)

$⌘**Manso de Velasco 1995 Cabernet Sauvignon**
Region: Chile, Curicó $14
Golds/Awards: Gold (BR)

Martin Ray 1993 Saratoga Cuvée Cabernet Sauvignon
Region: California $30
Golds/Awards: Gold (WWC-92 pts)

⌘**McGuigan Brothers 1994 Personal Reserve Cabernet**
Region: Australia, Southeast Region $19.99
Golds/Awards: Gold (WS)

$**Meeker 1993 Dry Creek Valley Gold Leaf Cuvée** (Cabernet Sauvignon)
Region: California, Sonoma County $15
Golds/Awards: Gold (OC)

Did You Know . . . ?
A 1996 Gallup poll determined that people were drinking 10% less alcohol than they did the year before. Only 58% of Americans drink alcohol, and the percentage of people who prefer wine is only 28%.

Cabernet Sauvignon   RED

$Meridian 1994 Cabernet Sauvignon
Region: California $11
Golds/Awards: Gold (PR, SD, OC)

Michel Schlumberger 1992 Schlumberger Reserve Cabernet Sauvignon
Region: California, Dry Creek Valley $35
Golds/Awards: Gold (CA)

Michel Schlumberger 1993 Cabernet Sauvignon
Region: California, Dry Creek Valley $19.50
Golds/Awards: Gold (CA)

Mirassou 1994 Harvest Reserve Cabernet Sauvignon
Region: California, Napa Valley $17.95
Golds/Awards: Gold (PR)

Monterey Peninsula 1987 Reserve Cabernet Sauvignon
Region: California, Monterey $25
Golds/Awards: Gold (AT)

Mount Veeder Winery 1993 Cabernet Sauvignon
Region: California $25
Golds/Awards: Gold (WWC-90 pts)

$Napa Ridge 1992 Reserve Cabernet Sauvignon
Region: California, Napa Valley $15
Golds/Awards: Gold (PR, WWC-90 pts)

$Napa Ridge 1993 Reserve Cabernet Sauvignon
Region: California, Napa Valley $15
Golds/Awards: Gold (NW)

$Napa Ridge 1995 Cabernet Sauvignon
Region: California, Napa Valley $9
Golds/Awards: Gold (WC); Best of Class (WC)

Did You Know . . . ?

The grain in a perfectly grown oak is so straight that the woodsman has only to give the wedge a tap and the wood splits almost perfectly into the desired 2-inch thickness for oak-barrel staves. This is the result of an oak's slow, steady maturation, with no growth spurts, over the course of about 200 years.

♪Neil Ellis 1993 Cabernet Sauvignon
Region: South Africa $16.99
Golds/Awards: Gold (WWC-90 pts); Cellar
Selection (WWC)

**$Nevada City 1994 Sierra Foothills Cabernet
Sauvignon**
Region: California, Nevada County $13
Golds/Awards: Gold (OC)

♪Orlando 1989 Jacaranda Ridge Cab. Sauvignon
Region: Australia, South Australia $35
Golds/Awards: Gold (IW)

Paradigm 1993 Cabernet Sauvignon
Region: California $30
Golds/Awards: Gold (WWC-92 pts); Cellar
Selection (WWC)

♪Parker 1994 Terra Rossa Cabernet Sauvignon
Region: Australia $24
Golds/Awards: Gold (WWC-91 pts); National
Champion Cabernet Sauvignon, Cellar Selection
(WWC)

**$Pedroncelli 1994 Three Vineyard Cabernet
Sauvignon**
Region: California, Dry Creek Valley $12.50
Golds/Awards: Gold (FF)

**$Pedroncelli 1995 Vintage Selection Cabernet
Sauvignon**
Region: California, Dry Creek Valley $10
Golds/Awards: Gold (OC)

Peju 1993 HB Vineyard Cabernet Sauvignon
Region: California $40
Golds/Awards: Gold (WWC-90 pts); Cellar
Selection (WWC)

Did You Know . . . ?
Carole Meridith, a wine-industry DNA detective, says it's
150 trillion times more likely that Cabernet Franc and
Sauvignon Blanc are the parents of Cabernet Sauvignon
than any other varieties. Cabernet Sauvignon probably
first appeared in the seventeeth century, an accident of
cross-pollination. Aren't you glad to know that?

Cabernet Sauvignon   RED

♫**Penfolds 1993 Bin 407 Cabernet Sauvignon**
Region: Australia, South Australia $17
Golds/Awards: Gold (AT)

♫**Penfolds 1993 Bin 707 Cabernet Sauvignon**
Region: Australia, South Australia $45
Golds/Awards: Gold (IW)

♫**Penley 1994 Cabernet Sauvignon**
Region: Australia, Coonawarra $40
Golds/Awards: Gold (IV)

♫**Petaluma 1993 Cabernet Sauvignon**
Region: Australia, Coonawarra $24.99
Golds/Awards: Gold (BR)

Plam 1993 Cabernet Sauvignon
Region: California, Napa Valley $35
Golds/Awards: Gold (PR, FF, WWC-92 pts);
Chairman's Award (FF); Cellar Selection (WWC)

Portteus 1993 Reserve Cabernet Sauvignon
Region: Washington $25
Golds/Awards: Gold (WWC-91 pts)

**Powers 1994 Mercer Ranch Vineyard Cabernet
Sauvignon**
Region: Washington $18
Golds/Awards: Gold (WWC-90 pts); Cellar
Selection (WWC)

Preston 1993 Cabernet Sauvignon Reserve
Region: Washington $21
Golds/Awards: Gold (AW)

Did You Know . . . ?
Equal pay for women in Australia, introduced in the
mid-1960s, changed the way Aussie wineries would
operate forever after. Wineries were forced to invest
money and research into mechanization alternatives.
As a result, it's more economical to grow and harvest
grapes in Australia now than it is in California.

Quail Ridge 1991 Cabernet Sauvignon Reserve
Region: California, Napa Valley $40
Golds/Awards: Gold (AT)

Raymond 1994 Cabernet Sauvignon Reserve
Region: California, Napa Valley $19
Golds/Awards: Gold (SD)

Renaissance 1994 Estate Cabernet Sauvignon
Region: California, North Yuba $16
Golds/Awards: Gold (CA)

Richardson 1994 Horne Vineyard Cabernet Sauvignon
Region: California, Sonoma Valley $18
Golds/Awards: Gold (WWC-90 pts)

Richardson 1995 Horne Vineyard Cabernet Sauvignon
Region: California, Sonoma Valley $18
Golds/Awards: Gold (SD, OC, SF); Four-Star Gold (OC)

Ridge 1991 Monte Bello Cabernet Sauvignon
Region: California, Santa Cruz $120
Golds/Awards: Gold (IW); Trophy for Best Bordeaux and Bordeaux-Style Wine (IW)

Ridge 1992 Monte Bello Cabernet Sauvignon
Region: California, Santa Cruz $80
Golds/Awards: Gold (WWC-94 pts); Cellar Selection (WWC)

Ridge 1993 Cabernet Sauvignon
Region: California $19
Golds/Awards: Gold (WWC-90 pts)

Robert Mondavi 1993 Cabernet Sauvignon
Region: California, Rutherford $20
Golds/Awards: Gold (AT, WWC-90 pts)

Did You Know . . . ?

Tea and well-made, tannic red wine have equally high levels of antioxidants, which are beneficial in preventing such illnesses as heart disease and cancer. It is thought that the alcohol in wine helps to stabilize the antioxidants and makes them easier for the body to absorb.

Cabernet Sauvignon   RED

Robert Mondavi 1993 Reserve Cabernet Sauvignon
Region: California $50
Golds/Awards: Gold (WWC-91 pts)

$Robert Mondavi 1994 Coastal Winery Cabernet Sauvignon
Region: California, North Coast $11
Golds/Awards: Gold (PR)

Rodney Strong 1993 Reserve Cabernet Sauvignon
Region: California, Northern Sonoma $30
Golds/Awards: Gold (OC); Double Gold (CA)

⌂Rosemount 1993 Show Reserve Cabernet Sauvignon
Region: Australia, Coonawarra $18.50
Golds/Awards: Gold (WS)

Rosenblum 1994 Yountville Vineyards Cabernet Sauvignon
Region: California, Napa Valley $20
Golds/Awards: Gold (NW)

Rosenblum 1995 Cabernet Sauvignon
Region: California, Napa Valley $33
Golds/Awards: Gold (SF)

Round Hill 1990 Van Asperen Signature Reserve Cabernet Sauvignon
Region: California, Napa Valley $30
Golds/Awards: Gold (WS)

Round Hill 1991 Van Asperen Signature Reserve Cabernet Sauvignon
Region: California $24
Golds/Awards: Double Gold (TG)

Did You Know . . . ?
Robert Mondavi is credited with doing more than anyone else to raise world consciousness about California
as the source for top-class wine. The Robert Mondavi
winery was at the forefront of developing varietal wines
based on Europe's most famous vine varieties.

Cabernet Sauvignon   RED

$Rutherford Vintners 1995 Barrel Select Cabernet Sauvignon
Region: California, Sonoma County $8.99
Golds/Awards: Double Gold (CA); Best of Class (CA)

St. Clement 1993 Cabernet Sauvignon
Region: California $23.50
Golds/Awards: Gold (WWC-91 pts)

St. Clement 1993 Howell Mountain Cabernet Sauvignon
Region: California $40
Golds/Awards: Gold (WWC-92 pts)

St. Francis 1992 Reserve Cabernet Sauvignon
Region: California $21.99
Golds/Awards: Gold (WWC-90 pts)

St. Francis 1993 Reserve Cabernet Sauvignon
Region: California $29
Golds/Awards: Gold (WWC-90 pts)

St. Hugo 1993 Coonawarra Cabernet Sauvignon
Region: Australia $17.99
Golds/Awards: Gold (VL)

$ Santa Digna 1995 Cabernet Sauvignon
Region: Chile, Curicó $6.99
Golds/Awards: Gold (BR)

Santa Rita 1994 Casa Réal, Old Vines Cabernet Sauvignon
Region: Chile $23
Golds/Awards: Gold (WWC-90 pts)

Seaview 1994 Edwards & Chaffey Cabernet Sauvignon
Region: Australia, McLaren Vale $21
Golds/Awards: Gold and Best of Category (SY)

Did You Know . . . ?

Wines produced in Chile's Maipo and Colchagua valleys, especially the Cabernets, benefit from a peculiar micro-climate that features sharp temperature swings between day and night, but virtually no risk of frost in the spring.

Cabernet Sauvignon RED

Sebastiani 1992 Cherryblock Old Vines Estate Bottled Cabernet Sauvignon
Region: California $40
Golds/Awards: Gold (SD)

$Sebastiani 1994 Cabernet Sauvignon
Region: California, Sonoma County $12.99
Golds/Awards: Gold (SD, FF)

Silverado 1993 Limited Reserve Cabernet Sauvignon
Region: California $48
Golds/Awards: Gold (WWC-93 pts)

Silver Oak 1991 Bonny's Vineyard Cabernet Sauvignon
Region: California $50
Golds/Awards: Gold (WWC-91 pts)

$Silver Ridge 1993 Cabernet Sauvignon
Region: California 9.99
Golds/Awards: Gold (NW); Best of Class (NW)

Soquel 1992 Cabernet Sauvignon
Region: California $18
Golds/Awards: Gold (WWC-90 pts)

Spottswoode 1993 Cabernet Sauvignon
Region: California $42
Golds/Awards: Gold (WWC-94 pts); Cellar Selection (WWC)

Stag's Leap 1993 Cask 23 Cabernet Sauvignon
Region: California $80
Golds/Awards: Gold (WWC-94 pts); Cellar Selection (WWC)

Stag's Leap 1993 Fay Cabernet Sauvignon
Region: California $40
Golds/Awards: Gold (AW, WWC-94 pts)

Did You Know . . . ?
Some Roman wines had great staying power. The famous Opimian wine, from the year of the consulship of Opimius, 121 BC, was being drunk when it was 125 years old.

Cabernet Sauvignon   RED

Stag's Leap 1993 Stag's Leap Vineyard Cabernet Sauvignon
Region: California
Golds/Awards: Gold (WWC-93 pts) $40

$Staton Hills 1992 Cabernet Sauvignon
Region: Washington, Yakima Valley
Golds/Awards: Gold (LA) $14.95

℗ **Stellenryck 1991 Cabernet Sauvignon**
Region: South Africa
Golds/Awards: Gold (VL) $16

$Stone Creek 1994 Special Selection Cabernet Sauvignon
Region: California
Golds/Awards: Gold (PR) $6.89

$Sutter Home 1992 Reserve Cabernet Sauvignon
Region: California, Napa Valley
Golds/Awards: Gold (OC) $11.95

Swanson 1993 Estate Cabernet Sauvignon
Region: California, Napa Valley
Golds/Awards: Gold (WS, WWC-93 pts) $22

$ ℗ **Swartland 1994 Cabernet Sauvignon**
Region: South Africa
Golds/Awards: Gold (WWC-90 pts); Best Buy (WWC) $9.99

$Taft Street 1995 Cabernet Sauvignon
Region: California
Golds/Awards: Gold (CA) $12

$Tessera 1995 Cabernet Sauvignon
Region: California
Golds/Awards: Gold (CA); Tie for Best of Region and Best of Class (CA) $9.99

Trefethen Vineyards 1994 Estate Cabernet Sauvignon
Region: California, Napa Valley
Golds/Awards: Double Gold (CA); Best of Class (CA) $24

Did You Know . . . ?
Plato advised no wine before the age of eighteen and moderation until thirty.

Cabernet Sauvignon   RED

$Trellis Vineyards 1995 Cabernet Sauvignon
Region: Cal., Sonoma C'nty/Alex. Valley $13.99
Golds/Awards: Gold (WC, SF)

Trentadue 1994 Estate Bottled Cabernet Sauvignon
Region: California, Dry Creek Valley $19
Golds/Awards: Gold (SD)

$Troon Vineyards 1995 Cabernet Sauvignon
Region: Oregon, Rogue Valley $13.50
Golds/Awards: Gold (OR)

$Turning Leaf 1993 Sonoma Reserve Wine-maker's Choice Barrel Aged Cabernet Sauvignon
Region: California, Sonoma County $10
Golds/Awards: Gold (OC)

$Twin Hills 1992 Cabernet Sauvignon
Region: California, Paso Robles $15
Golds/Awards: Gold (LA)

V. Sattui 1992 Reserve Cabernet Sauvignon
Region: California $60
Golds/Awards: Gold (WWC-92pts)
By mail-order only: (800) 799-2337

V. Sattui 1994 Morisoli Vineyard Cabernet Sauvignon
Region: California, Napa Valley $25
Golds/Awards: Double Gold (SF)
By mail-order only: (800) 799-2337

V. Sattui 1994 Preston Vineyard Cabernet Sauvignon
Region: California, Napa Valley $30
Golds/Awards: Gold (PR, NW, Springfest, Monterey Wine Fest, Wine Lovers International, Taster's Guild); Best of Class (NW)
By mail-order only: (800) 799-2337

Did You Know . . . ?
Wine critics agree: the 1994 vintage in California Cabernets was a great one. The only down side is that it was also a *small* one, so if you fall in love with a '94 Cab, call the winery and order a magnum.

V. Sattui 1994 Suzanne's Vineyard Cabernet Sauvignon
Region: California, Napa Valley $20
Golds/Awards: Double Gold (SF)
By mail-order only: (800) 799-2337

Venezia 1994 Meola Vineyards Cabernet Sauvignon
Region: California, Alexander Valley $20
Golds/Awards: Gold (PR, WC, FF); Best of Class (PR)

$Venezio Vineyard 1994 Cabernet Sauvignon
Region: California, El Dorado $10.50
Golds/Awards: Gold (OC)

Villa Mt. Eden 1993 Grand Reserve Cabernet Sauvignon
Region: California, Napa Valley $16
Golds/Awards: Gold (WWC-90 pts)

Villa Mt. Eden 1993 Signature Series Cabernet Sauvignon
Region: California $45
Golds/Awards: Gold (WWC-90 pts)

Villa Mt. Eden 1994 Grand Reserve Cabernet Sauvignon
Region: California, Napa Valley $18
Golds/Awards: Gold (WC, CA)

$ Vina Gracia 1994 Premium Cabernet Sauvignon
Region: Chile, Cachapoal Valley $12.99
Golds/Awards: Gold (VN, BR)

$ Vina Tarapaca 1992 Gran Reserva Cabernet
Region: Chile $15
Golds/Awards: Gold (WWC-90 pts)

$W.B. Bridgman 1993 Cabernet Sauvignon
Region: Washington $11.99
Golds/Awards: Gold (WWC-90 pts); Best Buy (WWC)

Did You Know . . . ?
It is generally agreed that Spanish settlers brought the vine to Chile some time in the 1550s.

Waterbrook 1994 Cabernet Sauvignon
Region: Washington $19.99
Golds/Awards: Gold (DA, WWC-92 pts); Cellar
Selection (WWC)

$Weinstock 1995 Cabernet Sauvignon
Region: California $10.99
Golds/Awards: Double Gold (CA); Best of Class (CA)

**$Wellington 1993 Mohrardt Ridge Vineyard
Cabernet Sauvignon**
Region: California $14
Golds/Awards: Gold (WWC-90 pts)

**$Wellington 1993 Random Ridge Cabernet
Sauvignon**
Region: California, Mount Veeder $15
Golds/Awards: Gold (SD)

Whitehall Lane 1994 Cabernet Sauvignon
Region: California $19
Golds/Awards: Gold (WWC-91 pts)

**Whitehall Lane 1994 Morisoli Vineyard Reserve
Cabernet Sauvignon**
Region: California $36
Golds/Awards: Gold (LA)

Whitehall Lane 1995 Cabernet Sauvignon
Region: California, Napa Valley $20
Golds/Awards: Gold (SF)

Windsor Vineyards 1993 Cabernet Sauvignon
Region: California, Sonoma County $20
Golds/Awards: Gold (NW, WWC-90 pts, CA)
By mail order only: (800) 333-9987

$Windsor Vineyards 1994 Cabernet Sauvignon
Region: California, Sonoma County $11
Golds/Awards: Gold (SD)
By mail order only: (800) 333-9987

Did You Know . . . ?
When oak-barrel staves are cut from a large tree, 70%
of the tree is wasted.

Yakima River 1992 Reserve Cabernet Sauvignon
Region: Washington $19.99
Golds/Awards: Gold (WWC-92 pts)

York Mountain 1991 Cabernet Sauvignon
Region: California, San Luis Obispo $16
Golds/Awards: Gold (LA)

$Zabaco 1993 Cabernet Sauvignon
Region: California, Sonoma County $9
Golds/Awards: Gold (FF)

ZD Wines 1994 Cabernet Sauvignon
Region: California $30
Golds/Awards: Double Gold (TG)

Did You Know . . . ?

In New England, some states still ban the sale of alcohol on Sundays, a remnant of the seventeenth-century "blue laws," drawn up by the Puritanical colonists who believed Sundays should remain sacred. The blue laws got their name because they were among the laws printed in the 1600s on blue paper.

Italian Varietals

If you're looking for a "new" red wine, don't overlook the great Italian varietals coming out of California and to a lesser degree Argentina. Transplanted Italian winemakers introduced these varieties to American soil and have started a trend that's meeting with commercial success and worldwide recognition. Italian-style wines stand up to hearty dishes such as beef, sausage, rabbit, and of course garlicky, tomato-sauced Italian cuisine.

Aglianico Not common in southern Italy, and even less common in California, this variety can produce deep ruby red wines with full flavor and powerful, intense aromas.

Barbera This was the fourth leading red wine variety grown in California until twenty-some years ago. Until recently it was relegated to the role of jug wine, or merely a blending agent to enhance its more powerful cousins, Nebbiolo and Sangiovese. But Barbera is now undergoing a change in reputation similar to that of Sauvignon Blanc, as fine California and Argentinean Barberas hit the market. In cooler regions Barbera becomes rich and complex; in hot climates it produces a light fruity wine.

Dolcetto Common in Italy, this grape produces easy-going, fruity, fragrant reds with flavors and aromas reminiscent of almonds and licorice.

Nebbiolo This is one of Italy's two finest grapes, Sangiovese being the other. It is responsible for some of that country's best wines, among them world-famous Barbaresco and Barolo. In both South and North America, Nebbiolo is making its presence known. A great Nebbiolo can be long-lived, tannic, acidic, alcoholic, richly textured, and big, big, big. Nebbiolo almost always requires aging in order to reach its full potential.

Sangiovese Because it ripens slowly and late, the Sangiovese variety can yield rich, alcoholic, long-lived red wines with cherry and plummy flavors. It can also be made into light, fresh and fruity, early-drinking reds.

$Abundance 1994 Vintner's Preferred Sangiovese
Region: California $9.99
Golds/Awards: Gold (NW); Best of Class (NW)

Adler Fels 1995 Sangiovese
Region: California, Mendocino County $16
Golds/Awards: Gold (SD)

Atlas Peak 1994 Reserve Sangiovese
Region: California, Napa Valley $24
Golds/Awards: Gold (AT, CA)

Atlas Peak 1995 Sangiovese
Region: California, Napa Valley $16
Golds/Awards: Gold (WC)

$Bargetto 1996 Dolcetto
Region: California, Central Coast $15
Golds/Awards: Gold (CA); Best of Class (CA)

Beaulieu 1995 Signet Collection Sangiovese
Region: California, Napa Valley $16
Golds/Awards: Gold (CA)

Bella Vista 1995 Sangiovese
Region: California, Solano County $20
Golds/Awards: Gold (WWC-90 pts)

Benziger 1994 Imagery Series Larga Vista Vineyards Sangiovese
Region: California, Dry Creek Valley $17.99
Golds/Awards: Gold (PR, LA, NW, WWC-92 pts); Best of Class (PR)

$Boeger 1994 Vineyard Select Barbera
Region: California, El Dorado $15
Golds/Awards: Gold (CA); Best of Region and Best of Class (CA)

Did You Know . . . ?
The Sangiovese vine is of ancient origin, as its name suggests. Literally translated, it means "blood of Jove." Some believe it was even known to the Etruscans.

Italian Varietals   RED

**Bonterra 1994 Organically Grown Grapes
Sangiovese**
Region: California, Mendocino County $22
Golds/Awards: Gold (PR, WWC-90 pts)

Cambria 1994 Tepusquet Sangiovese
Region: California, Santa Maria Valley $25
Golds/Awards: Gold (NW)

$Chameleon Cellars 1995 Sangiovese
Region: California $15
Golds/Awards: Gold (DA, PR)

**Coturri 1995 Poggio alla Pietra Vineyards
Sangiovese**
Region: California, Sonoma Valley $35
Golds/Awards: Gold (WWC-91 pts); Cellar
Selection (WWC)

$Folie à Deux 1995 Sangiovese
Region: California, Napa Valley $15
Golds/Awards: Gold (NW)

Indian Springs 1995 Sangiovese
Region: California, Nevada County $16
Golds/Awards: Gold (PR, NW); Best of Class (NW)

Martin Brothers 1994 Vecchio Nebbiolo
Region: California, Central Coast $20
Golds/Awards: Gold (WWC-94 pts)

Neb 1994 Nebbiolo
Region: California, Sonoma County $18
Golds/Awards: Gold (OC)

Orfila Vineyards 1995 Sangiovese
Region: California $18
Golds/Awards: Double Gold (TG); Gold (SF,
Monterey, Hilton Head, Wine Lovers International)

Did You Know . . . ?
Product endorsement was not unknown to Roman Italy.
Augustus's wife, Livia, gave a boost to the sale of wines
from the Fruili region by declaring that they were the
reason for her good health and ripe old age.

Italian Varietals RED

Rabbit Ridge 1994 Nebbiolo
Region: California $18
Golds/Awards: Gold (PR, OC); Four-Star Gold (OC)

Ramsay 1995 Aglianico
Region: California $21
Golds/Awards: Gold (CA); Best of Class (CA)

Renwood 1995 Linsteadt Vineyard Barbera
Region: California, Amador County $24
Golds/Awards: Gold (WWC-90 pts)

Robert Pepi 1994 Two-Heart Canopy Sangiovese
Region: California $18
Golds/Awards: Gold (PR)

Sebastiani 1994 Sonoma Cask Barbera
Region: California, Sonoma County $20
Golds/Awards: Gold (LA, OC, NW); Best of Class (NW); Best New World Barbera (NW)

Solis 1995 Estate Vineyard Sangiovese
Region: California, Santa Clara Valley $16.95
Golds/Awards: Gold (CA); Best of Class (CA)

Swanson 1994 Estate Bottled Sangiovese
Region: California, Napa Valley $22
Golds/Awards: Gold (DA)

Swanson 1995 Estate Bottled Sangiovese
Region: California, Napa Valley $24
Golds/Awards: Gold (FF); Double Gold (CA); Best of Class (CA)

$Temecula Crest 1995 Nebbiolo
Region: California, Temecula $15
Golds/Awards: Gold (NW); Best of Price Class (NW); Best New World Nebbiolo (NW)

Did You Know . . . ?
Men and women who consumed up to two drinks per day decreased their risk of stroke by 45%, according to a study of 1,200 Manhattanites.

Italian Varietals RED

Venezia 1995 Eagle Point Ranch Sangiovese
Region: California, Mendocino County $24
Golds/Awards: Double Gold (CA); Best of
California and Best of Class (CA)

Venezia 1995 Nuovo Mondo Sangiovese
Region: California $24
Golds/Awards: Double Gold (TG); Gold (SD, CA);
Best of Class (SD, CA)

Venezia 1995 Trione Vineyard Sangiovese
Region: California, Alexander Valley $24
Golds/Awards: Gold (WC, NW); Best of Class (WC)

$Vino Noceto 1995 Sangiovese
Region: California, Shenandoah Valley $12
Golds/Awards: Gold (CA); Best of Region and Best
of Class (CA)

> ### *Did You Know . . . ?*
> Wine writer Matt Kramer lists some "truths" about
> wine: (1) The final glass of wine from a bottle always
> tastes the best. (2) Expensive wine tastes better when
> someone else is paying. (3) All wines taste better in the
> winery tasting room/restaurant/friend's house than they
> do once they're on your table.

Merlot

Is there anyone who doesn't like Merlot? This charming varietal is soft, fruity, and has a supple personality characterized by an array of wonderful flavors and aromas, among them black cherries, plums, fruitcake, caramel, herbs, and sometimes a hint of orange peel. A typical Merlot may also often have high alcohol and a lush, chewy texture.

California, Washington State, and even Long Island, New York, are among the New World regions where the Merlot grape is thriving in the nineties, as well as New Zealand, Australia, and South America, particularly Chile, where amazing bargains can be found.

In the next few years consumers are apt to see this varietal more and more. It's enjoying such a surge in popularity that some call Merlot "the new Chardonnay," since it's easy to drink but offers the health benefits of red wine.

Because it has what Cabernet Sauvignon lacks, Merlot is often used to soften the latter in Bordeaux-style blends (also known as red Meritage). But increasingly, it's found the other way around: as the base varietal, with small amounts of Cabernet Sauvignon added to the Merlot to give it more structure and focus.

Less tannic than Cab, Merlot can be enjoyed sooner rather than cellared for years. Serve it with chicken, duck, ham, and turkey, as well as Mediterranean dishes and even spicy Chinese foods. Or sip it before dinner alongside soft cheeses.

Merlot   RED

Alderbrook 1995 Kunde Vineyard Merlot
Region: California, Sonoma Valley $22
Golds/Awards: Gold (PR, LA, NW, SF); Best
of Class (PR, NW)

Andrew Will 1994 Merlot
Region: Washington $25
Golds/Awards: Gold (WWC-90 pts); Cellar
Selection (WWC)

Andrew Will 1994 Reserve Merlot
Region: Washington $28
Golds/Awards: Gold (WWC-91 pts); Cellar
Selection (WWC)

Apex 1994 Merlot
Region: Washington, Columbia Valley $28.99
Golds/Awards: Gold (WWC-92 pts)

Arrowood 1993 Merlot
Region: California, Sonoma County $35.99
Golds/Awards: Gold (WWC-93 pts)

Bargetto 1995 Merlot
Region: California $18
Golds/Awards: Gold (WC)

Barnard Griffin 1994 Reserve Merlot
Region: Washington, Columbia Valley $24
Golds/Awards: Gold (WWC-92 pts)

**Bartholomew Park Winery 1995 Desnudos
Vineyard Merlot**
Region: California, Sonoma Valley $22
Golds/Awards: Gold (FF)

$Bel Arbor 1996 Vintner's Selection Merlot
Region: California/Chile $6.99
Golds/Awards: Gold (PR)

Did You Know . . . ?
The ancient Persians, according to Greek writer Herodo-
tus (490–425 BC), believed that any decision made
when sober had to be reconsidered when drunk.

Merlot   RED

Bella Vista 1995 Estate Merlot
Region: California, Solano County $18
Golds/Awards: Gold (LA, CA); Best of Region
and Best of Class (CA)

Benziger 1994 Estate Tribute Merlot
Region: California, Sonoma County $25
Golds/Awards: Gold (WWC-92 pts); Cellar
Selection (WWC)

Benziger 1995 Merlot
Region: California, Sonoma County $16
Golds/Awards: Four-Star Gold (OC); Gold (CA);
Best of Class (CA)

**Beringer 1993 Bancroft Ranch Estate Bottled
Merlot**
Region: California, Howell Mountain $40
Golds/Awards: Gold (SD, WWC-93 pts); Cellar
Selection (WWC)

Bridgeview 1995 Black Beauty Merlot
Region: Oregon $16.99
Golds/Awards: Gold (OR)

Byington 1994 Bradford Mountain Merlot
Region: California, Sonoma County $18
Golds/Awards: Gold (WWC-90 pts)

Cafaro 1993 Merlot
Region: California, Napa Valley $28
Golds/Awards: Gold (WWC-90 pts); Cellar
Selection (WWC)

Canoe Ridge Vineyard 1994 Merlot
Region: Washington, Columbia Valley $18
Golds/Awards: Gold (WWC-90 pts)

Did You Know . . . ?
Benziger offers a tram tour of their vineyards, where
visitors learn how grapes are grown, how rootstocks are
grafted, environmental farming practices, etc. Over-
whelmingly positive responses indicate that tourists
want to know more about wine than merely how it
tastes.

Merlot   RED

$ ⌂ Casa LaPostolle 1995 Cuvée Alexandre Estate Merlot
Region: Chile, Rapel Valley $15
Golds/Awards: Gold (SF)

$Cedar Brook Winery 1995 Merlot
Region: California, $8.99
Golds/Awards: Double Gold (CA); Best of Class (CA)

Charles Krug 1993 Reserve Merlot
Region: California, Napa Valley $21.50
Golds/Awards: Gold (NW)

$Charles Krug 1995 Merlot
Region: California, Napa Valley $15
Golds/Awards: Gold (LA)

$ ⌂ Chateau La Joya 1996 Merlot
Region: Chile, Colchagua Valley $9.99
Golds/Awards: Gold (BR)

Chateau St. Jean 1992 Reserve Merlot
Region: California, Sonoma County $35
Golds/Awards: Gold (LA)

Chateau St. Jean 1994 Merlot
Region: California $18
Golds/Awards: Double Gold (TG)

Chateau Ste. Michelle 1993 Cold Creek Merlot
Region: Washington, Columbia Valley $29.99
Golds/Awards: Gold (WS)

Chateau Ste. Michelle 1994 Chateau Reserve Merlot
Region: Washington, Columbia Valley $40
Golds/Awards: Platinum (WWC-96 pts); National Champion Merlot, Cellar Selection (WWC)

Chateau Ste. Michelle 1994 Merlot
Region: Washington, Columbia Valley $18
Golds/Awards: Double Gold (TG)

Did You Know . . . ?
An interesting website that features all the latest news about wine can be found at http://www.wineinstitute.org.

Chateau Ste. Michelle 1994 Cold Creek Vineyard Merlot
Region: Washington, Columbia Valley $28
Golds/Awards: Gold (FF, NW, WWC-92 pts); Chairman's Award (FF); Cellar Selection (WWC)

Chateau Ste. Michelle 1994 Indian Wells Vineyard Merlot
Region: Washington, Columbia Valley $30
Golds/Awards: Gold (FF, NW, WWC-90 pts); Best of Class (NW); Cellar Selection (WWC)

$Chateau Souverain 1994 Merlot
Region: California, Alexander Valley $13.50
Golds/Awards: Gold (AT)

Chateau Souverain 1995 Merlot
Region: California, Alexander Valley $16.50
Golds/Awards: Gold (SD, WC); Best of Class (SD)

CJ Pask 1995 Merlot
Region: New Zealand $18.99
Golds/Awards: Gold (IV)

$Columbia Crest 1994 Merlot
Region:.Washington, Columbia Valley $11
Golds/Awards: Gold (NW); Best of Class (NW); Best New World Merlot (NW)

Columbia Winery 1994 Red Willow Vineyard David Lake Signature Series Merlot
Region: Washington, Yakima Valley $23
Golds/Awards: Gold (WWC-90 pts); Cellar Selection (WWC)

Cottonwood Canyon 1994 Merlot
Region: California, Central Coast $24.50
Golds/Awards: Gold (WWC-90 pts)

Did You Know . . . ?
A lot of wineries suffered damage in the last major California earthquake, Loma Prieta, mostly in the form of packaged goods thrown to the floor.

Merlot   RED

Crichton Hall 1994 Merlot
Region: California, Napa Valley $24
Golds/Awards: Gold (WWC-90 pts)

$Domaine St. George 1994 Premier Cuvée
  Merlot
Region: California $11.99
Golds/Awards: Gold (IV)

Dry Creek Vineyard 1994 Reserve Merlot
Region: California, Dry Creek Valley $30
Golds/Awards: Gold (SF, WWC-90 pts)

Dry Creek Vineyard 1995 Twenty-Fifth
Anniversary Merlot
Region: California, Sonoma County $18.75
Golds/Awards: Gold (WC, OC); Best of
Class (WC); Four-Star Gold (OC)

Duckhorn 1994 Merlot
Region: California, Napa Valley $26
Golds/Awards: Gold (WWC-91 pts); Cellar
Selection (WWC)

Ehlers Grove 1995 Merlot Reserve
Region: California $25
Golds/Awards: Double Gold (TG)

$⌂Eikendal 1996 Merlot
Region: South Africa $13.99
Golds/Awards: Gold (VL)

$⌂Fairview 1994 Merlot
Region: South Africa $14.99
Golds/Awards: Gold (WWC-90 pts)

$Forest Glen 1995 Merlot
Region: California $9.99
Golds/Awards: Gold (NW); Best of Class (NW)

Did You Know . . . ?
Your bottle has been stored/transported improperly if:
(1) It has a slightly popped-up cork; (2) There's seepage
around the rim of the bottle; or (3) You see excessive air
space (more than 1/8 inch) beneath the cork.

Merlot   RED

Foxen 1994 Merlot
Region: California, South Central Coast $22
Golds/Awards: Gold (WWC-90 pts)

$Fox Hollow 1996 Merlot
Region: California $8.99
Golds/Awards: Gold (LA, WC); Best of Class (LA)

Geyser Peak 1994 Merlot
Region: California, Sonoma County $16
Golds/Awards: Gold (CA)

Geyser Peak 1994 Reserve Merlot
Region: California, Sonoma County $32
Golds/Awards: Gold (PR, WC); Best of Class (PR)

$Gold Hill 1994 Estate Bottled Merlot
Region: California, El Dorado $15
Golds/Awards: Gold (WC)

$Grand Cru 1996 Merlot
Region: California $7.99
Golds/Awards: Gold (NW)

Hamilton 1996 Ewell Reserve Merlot
Region: Australia, McLaren Vale $22.25
Golds/Awards: Gold (BR)

Hawthorne Mountain Vineyard Merlot
Region: Canada $13.49
Golds/Awards: Gold (WWC-90 pts)

Hyatt 1993 Reserve Merlot
Region: Washington, Yakima Valley $32
Golds/Awards: Gold (AT); Gold (Northwest
Enological Society)

Hyatt 1994 Reserve Merlot
Region: Washington, Yakima Valley $29.99
Golds/Awards: Gold (WWC-90 pts); Cellar
Selection (WWC)

Did You Know . . . ?
The UK is the number one market for American wines
from the Pacific Northwest.

Merlot

Jarvis 1994 Estate Grown Cave Fermented Merlot
Region: California, Napa Valley $45
Golds/Awards: Gold (LA)

Kendall-Jackson 1994 Grand Reserve Unfiltered Merlot
Region: California $42
Golds/Awards: Gold (SD, LA); Best of Class (LA)

Kenwood 1994 Jack London Vineyard Merlot
Region: California, Sonoma Valley $25
Golds/Awards: Gold (WWC-90 pts); Cellar Selection (WWC)

Kiona 1995 Merlot
Region: Washington $18
Golds/Awards: Gold (IV)

L'Ecole No. 41 1994 Merlot
Region: Washington, Columbia Valley $22
Golds/Awards: Gold (WWC-92 pts)

$Lorval Wines 1995 Merlot
Region: Texas $8.99
Golds/Awards: Gold (AW)

Louis M. Martini 1994 Reserve Merlot
Region: California, Russian River Valley $18
Golds/Awards: Gold (LA)

♫Magnotta 1991 Limited Edition Merlot
Region: Canada $18
Golds/Awards: Gold (VL, IV, WWC-91 pts); Best Buy (WWC)

> ### *Did You Know . . . ?*
> Karaoke for opera lovers? California's Jarvis, known for its cave winery complete with lasers, babbling brook, and crystals, is now sponsoring sing-along arias the first Saturday of every month at its Jarvis Conservatory in downtown Napa. The audience follows the lyrics with the help of subtitles.

Merlot

Matanzas Creek 1992 Journey Merlot
Region: California, Sonoma Valley $125
Golds/Awards: Gold (WWC-95 pts); Cellar
Selection (WWC)

Matanzas Creek 1993 Merlot
Region: California, Sonoma Valley $48
Golds/Awards: Gold (WS, WWC-90 pts)

$M.G. Vallejo 1995 Merlot
Region: California $6.99
Golds/Awards: Double Gold (TG)

Murphy-Goode 1995 Murphy Ranches Estate Merlot
Region: California, Alexander Valley, $18
Golds/Awards: Gold (CA)

$Nevada City 1994 Sierra Foothills Merlot
Region: California, Nevada County $14
Golds/Awards: Gold (OC)

Newton 1994 Merlot
Region: California, Napa Valley $28
Golds/Awards: Gold (WWC-90 pts)

$Page Mill 1994 O'Shaughnessy Vineyard Merlot
Region: California, Napa Valley $15
Golds/Awards: Gold (WWC-90 pts)

Pahlmeyer 1994 Merlot
Region: California, Napa Valley $28
Golds/Awards: Gold (WWC-92 pts); Cellar
Selection (WWC)

**$Patrick M. Paul 1993 Conner Lee Vineyards
Merlot**
Region: Washington, Columbia Valley $12
Golds/Awards: Gold (WWC-90 pts); Cellar
Selection and Best Buy (WWC)

Did You Know . . . ?
When taking the notoriously difficult examination to
become a Master of Wine, each candidate must describe, evaluate, and correctly identify up to twelve
unmarked wines. These wines can come from anywhere
in the world.

Merlot   RED

Plam 1994 Vintner's Reserve Merlot
Region: California, Napa Valley $25
Golds/Awards: Gold (NW, WWC-92 pts)

$Plum Creek Cellars 1994 Merlot
Region: Colorado $12.99
Golds/Awards: Gold (AW)

Ravenswood 1994 Merlot
Region: California, Carneros $26.50
Golds/Awards: Gold (WWC-90 pts)

Richardson 1995 Merlot
Region: California, Carneros $18
Golds/Awards: Gold (PR)

Robert Keenan 1994 Merlot
Region: California, Napa Valley $28
Golds/Awards: Gold (SF); Best Merlot (SF)

Robert Mondavi 1994 Unfiltered Merlot
Region: California, Napa Valley $22
Golds/Awards: Gold (NW)

**Robert Pecota 1994 Steven Andre Vineyard
Merlot**
Region: California, Napa Valley $25
Golds/Awards: Gold (WWC-90 pts)

Rodney Strong 1994 Merlot
Region: California, Sonoma County $16
Golds/Awards: Gold (OC, NW)

$Rutherford Ranch 1995 Merlot
Region: California, Napa Valley $11
Golds/Awards: Gold (CA); Best of Class (CA)

S. Anderson 1994 Reserve Merlot
Region: California, Napa Valley $28
Golds/Awards: Gold (WWC-95 pts)

Did You Know . . . ?
The earliest hangover cure appears in an early
Mesopotamian tablet, which recommends licorice,
beans, and wine. These are to be administered before
sunrise and before the inflicted one has been kissed.

Merlot   RED

St. Clement Vineyards 1994 Merlot
Region: California $24
Golds/Awards: Double Gold (TG)

St. Julian 1995 Merlot
Region: Michigan, Lake Michigan Shore $20
Golds/Awards: Gold (AW)

$ ⌂ Santa Carolina 1995 Reserve Merlot
Region: Chile, San Fernando Valley $8.99
Golds/Awards: Gold (SY)

$Sebastiani 1994 Sonoma Cask Merlot
Region: California, Sonoma County $14.99
Golds/Awards: Gold (AT, OC)

Sebastiani Estate 1994 Town Merlot
Region: California, Sonoma Valley $25
Golds/Awards: Gold (NW)

Selby 1994 Merlot
Region: California, Sonoma County $25
Golds/Awards: Gold (NW)

Seven Hills 1993 Merlot
Region: Washington, Walla Walla Valley $20
Golds/Awards: Gold (WS)

Seven Hills 1994 Seven Hills Vineyard Merlot
Region: Washington, Walla Walla Valley $24
Golds/Awards: Gold (WWC-90 pts); Cellar
Selection (WWC)

Seven Hills 1995 Klipson Vineyard Merlot
Region: Oregon $24
Golds/Awards: Gold (NE)

Seven Hills 1995 Seven Hills Vineyard Merlot
Region: Washington, Walla Walla Valley $24
Golds/Awards: Gold (OR)

Did You Know . . . ?
In Europe, wine bottles are reprocessed as many as
eight or nine times before they're crushed and remade.

Merlot   RED

Shafer 1994 Merlot
Region: California, Napa Valley $26
Golds/Awards: Gold (WWC-90 pts)

Silverado 1994 Merlot
Region: California, Napa Valley $20
Golds/Awards: Gold (WWC-90 pts); Cellar
Selection (WWC)

Silver Lake Winery 1993 Merlot Reserve
Region: Washington, Columbia Valley $25
Golds/Awards: Double Gold (TG); Gold (SD);
Best of Class (SD)

Stonestreet 1994 Estate Merlot
Region: California, Alexander Valley $30
Golds/Awards: Gold (LA)

Storrs 1994 Aron Michael Cuvée Merlot
Region: California, San Ysidro District $28
Golds/Awards: Double Gold (SF)

Swanson 1995 Estate Merlot
Region: California, Napa Valley $24
Golds/Awards: Gold (WC)

$Taft Street 1994 Merlot
Region: California, Sonoma County $14
Golds/Awards: Gold (PR)

Tefft Cellars 1994 Winemaker's Reserve Merlot
Region: Washington, Yakima Valley $25
Golds/Awards: Gold (WWC-92 pts); Cellar
Selection (WWC)

Villa Mt.Eden 1994 Grand Reserve Merlot
Region: California, Napa Valley $16
Golds/Awards: Gold (FF)

$⌂Vina Tarapaca 1995 Reserve Merlot
Region: Chile $9
Golds/Awards: Double Gold (TG)

Did You Know . . . ?
According to some estimates, 25% of all alcoholic beverages consumed in Canada are illegally imported. The
reason is because of the Canadian government's mark-
ups, which can be as high as 300+%.

Merlot   RED

Waterbrook 1994 Merlot
Region: Washington, Columbia Valley $19.99
Golds/Awards: Gold (WWC-93 pts)

**Whitehall Lane 1994 Leonardini Vineyard
Reserve Merlot**
Region: California, Napa Valley $32
Golds/Awards: Gold (WWC-94 pts)

Whitehall Lane 1995 Merlot
Region: California, Napa Valley $20
Golds/Awards: Gold (SD)

$Wildhurst 1995 Merlot
Region: California $12
Golds/Awards: Gold (WWC-90 pts); Best
Buy (WWC)

William Hill 1994 Merlot
Region: California, Napa Valley $18
Golds/Awards: Gold (PR)

Windsor 1994 Shelton Signature Merlot
Region: California, Sonoma County $23.55
Golds/Awards: Gold (WC, CA); Best of California
and Best of Class (CA)
By mail order only: (800) 333-9987

Woodward Canyon 1994 Merlot
Region: Washington, Columbia Valley $28
Golds/Awards: Gold (WWC-91 pts); Cellar
Selection (WWC)

℞**Yalumba 1993 Heggies Vineyard Merlot**
Region: Australia, Eden Valley $16
Golds & Awards: Gold (WS)

$York Mountain 1994 Merlot
Region: California, San Luis Obispo $14
Golds/Awards: Gold (WC)

**$Yorkville Cellars 1995 Organically Grown
Merlot**
Region: California, Mendocino County $15
Golds/Awards: Gold (WC)

Did You Know . . . ?
The average life expectancy of a cork tree is 170 years.

Miscellaneous Varietal Reds

There are many varietals of wine in the world, but the ones most of us see—and buy—in the store constitute a more modest selection. In fact, I was recently chatting with the owner of a small but excellent wine shop in Connecticut who complained that he never knows where to shelf the odd varietal. As a result, he often doesn't stock, say, the Malbec or the Rhône red.

I have a similar dilemma. All of the wines in this section were excellent enough to win the highest medal at one or more top competition. Yet they're not numerous enough to make up their own sections. Therefore, I've had to lump the less common reds all together.

Don't be put off by these offbeat varietals. Give them a try. You may fall in love with a type of red you've never experienced before and can get your winemonger to start stocking it.

Alicante Bouschet Often used as a blending agent, it makes a deep-purple-colored wine that tends to be high in alcohol with robust fruitiness.

Carignane A red Rhône grape capable of producing rich, spicy, earthy wines. Often used in Rhône-style blends.

Cinsault The Cinsault (often spelled Cinsaut) grape makes wines that are typically light, soft, and aromatic. Sometimes used to make rosés.

Durif An uncommon red wine grape that seems to do better in the New World than in its native France.

Gamay/Gamay Beaujolais American Gamays are no relation whatsoever to the French grape, Gamay Noir à Jus Blanc, of the Beaujolais region. And in fact, the French wine community is as grouchy about Americans calling their wine Gamay, Napa Gamay, or Gamay Beaujolais as they are with our generic term *champagne* for sparkling wines. Nevertheless, Gamay and Gamay Beaujolais, which are actually made from a grape that's related to Pinot Noir, as well as the unrelated Napa Gamay, made from a little-known French grape called

Valdiguié, are all reminiscent of a nice Beaujolais in that they are light, fruity, simple, and generally inexpensive. Gamays are meant to be consumed young.

Grenache Often used in spicy Rhône-style red blends, Grenache is also used to make light and fruity rosés.

Lemberger Mostly found in the state of Washington, this German red wine grape produces fresh and fruity, light red wines meant to be drunk young.

Malbec You're apt to see more and more of this varietal, particularly from Argentina and, to a lesser degree, California. Often used in Bordeaux-style red blends, Malbec at its best is richly concentrated with gamey, intense flavors and great aging potential because of its high tannin levels.

Petite Verdot Another classic Bordeaux red, Petite Verdot is fairly new to California and is usually used to make Red Meritage. It has many of the same strengths as Cabernet Sauvignon: rich color, hefty tannins, and excellent flavor concentration.

Pinotage A cross between Pinot Noir and Cinsault, this is South Africa's own wine grape, although New Zealand is beginning to plant some, and other countries may follow suit. It can produce either a Gamay-like light red, or a more serious, robust, Cabernet-style red that calls for serious aging in the bottle.

Mourvèdre A Rhône red varietal with plenty of structure, intense fruit, and blackberry perfume. Often used in Rhône-style blends.

Tannat Viejo A deeply colored and tannic red wine reminiscent of Nebbiolo and grown mostly in South America.

Valdiguié See Gamay.

Alban 1994 Reva Estate Grenache
Region: California $28
Golds/Awards: Gold (WWC-92 pts); Cellar
Selection (WWC)

$Baron Herzog 1996 Gamay
Region: California, Paso Robles $6.99
Golds/Awards: Gold (LA)

Chateau Lorane 1993 Durif
Region: Oregon $18
Golds/Awards: Gold (OR)

Edgewood Estate 1993 Malbec
Region: California, Napa Valley $18
Golds/Awards: Gold (PR, NW); Best of Class (NW)

$Fetzer 1995 Gamay Beaujolais
Region: California, Mendocino County $6.99
Golds/Awards: Gold (NW); Best of Class (NW)

$Fetzer 1996 Gamay Beaujolais
Region: California $6.99
Golds/Awards: Gold (LA, OC, CA); Best of
Class (CA)

$Galleano 1996 Carignane
Region: California, Cucamonga Valley $8
Golds/Awards: Gold (PR, FF, NW); Best of
Class (NW)

Geyser Peak 1994 Winemaker's Selection Malbec
Region: California, Alexander Valley $20
Golds/Awards: Gold (CA)

Geyser Peak 1995 Winemaker's Selection Malbec
Region: California, Alexander Valley $20
Golds/Awards: Gold (WC); Double Gold (CA);
Best of Class (CA)

Did You Know . . . ?
The first references to intoxication are an early Mesopotamian tablet that describes a man drunk on strong
wine: "He forgets his words and his speech becomes
confused, his mind wanders and his eyes have a set
expression."

**Geyser Peak 1995 Winemaker's Selection
Petite Verdot**
Region: California, Alexander Valley $20
Golds/Awards: Gold (WC, NW, CA); Best New
World Petite Verdot (NW); Best of Class (NW)

**$Glen Ellen 1996 Proprietor's Reserve Gamay
Beaujolais**
Region: California, Sonoma County $4.99
Golds/Awards: Gold (LA)

$Grove Street 1995 Malbec
Region: California and Argentina $7.50
Golds/Awards: Gold (NW); Best of Class (NW);
Best New World Malbec (NW)

Guenoc 1993 Petit Verdot
Region: California $18
Golds/Awards: Double Gold (TG)

Handley Cellars 1995 Pinot Mystere
Region: California, Anderson Valley $18
Golds/Awards: Gold (DA)

$Hart 1995 Mourvèdre
Region: California, South Coast $12
Golds/Awards: Gold (OC)

$ Hector Stagnari 1992 Tannat Viejo
Region: Uruguay $12
Golds/Awards: Gold (VL)

$J. Lohr 1996 Wildflower Valdiguié
Region: California, Monterey $8.50
Golds/Awards: Gold (LA, CA); Best of Class (LA)

Kanonkop 1995 Pinotage
Region: South Africa $19.99
Golds/Awards: Gold (WWC-90 pts); Cellar
Selection (WWC)

Did You Know . . . ?
Uruguayan wine? you ask. Stay tuned as South America's fourth most important wine-producing region develops with the help of incoming foreign capital.

Misc. Varietal Reds   RED

$Kiona 1993 Lemberger
Region: Washington, Yakima Valley $9.95
Golds/Awards: Gold (AT)

$Lake Sonoma Winery 1995 Cinsault
Region: California, Dry Creek Valley $14.95
Golds/Awards: Gold (NW)

**$Perry Creek 1995 Wenzell Vineyards
Mourvèdre**
Region: California, Sierra Foothills $12.50
Golds/Awards: Gold (DA, FF, NW); Chairman's
Award (FF); Best of Class (NW)

$Preston 1996 Gamay Beaujolais
Region: California, Dry Creek Valley $10.99
Golds/Awards: Gold (WWC-90 pts)

**$Rabbit Ridge 1995 Sceales Family Vineyard
Grenache**
Region: California, Alexander Valley $12.00
Golds/Awards: Gold (FF)

Ramsay 1995 Mourvèdre
Region: California $17
Golds/Awards: Gold (OC)

$River Run 1996 Wirz Vineyard Carignane
Region: California, Cienega Valley $13
Golds/Awards: Gold (LA); Best of Class (LA);
Division Sweepstakes (LA); Governor's Award (LA)

$Rosenblum 1995 Kenefick Ranch Carignane
Region: California, Napa Valley $15
Golds/Awards: Gold (CA); Best of Class (CA)

$ ⌂ Santa Julia 1994 Oak Reserve Malbec
Region: Argentina, Mendoza $6
Golds/Awards: Gold (BR)

Did You Know . . . ?
One of the biggest threats to vineyards in Argentina is
hail, which bruises grapes and renders them totally
useless. Santa Julia invested a large sum of money to
install hail nets over 42 hectares of their vines. Used in
northern Italy as well, these nets are 100% effective.

$Sebastiani Vineyards 1994 Old Vines Mourvèdre
Region: California $12.99
Golds/Awards: Gold (CA); Best of Class (CA)

$Solis 1995 Carignane
Region: California, Santa Clara Valley $10.50
Golds/Awards: Gold (CA); Best of Class (CA)

Thornton 1995 Limited Bottling Carignane
Region: California, South Coast $16
Golds/Awards: Gold (NW); Best of Class (NW);
Best New World Rhône-style Red (NW)

Topolos at Russian River 1995 Old Vines Alicante Bouschet
Region: California, Sonoma County $18
Golds/Awards: Gold (CA)

$Trentadue 1993 Carignane
Region: California, Sonoma County $10
Golds/Awards: Gold (WC); Best of Class (WC)

$V. Sattui 1996 Gamay Rouge
Region: California $12.25
Golds/Awards: Gold (FF); Chairman's Award (FF)
By mail-order only: (800) 799-2337

$♫Viu Manent 1996 Malbec
Region: Chile, Colchagua $8
Golds/Awards: Gold (BR)

$Windsor Vineyards 1995 Alexander Valley Private Reserve Carignane
Region: California, Sonoma County $14
Golds/Awards: Four-Star Gold (OC)
By mail order only: (800) 333-9987

Did You Know . . . ?
What to serve with a robust Argentinean Malbec? The winemaker at Viu Manent recommends smoked ham, pâtés, or pastas with rich sauces.

Native & Hybrid Reds

When I first heard the term *native American wine*, I assumed it was a wine made by Native Americans. The term refers to the grape, not the winemaker. In fact, nearly every region of the world has grapes that are native to it, just as most regions have all kinds of flora and fauna that originated there.

The wine grape is from the genus *Vitis*. The *species* of grape depends on where that grape originally grew, before the intervention of man. Native American grapes are different species from *Vitis vinifera*, called vinifera for short, the chief European grape that includes most of the wines in this book as well as most of the fine wines grown commercially in the world.

There are more than a dozen native American species. The most common red wine is the one your grandmother may have made in her backyard: Concord. Hardy native grapes have an advantage over their delicate French cousins in that they can grow almost anywhere, from Florida to Minnesota.

Researchers have been experimenting with French-American hybrids such as Chambourcin to produce wines that combine the best qualities of both species: the elegance of European wines, the tough pioneer hardiness of American.

Although one might not choose to serve a native American wine for a special occasion, the ones awarded gold medals for being well-made examples of their varietal are worthy of trying, particulary with local cuisine. Get ready, though, for a sensation you won't experience with vinifera wines. Some call it "foxy," others "musky," but it's a decidedly distinct quality that American grapes impart and one that takes a bit of getting used to. If you're in Wisconsin, Missouri, or some other nontraditional wine region (it so happens that wine is produced in every state in the continental U.S.), why not have some regional cuisine alongside the wine that nature provided?

Hermannhof 1992 Norton
Region: Missouri $19.99
Golds/Awards: Gold (WWC-90 pts); Cellar
Selection (WWC)

$Hoodsport 1995 Puget Sound Island Belle
Region: Washington, Puget Sound $9
Golds/Awards: Gold (AT)

Mount Pleasant 1994 Cynthiana
Region: Missouri $20
Golds/Awards: Gold (WWC-90 pts); Cellar
Selection (WWC)

$St. James Winery NV Concord Velvet Red
Region: Missouri $6
Golds/Awards: Gold (SD); Best of Class (SD)

$St. James 1993 Ozark Highlands Norton
Region: Missouri $13.99
Golds/Awards: Gold (AT)

$St. Julian 1994 Chambourcin
Region: Michigan, Lake Michigan Shore $9.50
Golds/Awards: Gold (AW)

$Stone Hill NV Hermannsberger Red Table Wine
Region: Missouri $8.49
Golds/Awards: Gold (NW); Best of Class (NW)

Did You Know . . . ?

Unwelcome imports from America to Europe: phylloxera louse (1860s), downey mildew (1878), and black rot
(1885), all of which nearly wiped out European vineyards. Welcome imports from America: native American
rootstocks, which were resistant to these diseases, and
onto which the European wine growers could graft
their vinifera vines.

Petite Sirah

This grape is no relation to Syrah, although it was once thought to be. In fact, the experts haven't come up with a definitive accounting of its mysterious origins.

What is known is that Petite Sirah has been growing in North and South America for a long time. Almost all Petite Sirah vines in California are much older than the state average, which of course is good, since the older the vine, the more concentrated the grapes.

Petite Sirah can produce red, almost black, wines that are extremely tannic but well balanced, with distinctive flavors and aromas that include black pepper. Its Rhône-like qualities make Petite Sirah an attractive blending agent for Zinfandel. But increasingly it is made into its own varietal wine that's full of character and aging potential.

I *love* Petite Sirah. Luckily, one can find gold medal examples of this varietal at really reasonable prices.

Try one with hard cheeses, lamb, beef, venison dishes, or other hearty fare.

Benziger 1994 Imagery Series Petite Sirah
Region: California, Paso Robles $17.99
Golds/Awards: Gold (SD)

$Bogle 1995 Petite Sirah
Region: California $8
Golds/Awards: Gold (NW); Best of Class (NW)

Concannon 1993 Reserve Petite Sirah
Region: California, Livermore Valley $24.95
Golds/Awards: Gold (AW, WWC-90 pts)

$Concannon 1994 Petite Sirah
Region: California, Central Coast $9.95
Golds/Awards: Gold (AW, IW, SY)

Concannon 1994 Reserve Petite Sirah
Region: California, Livermore Valley $17.95
Golds/Awards: Gold (WC)

$Concannon 1995 Select Vineyard Petite Sirah
Region: California $9.95
Golds/Awards: Gold (WC, LA); Best of Class (WC, LA)

$David Bruce 1995 Petite Syrah
Region: California, San Luis Obispo $14
Golds/Awards: Gold (LA, OC, WWC-90 pts); Cellar Selection (WWC)

David Bruce 1995 Shell Creek Vineyard Reserve Petite Syrah
Region: California, Paso Robles $18
Golds/Awards: Gold (DA, OC, WWC-95 pts); Cellar Selection and Best Buy (WWC)

Did You Know . . . ?

American peacekeepers in Bosnia are restricted from consuming any type of alcohol, including at the local pubs and restaurants. However, the major-general is exempt from the prohibition he's imposed on his troops, since a loophole in the rules allows for alcoholic drinks to be consumed in important meetings and negotiations where it's customary to seal the deal with drink.

Petite Sirah   RED

Foppiano 1993 Centennial Selection, La Grande Anniversaire Petite Sirah
Region: California $24
Golds/Awards: Gold (WWC-91 pts)

$Granite Springs 1995 Petite Sirah
Region: California, El Dorado $13
Golds/Awards: Gold (SF); Double Gold (CA);
Best of Class (CA)

$Guenoc 1994 Petite Sirah
Region: California, North Coast $14.50
Golds/Awards: Gold (DA)

La Jota 1994 Petite Sirah
Region: California $24
Golds/Awards: Gold (WWC-92 pts); Cellar
Selection (WWC)

$Parducci 1994 Petite Sirah
Region: California $9.99
Golds/Awards: Gold (IW)

Rosenblum 1995 Kenefick Ranch Petite Sirah
Region: California, Napa Ranch $17
Golds/Awards: Gold (OC)

Stag's Leap 1993 Reserve Petite Syrah
Region: California $45
Golds/Awards: Gold (WWC-93 pts)

$Windsor 1994 Petite Sirah
Region: California, North Coast $11
Golds/Awards: Gold (NW); Best of Class (NW);
Best New World Petite Sirah (NW)
By mail order only: (800) 333-9987

Did You Know . . . ?
A California couple by the name of *Weinstock* (you
can't make stuff up this good) loved wine collecting so
much that they converted their 20-by-40-foot living
room into a wine cellar. Seem kind of cool and damp in
here, honey?

Pinot Noir

Often described in poetic, sensual terms, a great Pinot Noir has subtlety, elegance, complexity, and finesse. On the palate it can be lush, broad, and seductive, with essences of raspberries, strawberries, loganberries, cherries, herbs, earth, and bouquets of fresh wildflowers such as violets.

But more than these wonderful qualities, which winemakers the world over try to achieve with their Pinot Noirs, the grape's most dominant feature is how exasperating it is to grow. Winemakers spend their entire careers wrestling with this thin-skinned, fragile grape that's susceptible to various maladies and vulnerable to frost. For these and other reasons, Pinot Noirs tend to be expensive.

Pinot Noir is made in almost every country where ambitious winemakers ply their trade. It's the sole grape of which France's red burgundy is made. California, Washington, and especially Oregon, with a climate very similar to Burgundy's, are doing wonders with this fickle grape. Canada, Australia, South Africa, and New Zealand are also attempting to master it, with Australia the real wild card, since many of its recently planted Pinot Noir vines are now coming of age.

Because Pinot Noir loses its tannins quickly, most bottles should be consumed within a couple years of the vintage, no more than seven or eight years max.

Have Pinot Noir with swordfish, fresh tuna steak, roast chicken or turkey, or game such as pheasant.

Adelaida 1994 HMR Vineyard Pinot Noir
Region: California, South Central Coast $24
Golds/Awards: Gold (WWC-91 pts)

Adelsheim 1994 Seven Springs Vineyard Pinot Noir
Region: Oregon, Willamette Valley $30
Golds/Awards: Gold (WWC-90 pts); Cellar Selection (WWC)

Alderbrook 1995 Pinot Noir
Region: California $18
Golds/Awards: Gold (AW)

Amity 1994 Winemaker's Reserve Pinot Noir
Region: Oregon, Willamette Valley $30
Golds/Awards: Gold (OR)

Au Bon Climat 1994 Pinot Noir
Region: California, Santa Maria Valley $18
Golds/Awards: Gold (IW); Tie for Best Burgundy or Pinot Noir (IW)

Autumn Wind 1994 Reserve Pinot Noir
Region: Oregon $30
Golds/Awards: Gold (WWC-90 pts); Cellar Selection (WWC)

$Bellerose 1995 Pinot Noir
Region: California, North Coast $10.25
Golds/Awards: Double Gold (CA); Best of Class (CA)

Benton Lane 1994 Reserve Pinot Noir
Region: Oregon $28.50
Golds/Awards: Gold (WWC-90 pts); Cellar Selection (WWC)

Benziger 1995 Pinot Noir
Region: California $16
Golds/Awards: Gold (WC); Best of Class (WC)

Did You Know . . . ?
Chinese premier Li Peng is directing a massive movement away from the consumption of grain spirits to wine. There goes the world's wine supply!

Pinot Noir   RED

Beringer 1994 Stanly Ranch Pinot Noir
Region: California, Carneros $30
Golds/Awards: Gold (WWC-92 pts); Cellar
Selection (WWC)

**Bernardus 1994 Bien Nacido Vineyard
Pinot Noir**
Region: California, South Central Coast $30
Golds/Awards: Gold (WWC-90 pts)

$Bridgeview 1996 Pinot Noir
Region: Oregon $10.99
Golds/Awards: Gold (NE)

**Byington 1994 Special Reserve Vineyards
Pinot Noir**
Region: California, Santa Cruz Mountains $20
Golds/Awards: Gold (WWC-91 pts)

Byron 1993 Reserve Pinot Noir
Region: California, South Central Coast $22.50
Golds/Awards: Gold (WWC-90 pts)

Byron 1994 Pinot Noir
Region: California, South Central Coast $17
Golds/Awards: Gold (WWC-90 pts)

Byron 1994 Reserve Pinot Noir
Region: California, Santa Barbara County $24
Golds/Awards: Gold (CA); Best of California and
Best of Class (CA)

Calera 1992 Jensen Pinot Noir
Region: California, Mt. Harlan $35
Golds/Awards: Gold (WWC-93 pts); Cellar
Selection (WWC)

Calera 1992 Mills Pinot Noir
Region: California, Mt. Harlan $35
Golds/Awards: Gold (WWC-92 pts); Cellar
Selection (WWC)

Did You Know . . . ?
Before Bernardus owner Ben Pon got into fine-wine
making, he was a race-car driver for Porsche.

Pinot Noir   RED

Calera 1993 Selleck Pinot Noir
Region: California, Mt. Harlan $38
Golds/Awards: Gold (WWC-93 pts)

Calera 1994 Pinot Noir
Region: California, Central Coast $16
Golds/Awards: Gold (OC)

Cambria 1994 Julia's Vineyard Pinot Noir
Region: California, Santa Maria Valley $27
Golds/Awards: Gold (AT)

Cambria 1994 Reserve Pinot Noir
Region: California, Santa Maria Valley $42
Golds/Awards: Gold (IV, WWC-90 pts); Cellar
Selection (WWC)

**Carneros Creek 1994 Signature Reserve
Pinot Noir**
Region: California, Carneros $35
Golds/Awards: Gold (PR)

**$Carneros Creek 1994 Fleur de Carneros
Pinot Noir**
Region: California, Carneros $12
Golds/Awards: Gold (IW, NW)

$Castle Vineyards 1995 Pinot Noir
Region: California, Carneros $14
Golds/Award: 4-Star Gold (OC, CA); Best of Class (CA)

Chalone 1992 Estate Pinot Noir
Region: California, Chalone $26
Golds/Awards: Gold (WWC-90 pts); Cellar
Selection (WWC)

Chateau Benoit 1994 Estate Reserve Pinot Noir
Region: Oregon, Willamette Valley $25
Golds/Awards: Gold (WWC-92 pts); Cellar
Selection (WWC)

Did You Know . . . ?
The eruption of Mount Vesuvius on August 24, 79 AD,
was tragic for Pompeii inhabitants, but fortunate for us,
since it preserved detailed evidence of the processes
involved in the production, sale, and consumption of
wine at that time.

Pinot Noir   RED

Chateau St. Jean 1994 Pinot Noir
Region: California, Sonoma County $18
Golds/Awards: Gold (WWC-90 pts); Cellar
Selection (WWC)

Chimere 1994 Bien Nacido Vineyard Pinot Noir
Region: : California, South Central Coast $24
Golds/Awards: Gold (WWC-92 pts)

Chimere 1994 Unfiltered Pinot Noir
California, California's South Central Coast $18
Golds/Awards: Gold (WWC-90 pts)

$Claudia Springs 1994 Pinot Noir
Region: California, Anderson Valley $13
Golds/Awards: Gold (PR)

Claudia Springs 1995 Pinot Noir
Region: California. Anderson Valley $16
Golds/Awards: Gold (FF)

Clos LaChance 1994 Pinot Noir
Region: California, Santa Cruz Mountains $20
Golds/Awards: Gold (WWC-90 pts); Cellar
Selection (WWC)

℞**Coldstream Hills 1995 Reserve Pinot Noir**
Region: Australia, Yarra Valley $32
Golds/Awards: Gold (SY)

**Cooper Mountain 1994 Estate Reserve
Pinot Noir**
Region: Oregon, Willamette Valley $29.75
Golds/Awards: Gold (WWC-91 pts); Cellar
Selection (WWC)

Cosentino 1995 Pinot Noir
Region: California, Napa Valley $24
Golds/Awards: Gold (WWC-90 pts)

Did You Know . . . ?
Because of the Muslim religion, which prohibits alcohol,
wine is no longer produced in much of the land most
closely associated with the origins of viticulture: the
Near and Middle East, North Africa, and parts of Asia.

Cristom 1994 Marjorie Vineyard Pinot Noir
Region: Oregon, Willamette Valley $27
Golds/Awards: Gold (WWC-92 pts); Cellar
Selection (WWC)

Cristom 1994 Reserve Pinot Noir
Region: Oregon, Willamette Valley $27
Golds/Awards: Gold (WWC-92 pts)

David Bruce 1994 Pinot Noir
Region: California, Russian River Valley $25
Golds/Awards: Gold (LA, NW, WWC-92 pts);
Best of Class (LA); Cellar Selection (WWC)

David Bruce 1994 Chalone Pinot Noir
Region: California $30
Golds/Awards: Gold (DA, NW, WWC-92 pts);
Double Gold (TG)

Davis Bynum 1995 Pinot Noir
Region: California $16
Golds/Awards: Gold (CA)

Domaine Drouhin 1994 Lauréne Pinot Noir
Region: Oregon, Willamette Valley $42
Golds/Awards: Gold (WWC-94 pts); Cellar
Selection (WWC)

**Domaine Serene 1994 Evenstad Reserve
Pinot Noir**
Region: Oregon $30
Golds/Awards: Gold (PR, WWC-91 pts); Best
of Class (PR)

Domaine Serene 1994 Reserve Pinot Noir
Region: Oregon $20
Golds/Awards: Gold (WWC-90 pts)

Did You Know . . . ?
In 1979 a French-sponsored tasting comparing French
wines with their New World counterparts turned out a
surprising star: an Oregonean Pinot Noir. So impressed
was Beaune merchant Robert Drouhin that he purchased land in Oregon and started his own Oregon
winery. Oregon's reputation has grown ever since.

Duck Pond 1994 Fries Family Reserve Pinot Noir
Region: Oregon, Willamette Valley $25
Golds/Awards: Gold (WWC-91 pts); Cellar Selection (WWC)

Elk Cove 1994 La Boheme Vineyard Pinot Noir
Region: Oregon, Willamette Valley $35
Golds/Awards: Gold (WWC-90 pts); Cellar Selection (WWC)

Elkhorn Peak Cellars 1995 Fagan Creek Pinot Noir
Region: California, Napa Valley $24
Golds/Awards: Gold (NW)

Erath 1994 Weber Vineyard Reserve Pinot Noir
Region: Oregon, Willamette Valley $25
Golds/Awards: Gold (WWC-91 pts)

$Estancia 1995 Pinot Noir
Region: California, Monterey $10.50
Golds/Awards: Gold (OC)

Étude 1994 Pinot Noir
Region: California, Carneros $28
Golds/Awards: Gold (WWC-92 pts)

Evesham Wood 1994 Temperance Hill Vineyard Pinot Noir
Region: Oregon, Willamette Valley $24
Golds/Awards: Gold (WWC-91 pts); Cellar Selection (WWC)

Fess Parker 1995 American Tradition Reserve Pinot Noir
Region: California, Santa Barbara County $28
Golds/Awards: Gold (NW); Best of Class (NW); Best New World Pinot Noir (NW)

Did You Know . . . ?
The Brits love our wine. The UK moved from the fifth to the fourth largest market for American wines in 1996. Twenty percent more American wine was sold in the UK in 1996 than the year before.

Pinot Noir   RED

$Fetzer 1994 Bien Nacido Vineyard Reserve Pinot Noir
Region: California, Mendocino $14.99
Golds/Awards: Gold (LA, NW); Best of Class (LA)

$Fetzer 1995 Barrel Select Pinot Noir
Region: California $12.99
Golds/Awards: Gold (NW); Best of Class (NW)

$Firesteed 1996 Pinot Noir
Region: Oregon $9.99
Golds/Awards: Gold (OR)

$Foris 1995 Pinot Noir
Region: Oregon, Rogue Valley $11
Golds/Awards: Gold (OR)

Gary Farrell 1994 Rochioli Vineyard Pinot Noir
Region: California, Russian River Valley $50
Golds/Awards: Gold (WWC-90 pts); Cellar Selection (WWC)

Gary Farrell 1995 Allen Vineyard Pinot Noir
Region: California, Russian River Valley $40
Golds/Awards: Gold (LA, NW)

Gary Farrell 1995 Olivet Lane Pinot Noir
Region: California, Russian River Valley $30
Golds/Awards: Gold (PR, OC, Citrus Fair)

Gary Farrell 1995 Pinot Noir
Region: Cal., Mendocino & Anderson Valley $30
Golds/Awards: Gold (PR, CA); Best of Class (PR)

Gary Farrell 1995 Rochioli Vineyard Pinot Noir
Region: California, Russian River Valley $50
Golds/Awards: Gold (FF, OC, Citrus Fair)

Handley Cellars 1994 Reserve Pinot Noir
Region: California, Anderson Valley $22
Golds/Awards: Gold (NW)

> ### *Did You Know . . . ?*
> California accounts for 98 percent of wine production in the United States.

Hartford Court 1994 Arrendell Vineyard Pinot Noir
Region California, Russian River Valley $40
Golds/Awards: Gold (WWC-90 pts)

Hartford Court 1994 Dutton Ranch-Sanchietti Vineyard Pinot Noir
Region California, Russian River Valley $35
Golds/Awards: Gold (WWC-91 pts); Cellar Selection (WWC)

Henry Estate 1993 Barrel Select Pinot Noir
Region: Oregon $18
Golds/Awards: Double Gold (TG)

$Indian Creek Winery 1994 Pinot Noir
Region: Idaho $14.95
Golds/Awards: Gold (NW); Best of Class (NW)

Kalin 1992 Cuvée DD Pinot Noir
Region: California, Sonoma County $30
Golds/Awards: Gold (WWC-92 pts)

Kendall-Jackson 1994 Grand Reserve Pinot Noir
Region: California $30
Golds/Awards: Gold (NW)

La Crema 1995 Pinot Noir
Region: California, Sonoma Coast $21
Golds/Awards: Gold (FF); Chairman's Award (FF)

La Crema 1995 Reserve Pinot Noir
Region: California, Sonoma Coast $28
Golds/Awards: Gold (SF)

Lange 1994 Pinot Noir
Region: Oregon, Willamette Valley $18
Golds/Awards: Gold (WWC-90 pts)

Did You Know . . . ?
Goofy, Dopey, and Sleepy must have been there. A recent banquet at Walt Disney World's Cinderella Castle in Lake Buena Vista, Florida, marked the first time the public was offered wine within the amusement park. Kendall-Jackson's Artisan & Estates wines were served.

Pinot Noir   RED

Lange 1994 Reserve Pinot Noir
Region: Oregon, Willamette Valley $40
Golds/Awards: Gold (WWC-93 pts); Cellar
Selection (WWC)

Laurier 1995 Pinot Noir
Region: California, Sonoma County $17.99
Golds/Awards: Gold (NW)

⌂**Martinborough 1994 Reserve Pinot Noir**
Region: New Zealand, Martinborough $38
Golds/Awards: Gold and Best of Category (SY); Best
Pinot Noir (Perth); Best Soft Finish Red (Canberra)

$McHenry 1993 Massaro Vineyard Pinot Noir
Region: California, Carneros $15
Golds/Awards: Gold (WWC-91 pts); Best Buy (WWC)

$Meridian 1995 Pinot Noir
Region: California, Santa Barbara County $14
Golds/Awards: Gold (SD, NW, Monterey Wine
Festival); Best of Class (SD); Red Wine Sweepstakes
(Monterey)

Meridian 1995 Reserve Pinot Noir
Region: Cal., San Luis Obispo/Santa Barbara $17
Golds/Awards: Gold (NW, WC, OC); Best of
Class (WC)

Mirassou 1995 Harvest Reserve Pinot Noir
Region: California, Monterery $16
Golds/Awards: Gold (SF)

Morgan 1995 Pinot Noir
Region: California, California $18
Golds/Awards: Gold (WWC-92 pts); Best
Buy (WWC)

$Napa Ridge 1995 Pinot Noir
Region: California, North Coast $10
Golds/Awards: Gold (DA, SD)

Did You Know . . . ?
The planting of vineyards has always symbolized victory
and the determination to settle. For example, when the
Christians drove the Moors from medieval Spain, they
planted vines behind them.

Pinot Noir   RED

Navarro 1994 Methode Ancienne Pinot Noir
Region: California, Anderson Valley $18
Golds/Awards: Gold (WC, FF)

**Oak Knoll 1994 Silver Anniversary Reserve
Pinot Noir**
Region: Oregon, Willamette Valley $20
Golds/Awards: Gold (WWC-90 pts); Cellar
Selection (WWC)

Panther Creek 1994 Bednarik Vnyd. Pinot Noir
Region: Oregon, Willamette Valley $35
Golds/Awards: Gold (WWC-92 pts)

Paraiso Springs 1994 Pinot Noir
Region: California, Monterey $17
Golds/Awards: Gold (WWC-90 pts)

Pepperwood Springs 1995 Pinot Noir
Region: California, Anderson Valley $20
Golds/Awards: Gold (WC)

Ponzi 1993 Reserve Pinot Noir
Region: Oregon, Willamette Valley $26.99
Golds/Awards: Gold (WWC-92 pts)

Ponzi 1994 Reserve Pinot Noir
Region: Oregon, Willamette Valley $35
Golds/Awards: Gold (WWC-92 pts); Cellar
Selection (WWC)

**Rabbit Ridge 1995 Frank Johnson Vineyard
Pinot Noir**
Region: California, Sonoma County $16
Golds/Awards: Gold (WC, NW)

Redhawk 1994 Estate Reserve Pinot Noir
Region: Oregon, Willamette Valley $25
Golds/Awards: Gold (WWC-91 pts); Cellar
Selection (WWC)

Did You Know . . . ?
Navarro is one of an increasing number of wineries
committed to earth-friendly farming practices. They
share their vineyards with geese, which dine on slugs
and snails. They don't spray, even with organic pesti-
cides; they rely on beneficial insects to devour pests.

Robert Mondavi 1992 Napa Reserve Pinot Noir
Region: California, Napa Valley $45
Golds/Awards: Gold (IW)

Robert Mondavi 1994 Reserve Pinot Noir
Region: California, Carneros $35
Golds/Awards: Gold (WWC-90 pts)

Rochioli 1993 Pinot Noir
Region: California, Russian River Valley $18
Golds/Awards: Gold (IW); Tie for Best Burgundy
or Pinot Noir (IW)

Rochioli 1994 Estate Pinot Noir
Region: California, Russian River Valley $22
Golds/Awards: Gold (WWC-90 pts)

**Rodney Strong 1994 River East Vineyard
Pinot Noir**
Region: California, Russian River Valley $16
Golds/Awards: Gold (PR)

**St. Innocent 1994 Seven Springs Vineyard
Pinot Noir**
Region: Oregon, Willamette Valley $28.50
Golds/Awards: Gold (WWC-90 pts); Cellar
Selection (WWC)

**St. Innocent 1994 Temperance Hill Vineyard
Pinot Noir**
Region: Oregon, Willamette Valley $32.50
Golds/Awards: Gold (WWC-92 pts)

Sanford 1994 Pinot Noir
Region: California, Central Coast $19
Golds/Awards: Gold (SY)

Sanford 1995 Pinot Noir
Region: California, Central Coast $25
Golds/Awards: Gold (WC)

Did You Know . . . ?
During Cicero's time, campaign rhetoric frequently
stooped as low as it does today, relying on character
assassination to boost or destroy reputations. Cicero's
team painted a picture of Mark Antony as having a
riotous home life where drinking began at 9 a.m.

Pinot Noir   RED

Santa Barbara 1995 Reserve Pinot Noir
Region: California $40
Golds/Awards: Gold (IV)

Schug 1994 Heritage Reserve Pinot Noir
Region: California, Carneros $30
Golds/Awards: Gold (WWC-90 pts); Cellar
Selection (WWC)

Secret House 1995 Pinot Noir
Region: Oregon, Willamette Valley $18
Golds/Awards: Gold (OR)

Siduri 1995 Pinot Noir
Region: Oregon $30
Golds/Awards: Gold (WWC-92 pts)

Signorello 1994 Las Amigas Vineyard Pinot Noir
Region: California, Carneros $35
Golds/Awards: Gold (WWC-90 pts)

Silvan Ridge 1994 Pinot Noir
Region: Oregon, Willamette Valley $22
Golds/Awards: Double Gold (TG); Gold (WS)

Sokol Blosser 1994 Redland Pinot Noir
Region: Oregon, Willamette Valley $35
Golds/Awards: Gold (WWC-92 pts); Cellar
Selection (WWC)

Stephen Ross 1995 Edna Ranch Pinot Noir
Region: California, South Central Coast $18
Golds/Awards: Gold (WWC-91 pts)

Sterling 1995 Carneros Pinot Noir
Region: California, Napa Valley $16
Golds/Awards: Gold (SF)

Stonestreet 1994 Pinot Noir
Region: California, Russian River Valley $30
Golds/Awards: Gold (AT, WC, NW)

Did You Know . . . ?
One of the ways paleoethnobotonists (those who study
botanical remains) are able to determine which ancient
cultures made wine from domesticated grapes is by
studying the pips, or seeds, that have been fossilized or
are found in the form of charcoal at burial sites.

Pinot Noir   RED

$Talus 1995 Pinot Noir
Region: California $7.99
Golds/Awards: Gold (SD)

Torii Mor 1994 Reserve Pinot Noir
Region: Oregon, Willamette Valley $28
Golds/Awards: Gold (WWC-93 pts)

Tualatin 1994 Estate Reserve Pinot Noir
Region: Oregon, Willamette Valley $20
Golds/Awards: Gold (WWC-90 pts); Cellar
Selection (WWC)

$Tualatin 1995 Pinot Noir
Region: Oregon, Willamette Valley $12.50
Golds/Awards: Gold (WC)

Tyee Wine Cellars 1994 Pinot Noir
Region: Oregon, Willamette Valley $17.95
Golds/Awards: Gold (SD, OR); Best of
Show Red (OR)

Villa Mt. Eden 1995 Grand Reserve Pinot Noir
Region: California; Santa Maria Valley $16
Golds/Awards: Gold (WC)

$Villa Mt. Eden 1995 Cellar Select Pinot Noir
Region: California $9.50
Golds/Awards: Gold (AW, OC)

Whitford Cellars 1993 Estate Pinot Noir
Region: California, Napa Valley $16
Golds/Awards: Gold (SF)

**Wild Horse 1994 Cheval Sauvage Proprietary
Selection Pinot Noir**
Region: California, Central Coast $35
Golds/Awards: Gold (SD)

Wild Horse 1995 Pinot Noir
Region: California, Central Coast $18
Golds/Awards: Gold (FF)

Did You Know . . . ?
It takes about 600 grapes to make a bottle of wine.

Pinot Noir   RED

$Windsor 1994 Private Reserve Pinot Noir
Region: California, Russian River Valley $13
Golds/Awards: Gold (NW)
By mail order only: (800) 333-9987

**Windsor 1994 Shelton Signature Series
Pinot Noir**
Region: California $16
Golds/Awards: Gold (WC, NW, CA); Best of
California and Best of Class (CA)
By mail order only: (800) 333-9987

$Windsor 1995 Private Reserve Pinot Noir
Region: California, North Coast $13
Golds/Awards: Gold (CA)
By mail order only: (800) 333-9987

**Yamhill Valley Vineyards 1994 Reserve
Pinot Noir**
Region: Oregon $33
Golds/Awards: Gold (NE)

ZD Wines 1994 Pinot Noir
Region: California, Carneros $25
Golds/Awards: Gold (NW)

ZD Wines 1995 Pinot Noir
Region: California, Carneros $25
Golds/Awards: Gold (WC)

Did You Know . . . ?
Want a great gift idea? Windsor will custom-print labels
for your wedding, birthday, clients—you name it. But
such generosity got one LA man in trouble. He had two
bottles inscribed for Valentine presents: one for his
wife, one for his girlfriend. "With all my love for
Barbara," declared one. "With all my love to Jennifer,"
gushed the other. They were both signed, "Forever and
ever, Ray." Unfortunately, he reversed addresses for his
shipment to the two waiting lovebirds, and you'll have
to guess the end of the story.

Red Blends

This is my favorite section of the book. I *love* red wine blends. In this section are all kinds of red blends made from Bordeaux grapes, Rhône grapes, combinations of the two, with sometimes Italian red grapes or other less common varieties thrown in for good measure. These wines are exciting, different, innovative, and always delicious—otherwise they wouldn't have won a gold medal. If you're bored with Cabernet Sauvignon, check out red blends. I guarantee you'll love them, perhaps more than single-variety wines.

Meritage, or Bordeaux-style blends Meritage is a trademarked name coined by American wineries to solve a marketing problem. To call a wine by its varietal name, say, Cabernet Sauvignon, that wine is required to be composed of a minimum of 75 percent Cabernet Sauvignon. When that wasn't the case, high-class wineries had to call their red or white gems "table wine," or give the wine some proprietary name that gave consumers no clue as to what was in the bottle.

To use the name Meritage, red wines have to be made up of two or more of the following Bordeaux grape varieties: Cabernet Sauvignon, Merlot, Cabernet Franc, Petit Verdot, Malbec, Gros Verdot, or Carmenère.

Bordeaux-style red blends tend to be long-lived, big, chewy, full-bodied wines, and are often quite pricy.

Rhône-style blends A group of adventurous California winemakers, collectively known as the Rhône Rangers, have been trying to recreate the wonderful reds of France's Rhône Valley, using grapes such as Syrah, Carignane, Grenache, Mourvèdre, and Alicante Bouschet. These wines will often be rich and spicy, and they're usually less expensive than Bordeaux-style red blends.

Atlas Peak 1993 Consenso (Cabernet/Sangiovese)
Region: California, Napa Valley $22
Golds/Awards: Gold (LA, CA); Best of Class (CA)

Beaulieu 1993 Tapestry Reserve (Bordeaux-style
blend)
Region: California, Napa Valley $20
Golds/Awards: Gold (AT, OC)

Beaulieu 1994 Tapestry Reserve (Bordeaux-style
blend)
Region: California, Napa Valley $20
Golds/Awards: Gold (SF)

Benziger 1993 Tribute Red Estate (Bordeaux-style
blend)
Region: California, Dry Creek Valley $23
Golds/Awards: Gold (LA, FF, NW); Chairman's Award (FF)

Benziger 1994 Tribute Red (Bordeaux-style blend)
Region: California, Sonoma $25
Golds/Awards: Gold (SF)

$Beringer 1992 Meritage
Region: California, Knights Valley $14
Golds/Awards: Gold (AT)

Beringer 1993 Knights Valley Alluvium
(Bordeaux-style blend)
Region: California, Knights Valley $25
Golds/Awards: Gold (LA); Double Gold (SF)

Bernardus 1993 Marinus (Bordeaux-style blend)
Region: California $24
Golds/Awards: Gold (WWC-90 pts)

$Boeger 1994 Majeure Reserve (Rhône-style blend)
Region: California, El Dorado $9
Golds/Awards: Gold (LA)

Did You Know . . . ?
The same aerial-photography techniques used for
decades by U.S. intelligence agencies are now being
employed by intelligent, high-tech winegrowers. Aerial
mapping can reveal physical and chemical changes
occurring in their vineyards.

Red Blends   RED

Bonny Doon 1994 Le Cigare Volant (Rhône-style blend)
Region: California $20
Golds/Awards: Gold (WWC-90 pts); Cellar Selection (WWC)

$Ca' del Solo 1994 Big House Red (Rhône-style blend)
Region: California $8.50
Golds/Awards: Gold (IW)

℞**Chapel Hill 1994 The Vicar Cabernet Shiraz**
Region: Australia, South Australia $17
Golds/Awards: Gold (SY, Perth & Brisbane Wine Shows)

Charles B. Mitchell Vineyards 1995 Grand Reserve (Bordeaux-style blend)
Region: California, El Dorado $28
Golds/Awards: Gold (CA)

Charles Krug 1992 Generations (Bordeaux-style blend)
Region: California, Napa Valley $30
Golds/Awards: Gold (NW)

Chateau Ste. Michelle 1993 Meritage
Region: Washington $30
Golds/Awards: Gold (WWC-93pts)

Clos Du Bois 1993 Marlstone (Bordeaux-style blend)
Region: California, Alexander Valley $21
Golds/Awards: Gold (CA); Best of Class (CA)

Concannon 1993 Assemblage Red (Bordeaux-style blend)
Region: California, Alexander Valley $20
Golds/Awards: Double Gold (TG); Gold (WWC-90 pts)

Did You Know . . . ?
Archaeologists digging in Pompeii have discovered evidence of thriving viticulture. With the blessing of the Italian government, two Italian vintners, the Mastroberardino brothers, are planting grapevines inside the city's old wall corresponding to those ancient vineyards.

Red Blends   RED

$Concannon 1994 Raboli Field Blend (Mixed red blend)
Region: California, Livermore Valley $12.95
Golds/Awards: Gold (LA)

Conn Creek 1993 Anthology (Bordeaux-style blend)
Region: California, Napa Valley $30
Golds/Awards: Gold (OC)

Cosentino 1993 The Poet Red Meritage
Region: California, Napa Valley $26
Golds/Awards: Gold (NW)

Cosentino 1993 M. Coz (Bordeaux-style blend)
Region: California $45
Golds/Awards: Gold (WWC-90 pts)

Cosentino 1994 Unfined and Unfiltered M. Coz (Bordeaux-style blend)
Region: California, Napa Valley $60
Golds/Awards: Double Gold (SF); Best of Show Red (SF)

Cuneo 1992 Cana's Feast (Bordeaux-style blend)
Region: Oregon $25
Golds/Awards: Gold (WWC-91 pts)

Dark Star Cellars 1995 Ricordati (Bordeaux-style blend)
Region: California, Paso Robles $20
Golds/Awards: Gold (OC)

De Lorimier 1994 Mosaic Meritage
Region: California $20
Golds/Awards: Gold (SD, WC); Best of Class (WC)

Dry Creek Vineyard 1994 Red Meritage
Region: California $25
Golds/Awards: Double Gold (TG)

$Eberle 1995 Côtes-du-Robles (Rhône-style blend)
Region: California, Paso Robles $13
Golds/Awards: Gold (PR, SD, FF); Best of Class (PR)

Did You Know . . . ?
A large oak tree can produce about nine barrels. A smaller tree, about four.

Red Blends   RED

⌂**Eikendal 1992 Classique** (Bordeaux-style blend)
Region: South Africa $16
Golds/Awards: Gold (WWC-90 pts)

$⌂**Eikendal 1996 Classique** (Bordeaux-style blend)
Region: South Africa $13.99
Golds/Awards: Gold (VL)

Ferrari Carano 1991 Reserve Red (Bordeaux-style blend)
Region: California $47
Golds/Awards: Gold (WWC-92 pts)

Fife 1994 Max Cuvée (Rhône-style blend)
Region: California $18.50
Golds/Awards: Gold (WWC-91 pts); Cellar
Selection (WWC)

Firestone 1993 Red Reserve (Bordeaux-style blend)
Region: California, Santa Ynez $30
Golds/Awards: Gold (AT, OC, NW); Best U.S. Red
(AT); Best of Show (AT)

Flora Springs 1993 Trilogy (Bordeaux-style
blend)
Region: California $30
Golds/Awards: Gold (WWC-91 pts))

Flora Springs 1994 Trilogy (Bordeaux-style
blend)
Region: California $35
Golds/Awards: Double Gold (TG)

Franciscan 1993 Magnificat (Bordeaux-style
blend)
Region: California $22.50
Golds/Awards: Gold (WWC-91 pts)

**Geyser Peak Trione Cellars 1993 Reserve
Alexandre Red Meritage**
Region: California, Alexander Valley $28
Golds/Awards: Gold (WS)

Did You Know . . . ?
While California winegrowers have to contend with
squirrels and bunnies, their counterparts in many South
African wineries have to cope with pesky baboons.

Red Blends   RED

Geyser Peak 1994 Trione Cellars Reserve Alexandre Red Meritage
Region: California, Alexander Valley $28
Golds/Awards: Gold (DA, PR, AW, IV, FF, Grand Harvest Awards, Citrus Fair); Best of Class (PR); Double Gold (TG); Chairman's Award (FF)

$Granite Springs 1994 Carousel Series (Bordeaux-style blend)
Region: California $12
Golds/Awards: Gold (CA); Best of Class (CA)

$Guenoc 1994 Red Meritage
Region: California, Lake County $15
Golds/Awards: Gold (SD, FF); Double Gold (CA); Best of Class (CA)

Hamilton 1995 Ewell Cabernet/Merlot
Region: Australia $20
Golds/Awards: Gold (IV)

Havens 1994 Bourriquot (Bordeaux-style blend)
Region: California, Napa Valley $25
Golds/Awards: Gold (OC)

Hedges 1992 Red Mountain Reserve Red (Bordeaux-style blend)
Region: Washington $25
Golds/Awards: Gold (WWC-91 pts)

Henschke 1993 Keyneton Estate (Shiraz/Cabernet/Malbec)
Region: Australia, Barossa $30
Golds/Awards: Gold (WS)

$Horton 1993 Montdomaine Heritage (Bordeaux-style blend)
Region: Virginia $15
Golds/Awards: Gold (WWC-90 pts)

Did You Know . . . ?
When shopping for eating grapes, you might choose big, juicy ones. For wine, however, smaller berries contribute to better wine quality, especially for reds.

Red Blends   RED

$ ⌕Jacob's Creek 1995 Shiraz Cabernet
Region: Australia $6.99
Golds/Awards: Gold (VL)

$Jekel 1990 Red Meritage
Region: California $10
Golds/Awards: Gold (WWC-90 pts); Best Buy (WWC)

$Jekel 1991 Sanctuary Estate Red Meritage
Region: California, Arroyo Seco $10
Golds/Awards: Gold (NW); Best of Class (NW)

$Jory 1995 Black Hand (Mano Nera)
(Rhône/Italian blend)
Region: California $15
Golds/Awards: Gold (AT); '96 Gold, Best of
Class (CA)

$Jory 1996 Purple Gang (Mixed red blend)
Region: California $15
Golds/Awards: Gold (LA, CA)

Joseph Phelps 1994 Insignia (Bordeaux-style
blend)
Region: California, Napa Valley $60
Golds/Awards: Gold (OC)

Joseph Phelps 1994 Le Mistral (Bordeaux-style
blend)
Region: California $18
Golds/Awards: Gold (WWC-92 pts); Cellar
Selection (WWC)

Justin 1994 Isosceles (Bordeaux-style blend)
Region: California, Paso Robles $32.50
Golds/Awards: Gold (LA, CA); Best of Class (CA)

⌕**Kanonkop 1992 Paul Sauer** (Bordeaux-style
blend)
Region: South Africa, Stellenbosch $23.99
Golds/Awards: Gold (WS); Top Wine (1994
Brussels); Best Blended Red Wine (1994 WS)

Did You Know . . . ?
In France, McDonald's serves wine. Let's see . . . What
would best complement Le Big Mac?

Lambert Bridge 1994 Crane Creek Cuvée
(Bordeaux-style blend)
Region: California, Dry Creek Valley $28
Golds/Awards: Gold (SD); Double Gold (SF); Best
of Class (SD)

Langtry 1993 Meritage
Region: California, Guenoc Valley $41
Golds/Awards: Gold (AT); Double Gold (TG)

Langtry 1994 Meritage
Region: California, Napa Valley $41
Golds/Awards: Gold (SD, OC)

⌐**Lindemans 1992 Coonawarra Pyrus** (Bordeaux-
style blend)
Region: Australia, Coonawarra $22
Golds/Awards: Gold (WWC-92 pts)

⌐**Lindemans 1992 Limestone Ridge Vineyard
Cabernet-Shiraz-Merlot**
Region: Australia $22
Golds/Awards: Gold (WWC-91 pts)

⌐**Lindemans 1993 Coonawarra Pyrus Meritage**
Region: Australia, Coonawarra $22
Golds/Awards: Gold (FF)

⌐**Lindemans 1993 Limestone Ridge Vineyard
Shiraz- Cabernet**
Region: Australia, Coonawarra $27.99
Golds/Awards: Gold (SY)

$⌐**Lindemans 1994 Padthaway Cabernet-Merlot**
Region: Australia, South Australia $14.99
Golds/Awards: Gold (AT)

$**Madrona 1995 Estate Bottled Shiraz/Cabernet**
Region: California, El Dorado $10
Golds/Awards: Gold (OC)

> ### *Did You Know . . . ?*
> In Australia the sale of wine is fairly unrestricted com-
> pared with U.S. laws. Movement between states is un-
> hindered, and wine producers can sell their wine to
> whomever they wish, wherever they wish.

Red Blends   RED

⌐Matua Valley 1994 Ararimu Cabernet Merlot
Region: New Zealand, Hawkes Bay $18.99
Golds/Awards: Gold (WS)

⌐Meerlust 1992 Rubicon (Bordeaux-style blend)
Region: South Africa $22
Golds/Awards: Gold (WWC-91 pts)

Merryvale 1993 Profile (Bordeaux-style blend)
Region: California, Napa Valley $48
Golds/Awards: Gold (NW); Best of Class (NW);
Best New World Meritage-Type Red (NW)

**⌐Mission Hill 1995 Grand Reserve Merlot
Cabernet Sauvignon**
Region: Canada, British Columbia   (Can $) 24.95
Golds/Awards: Gold (IV)

Mount Veeder Winery 1992 Reserve (Bordeaux-
style blend)
Region: California $40
Golds/Awards: Gold (WWC-92 pts)

**Oakville Ranch 1993 Robert's Blend Red Table
Wine** (Bordeaux-style blend)
Region: California $42
Golds/Awards: Gold (WWC-90 pts)

Opus One 1993 (Bordeaux-style blend)
Region: California $85
Golds/Awards: Platinum (WWC-96 pts); Red
Meritage National Champion and Cellar Selection
(WWC)

Opus One 1992 (Bordeaux-style blend)
Region: California, Napa Valley $95
Golds/Awards: Gold (IW)

Palmer 1994 Select Reserve Red (Bordeaux-style
blend)
Region: New York $19.99
Golds/Awards: Double Gold (TG)

Did You Know . . . ?
Half of Opus One's case production of 20,000 is sold by
the glass.

$Paul Thomas 1995 Cabernet-Merlot
Region: Washington $11
Golds/Awards: Gold (NW); Best of Class (NW)

꒰**Penfolds 1993 Bin 389 Cabernet/Shiraz**
Region: Australia, South Australia $19
Golds/Awards: Gold (IW)

꒰**Penley 1993 Shiraz-Cabernet**
Region: Australia, Coonawarra $25
Golds/Awards: Gold (WS)

꒰**Penley 1994 Shiraz-Cabernet**
Region: Australia, Coonawarra $25
Golds/Awards: Gold (IV)

꒰**Peter Lehmann 1991 Mentor**
Region: Australia $28
Golds/Awards: Gold (WWC-93 pts); Proprietary
Red Blend Champion, Cellar Selection (WWC)

Prince Michel 1990 Le Ducq (Bordeaux-style
blend)
Region: California, Napa Valley $50
Golds/Awards: Gold (WWC-90 pts); Cellar
Selection (WWC)

Prince Michel 1991 Le Ducq (Bordeaux-style
blend)
Region: California, Napa Valley $65
Golds/Awards: Gold (NW)

$Quivera 1995 Dry Creek Cuvée (Rhône-style
blend)
Region: Califonia, Dry Creek Valley $13
Golds/Awards: Gold (WC, LA)

**Rabbit Ridge 1994 Avventura Reserve Migliore
di Vigneto** (Bordeaux-Italian blend)
Region: California, Sonoma County $25
Golds/Awards: Four-Star Gold (OC)

> ***Did You Know . . . ?***
> The average number of useful harvests a cork tree will
> yield in its lifetime is fifteen.

Red Blends   RED

$River Run 1995 Côte d'Aromas (Rhône-style blend)
Region: California $15
Golds/Awards: Gold (NW); Best of Class (NW)

⚲**Rosemount 1994 G.S.M.**
(Grenache/Syrah/Mourvèdre)
Region: Australia $16
Golds/Awards: Gold (WWC-91 pts)

⚲**Rosemount 1994 Mountain Blue No. 1**
(Bordeaux-style blend)
Region: Australia $16
Golds/Awards: Gold (WWC-90 pts); Cellar
Selection (WWC)

⚲**Rosemount 1994 Mountain Blue Shiraz**
Cabernet Sauvignon
Region: Australia, Mudgee $25
Golds/Awards: Gold (SY, NW, WWC-90 pts); Best
of Class (NW); Cellar Selection (WWC-90 pts)

$⚲**Rosemount Estates 1996 Grenache Shiraz**
Region: Australia, Southeast Region $8.95
Golds/Awards: Gold (PR); Double Gold (SF)

Rosenblum 1994 Holbrook Mitchell Trio
Meritage
Region: California, Napa Valley $38
Golds/Awards: Gold (LA)

⚲**Rust en Verde 1992 Estate Red** (Cabernet /Shiraz)
Region: South Africa $25
Golds/Awards: Gold (WWC-92 pts)

St. Clement 1994 Oroppas (Bordeaux-style blend)
Region: California $30
Golds/Awards: Gold (WWC-92 pts, CA); Cellar
Selection (WWC); Best of Class (CA)

$**Sierra Vista 1996 Fleur de Montagne** (Rhône-style
blend)
Region: California, El Dorado $13.50
Golds/Awards: Gold (SD, LA, OC)

+--+
| *Did You Know . . . ?* |
| There are no wine grapes native to Australia. |
+--+

Red Blends RED

Silver Lake Winery 1993 Red Wine Reserve
(Bordeaux-style blend)
Region: Washington $15.99
Golds/Awards: Double Gold (TG)

Sterling 1993 Reserve SVR (Bordeaux-style blend)
Region: California, Napa Valley $40
Golds/Awards: Gold (OC)

Stonestreet 1992 Legacy (Bordeaux-style blend)
Region: California $40
Golds/Awards: Gold (WWC-91 pts)

Stonestreet 1993 Legacy (Bordeaux-style blend)
Region: California $40
Golds/Awards: Gold (WWC-90 pts)

Swanson 1994 Estate Alexis (Cab. Sauvignon/
Syrah/Merlot)
Region: California, Napa Valley $33
Golds/Awards: Gold (FF, OC); Chairman's Award (FF)

$Vigil Vineyard 1995 Terra Vin (Rhône-style
blend)
Region: California $12
Golds/Awards: Gold (CA); Best of Class (CA)

Windsor 1993 Private Reserve Red Meritage
Region: California, Mendocino $16.50
Golds/Awards: Gold (NW)
By mail order only: (800) 333-9987

⌂**Wolf Blass 1993 Black Label Cabernet Shiraz**
Region: Australia, South Australia $30
Golds/Awards: Gold (SY)

$Worden 1994 Cabernet/Merlot
Region: Washington $15
Golds/Awards: Gold (LA)

Did You Know . . . ?
The single most expensive bottle ever sold at wine
auction was a French Bordeaux blend, a Château Lafite,
vintage 1787, that once may have belonged to Thomas
Jefferson. It sold for $156,450 in 1986.

Syrah/Shiraz

One of the great grapes of the Rhône, Syrah, called Shiraz in Australia, produces dark, dense, deeply flavorful red wines that hint of pepper and other exotic spices. Australian Shiraz became wildly popular with Americans in the last decade and helped to catapult that country into the international competitive world of wine. California Syrahs are in greater demand as well.

The Australians are fond of blending their Shiraz with Cabernet Sauvignon and other Bordeaux varietals. In California, one is more apt to see Syrah in spicy Rhône-style blends.

South Africa produces some Syrah, called Shiraz, and Argentina also grows a small amount, which they call Balsamia.

Whatever you call it, Syrah/Shiraz is usually big and full-flavored, and therefore will marry best with foods that can stand up to its weight. Try it with rich meat stews, barbecued meat or vegetables, chili, roast goose, or duck and turkey with all of the trimmings.

Syrah/Shiraz   RED

Bella Vista 1995 Estate Syrah
Region: California, Solano County $18
Golds/Awards: Gold (LA)

Benziger 1994 Syrah
Region: California, Central Coast $17
Golds/Awards: Gold (WC, CA); Best of Class (CA)

Bonterra Organically Grown 1994 Syrah
Region: California, Mendocino County $22
Golds/Awards: Gold (WC, OC); Four-Star Gold
(OC)

꼬**Charles Melton 1995 Shiraz**
Region: Australia, Barossa Valley $35
Golds/Awards: Gold (SY)

꼬**Chateau Reynella 1994 Basket Pressed Shiraz**
Region: Australia, McLaren Vale $22.50
Golds/Awards: Gold (IW, SY)

$Columbia 1995 Syrah
Region: Washington, Yakima Valley $13
Golds/Awards: Double Gold (SF)

Columbia Crest 1994 Reserve Syrah
Region Washington $17
Golds/Awards: Gold (WWC-95 pts); Cellar
Selection and Best Buy (WWC)

꼬**Coriole 1994 Lloyd Reserve Shiraz**
Region: Australia, McLaren Vale $38
Golds/Awards: Gold (SY)

꼬**D'Arenberg 1994 The Dead Arm Shiraz**
Region: Australia, South Australia $45
Golds/Awards: Gold (IW)

꼬**Eileen Hardy 1994 Shiraz**
Region: Australia, South Australia $45
Golds/Awards: Gold (AT); Double Gold (SF); Best Shiraz
(SF)

Did You Know . . . ?
Besides their reputation as brilliant innovators, Australian winemakers are known for their extreme work
ethic, ignoring evenings and weekends during harvest.

Syrah/Shiraz   RED

$ ℞ Fairview Estate 1993 Shiraz Reserve
Region: South Africa, Paarl $14.99
Golds/Awards: Gold (WS)

Fess Parker 1994 Syrah
Region: California, Santa Barbara $18
Golds/Awards: Gold (AT)

Fess Parker 1994 American Tradition Reserve Syrah
Region: California, Santa Barbara County $28
Golds/Awards: Gold (CA)

℞ Georgia's Paddock 1993 Shiraz
Region: Australia, Victoria $45
Golds/Awards: Gold (IW)

$ Geyser Peak 1994 Shiraz
Region: California, Sonoma County $14
Golds/Awards: Gold (NW)

Geyser Peak 1994 Reserve Shiraz
Region: California, Sonoma County $32
Golds/Awards: Gold (FF, NW, WWC-90 pts); Best of Class (NW); Cellar Selection (WWC)

$ Geyser Peak 1995 Shiraz
Region: California, Sonoma County $15
Golds/Awards: Gold (PR, WC, NW, SF); Best of Class (PR, WC); Grand Champion (PR); Best Red Wine (PR)

Glen Fiona 1995 Syrah
Region: Washington $30
Golds/Awards: Gold and Grand Award Trophy (NE)

℞ Henschke 1994 Mount Edelstone Shiraz
Region: Australia, Keyneton/Barossa $49
Golds/Awards: Gold (SY)

Did You Know . . . ?

Rusty Figgins, owner/winemaker at Glen Fiona, grew up in a winemaking family and trained in Australia. His *very first vintage* of Syrah, the 1995, won both a gold medal and the Grand Award at the Northwest Enological Society wine judging. Way to go, Rusty!

Syrah/Shiraz   RED

$Indian Springs 1995 Syrah
Region: California, Nevada County $15
Golds/Awards: Gold (CA); Best of Class (CA)

$J. Lohr 1994 South Ridge Syrah
Region: California, Napa Valley $14
Golds/Awards: Gold (IW)

Jade Mountain 1993 Syrah
Region: California, Paso Robles $18
Golds/Awards: Gold (IW)

⏚Lawson's 1991 Shiraz
Region: Australia, Southeast Region $25
Golds/Awards: Gold (IW, WS); Best Rhône-Style (IW, SY)

⏚Lawson's 1994 Padthaway Shiraz
Region: Australia $24.99
Golds/Awards: Gold (VL)

$⏚Leasingham 1994 Classic Clare Shiraz
Region: Australia, Clare Valley $11.25
Golds/Awards: Gold (WS); Best Aus. Red,
Best Shiraz (WS)

⏚Marienberg 1994 Shiraz
Region: Australia $38
Golds/Awards: Gold (IV)

Mc Crea 1994 French Barrel Syrah
Region: Washington $35
Golds/Awards: Gold (WWC-92 pts); Cellar
Selection (WWC)

Mc Crea 1994 Syrah
Region; Washington $35
Golds/Awards: Gold (WWC-93 pts); Cellar
Selection (WWC)

$McDowell Valley Vineyards 1995 Estate Syrah
Region: California, Mendocino $15
Golds/Awards: Gold (SF)

Did You Know . . . ?
The average length of time Americans age their wine is
eighteen minutes (from the store to their home).

Syrah/Shiraz   RED

McGuigan Brothers 1994 Personal Reserve Shiraz
Region: Australia, South Australia $19.99
Golds/Awards: Gold (IW)

Orfila Vineyards 1994 Val de la Mer Syrah
Region: California, San Diego $22
Golds/Awards: Gold (AW, Tennessee International); Double Gold (TG)

Penfolds 1994 Bin 28 Kalimira Shiraz
Region: Australia, South Australia $16.99
Golds/Awards: Gold (FF); Best of Category (FF)

Peter Lehmann 1992 Stonewell Shiraz
Region: Australia, Barossa Valley $40
Golds/Awards: Gold (SY)

Plantagenet 1994 Mount Barker Shiraz
Region: Australia $24
Golds/Awards: Gold (IW)

$R.H. Phillips 1995 EXP Syrah
Region: California, Dunnigan Hills $12
Golds/Awards: Gold (CA); Best of Class (CA)

Rosemount 1993 Balmoral Syrah
Region: Australia, McLaren Vale $35
Golds/Awards: Gold (IW)

Rosemount 1994 Balmoral Syrah
Region: Australia, McLaren Vale $35
Golds/Awards: Gold (WWC-94 pts)

Rosemount 1994 Show Reserve Syrah
Region: Australia, McLaren Vale $18.50
Golds/Awards: Gold (SY)

Rothbury Estate 1994 Reserve Bottling Shiraz
Region: Australia, Hunter Valley $18
Golds/Awards: Gold (SY)

Did You Know . . . ?
England buys cheaper Aussie wine than do Americans. The price of Australian wine sold here averages 50 percent more than it does in the UK.

Syrah/Shiraz   RED

♫**St. Hallett 1993 Old Block Shiraz**
Region: Australia $22
Golds/Awards: Gold (WWC-90 pts)

Santa Barbara 1995 Syrah
Region: California, Santa Barbara County $16
Golds/Awards: Gold (PR, NW, WWC-90 pts); Best
of Class, Best New World Shiraz (NW); Cellar
Selection, Best Buy (WWC)

Sierra Vista 1994 Red Rock Ridge Syrah
Region: California, El Dorado $16.50
Golds/Awards: Gold (WWC-90 pts)

♫**Stellenzicht 1994 Syrah**
Region: South Africa $48
Golds/Awards: Gold (WWC-92 pts)

Thackrey 1994 Orion Rossi Vineyard Syrah
Region: California $30
Golds/Awards: Gold (WWC-94 pts); Cellar
Selection (WWC)

♫**Tim Adams 1994 Aberfeldy Shiraz**
Region: Australia, South Australia $17.90
Golds/Awards: Gold (IW)

♫**Tyrrell's 1990 Vat 9 Shiraz**
Region: Australia, Hunter Valley $29.99
Golds/Awards: Gold (IW)

♫**Vasse Felix 1995 Shiraz**
Region: Australia, Margaret River $21
Golds/Awards: Gold (SY)

$Wellington 1994 Alegria Vineyard Syrah
Region: California, Russian River Valley $15
Golds/Awards: Gold (WWC-90 pts); Best Buy
(WWC)

Did You Know . . . ?
Georg Riedel, famous designer of wine glasses specific
to each varietal, has determined that Shiraz (Australian)
and Syrah (French) are so distinct from one another
that they require two different glass shapes.

$Wellington 1995 Alegria Vineyard Syrah
Region: California, Russian River Valley $15
Golds/Awards: Gold (SD); Best of Class (SD)

Wolf Blass 1993 President's Selection Shiraz
Region: Australia, South Australia $18
Golds/Awards: Gold (IW)

Zaca Mesa 1995 Syrah
Region: California, Santa Barbara $18
Golds/Awards: Gold (SF, CA); Best of Class (CA)

Did You Know . . . ?

One famous New Orleans wine collector had spent the majority of his life building a world-class cellar full of expensive rarities. He lost it all in a divorce. Another collector, well-known in exclusive wine auction circles for his big Texan taste and pocketbook, lost *his* entire wine collection. This time it wasn't to a dame, but to God. He found religion and sold off everything to raise money for his church.

Zinfandel

This exotic red-wine grape has taken the New World by storm. California is where most Zinfandel is cultivated these days, with Australia and South Africa new entrants in the field. Thanks to DNA testing, it's been determined that Zinfandel is actually the same as Italy's Primativo grape.

One reason this varietal has so much popular appeal is that it lends itself to any number of styles. Zinfandel can be fruity, light, Beaujolais-like, or medium bodied with definite character, or extremely rich, intensely flavored, tannic, and long-lived, like a great Cabernet Sauvignon. Some winemakers also make it into a sweet dessert wine.

Zinfandel has an easily recognizable varietal character: aromas and flavors of black pepper and brambles, with cherries, blackberries, and raspberries, and a lush, supple texture.

It is also the grape used to make White Zinfandel (which is actually pink), one of the most consumed varietals in the United States.

Because of its well-flavored, spicy nature, serve it with equally sturdy dishes, such as ratatouille, anchovy and olive antipasti, and steak with mustard sauce.

Alderbrook 1995 Gamba Vineyard Zinfandel
Region: California, Russian River Valley $18
Golds/Awards: Gold (AT)

Benziger 1994 Old Vines Zinfandel
Region: California, Sonoma County $16
Golds/Awards: Gold (PR, SD); Best of Class (SD)

Benziger 1995 Old Vines Zinfandel
Region: California, Sonoma County $17
Golds/Awards: Double Gold (CA); Tie for Best
of California and Best of Class (CA)

$Beringer 1993 Zinfandel
Region: California $12
Golds/Awards: Double Gold (TG)

$Boeger 1995 Walker Zinfandel
Region: California, El Dorado $15
Golds/Awards: Double Gold (SF)

$Castoro Cellars 1994 Zinfandel
Region: California, Paso Robles $9.95
Golds/Awards: Gold (DA, FF)

$Castoro Cellars 1995 Zinfandel
Region: California, Paso Robles $9.95
Golds/Awards: Gold (SD, SF)

$Castoro Cellars 1995 Guibbini Vnyrd Estate Zin.
Region: California, Paso Robles $14
Golds/Awards: Gold (OC)

Cline 1995 Ancient Vines Zinfandel
Region: California $18
Golds/Awards: Gold (WWC-90 pts)

Cosentino 1995 The Zin Zinfandel
Region: California $22
Golds/Awards: Gold (CA); Best of Class (CA)

De Loach 1995 Estate Bottled O.F.S. Zinfandel
Region: California, Russian River Valley $25
Golds/Awards: Gold (DA, PR, WWC-92 pts); Best of
Class (PR)

Did You Know . . . ?
Zin has been popular in the U.S. since Gold Rush days,
when it was the miners' drink of choice in saloons.

De Loach 1995 Papera Ranch Zinfandel
Region: California, Russian River Valley $18
Golds/Awards: Gold (WWC-90 pts)

De Loach 1995 Pelletti Ranch Zinfandel
Region: California, Russian River Valley $18
Golds/Awards: Gold (WWC-92 pts)

De Rose 1993 Cedolini Vineyard Dry Farm Hillside Reserve Zinfandel
Region: California, Cienega Valley $20
Golds/Awards: Gold (AT, BT)

Dickerson 1994 Limited Reserve Zinfandel
Region: California, Napa Valley $24.99
Golds/Awards: Gold (WWC-90 pts); Cellar Selection (WWC)

Dry Creek Vineyard 1994 Reserve Zinfandel
Region: California, Sonoma County $20
Golds/Awards: Gold (NW, WWC-90 pts)

Edmeades 1994 Zinfandel
Region: California, Mendocino County $16
Golds/Awards: Gold (AT)

Edmeades 1995 Zinfandel
Region: California, Mendocino County $19
Golds/Awards: Gold (PR, IV, LA, NW)

Edmeades 1995 Eaglepoint Vineyard Zinfandel
Region: California, Mendocino County $19
Golds/Awards: Gold (PR)

Estate Baccala 1995 Zinfandel
Region: California, Mendocino $16
Golds/Awards: Gold (FF); Chairman's Award (FF)

Fanucchi 1995 Wood Road Old Vines Zinfandel
Region: California, Russian River Valley $26
Golds/Awards: Gold (SF)

Did You Know . . . ?
Small and middle-tier wineries (less than 50,000 cases) get as much as 20 percent of their business from direct shipping to customers. New laws prohibiting such shipments in certain states are taking an economic toll on these wineries.

Zinfandel   RED

$Fetzer 1994 Barrel Select Zinfandel
Region: California, Mendocino County $8.99
Golds/Awards: Gold (OC)

$Gallo Sonoma 1994 Frei Ranch Vineyard Zinfandel
Region: California, Sonoma County $14
Golds/Awards: Gold (AT)

$Gallo Sonoma 1995 Chiotti Vineyard Zinfandel
Region: California, Dry Creek Valley $14
Golds/Awards: Gold (PR, IV)

Gary Farrell 1995 Zinfandel
Region: California, Russian River Valley $20
Golds/Awards: Gold (DA, SD, WC, LA, OC, NW, CA, WWC-91 pts, Citrus Fair); Best of Class (NW, CA); Best New World Zinfandel (NW); Sweepstakes Red (NW, CA)

Gary Farrell 1995 Grist Ranch Zinfandel
Region: California, Dry Creek Valley $24
Golds/Awards: Gold (LA, OC)

$Geyser Peak 1995 Zinfandel
Region: California, Sonoma County $14
Golds/Awards: Gold (NW)

Greenwood Ridge 1995 Scherrer Vineyard Zinfandel
Region: California, Sonoma County $16
Golds/Awards: Gold (DA, NW, CA); Best of Class (NW, CA)

$Grey Wolf Cellars 1995 Zinfandel
Region: California, Paso Robles $13
Golds/Awards: Gold (WWC-90 pts); Best Buy (WWC)

Grgich Hills 1994 Zinfandel
Region: California, Sonoma County $18
Golds/Awards: Gold (LA); Best of Class (LA)

Did You Know . . . ?
The first-known vintage produced in California was 1782.

$Guenoc 1995 Zinfandel
Region: California $11
Golds/Awards: Gold (NW); Best of Class (NW)

$Gundlach-Bundschu 1995 Morse Vineyard Zinfandel
Region: California, Sonoma Valley $14
Golds/Awards: Gold (SD); Best of Class (SD)

Hartford Court 1995 Hartford Vineyard Zinfandel
Region: California, Russian River Valley $40
Golds/Awards: Gold (OC, NW); Double Gold (SF); Best Zinfandel (SF)

Haywood 1994 Los Chamizal Vineyards Zinfandel
Region: California, Sonoma Valley $16
Golds/Awards: Gold (WWC-90 pts)

Haywood 1994 Rocky Terrace Zinfandel
Region: California, Sonoma Valley $22
Golds/Awards: Gold (WWC-92 pts)

Hendry 1994 Block 7 Zinfandel
Region: California, Napa Valley $17
Golds/Awards: Gold (WWC-90 pts)

Hidden Cellars 1995 Mendocino Heritage Sorcery (Zinfandel)
Region: California, Mendocino $25
Golds/Awards: Gold (OC)

Kendall-Jackson 1994 Grand Reserve Zinfandel
Region: California $25
Golds/Awards: Gold (IV, FF, OC); Chairman's Award (FF)

$Kenwood 1992 Zinfandel
Region: California, Sonoma Valley $12
Golds/Awards: Gold (IW)

Did You Know . . . ?
Zinfandels tend to have rootstock that's older, from 30 to 100 years, than other American varieties. The reason is because Zin rootstocks weren't victims of the root louse, phylloxera, that wiped out most other varieties.

Kenwood 1993 Nuns Canyon Zinfandel
Region: California, Sonoma Valley $19
Golds/Awards: Gold (IW)

$Konrad Estate 1993 Estate Bottled Zinfandel
Region: California, Mendocino County $14.50
Golds/Awards: Gold (PR); Best of Class (PR)

$Kunde 1995 Century Vines Zinfandel
Region: California, Sonoma Valley $15
Golds/Awards: Gold (WWC-91 pts)

La Crema 1995 Reserve Zinfandel
Region: California, Sonoma County $24
Golds/Awards: Gold (NW, CA)

Lake Sonoma Winery 1994 Old Vine Reserve Zinfandel
Region: California, Dry Creek Valley $17.95
Golds/Awards: Gold (PR); Double Gold (TG)

Lamborn Family Vineyards 1994 The Queen's Vintage Zinfandel
Region: California, Napa Valley $17
Golds/Awards: Gold (WWC-90 pts)

Lamborn Family Vineyards 1995 The French Connection Zinfandel
Region: California, Napa Valley $18
Golds/Awards: Gold (WWC-91 pts); Cellar Selection (WWC)

Lolonis 1994 Private Reserve Zinfandel
Region: California, Redwood Valley $19
Golds/Awards: Gold (SD)

$Madrona 1995 Estate Bottled Zinfandel
Region: California, El Dorado $10
Golds/Awards: Gold (OC)

Did You Know . . . ?
World War II devastated European wineries, and is one of the factors that played a part in the rise and development of the American wine business.

Zinfandel   RED

McIlroy Wines 1995 Porter Bass Vineyard Zinfandel
Region: California, Russian River Valley $19
Golds/Awards: Gold (PR)

$Mietz Cellars 1995 Zinfandel
Region: California, Sonoma County $15
Golds/Awards: Gold (NW)

Nalle 1995 Zinfandel
Region: California, Dry Creek Valley $17.49
Golds/Awards: Gold (WWC-90 pts)

$Napa Ridge 1995 Coastal Zinfandel
Region: California, Central Coast $9
Golds/Awards: Gold (CA); Best of Class (CA)

Navarro 1995 Zinfandel
Region: California, Mendocino County $18
Golds/Awards: Gold (WC)

$Nevada City 1995 Sierra Foothills Zinfandel
Region: California, Nevada County $12
Golds/Awards: Gold (OC)

$Pedroncelli 1994 Mother Clone Zinfandel
Region: California, Dry Creek Valley $11.50
Golds/Awards: Gold (NW)

$Pedroncelli 1994 Pedroni-Bushnell Vineyard Zinfandel
Region: California, Dry Creek Valley $11.50
Golds/Awards: Gold (PR, NW)

Pezzi King 1995 Zinfandel
Region: California, Dry Creek Valley $22
Golds/Awards: Gold (WWC-90 pts)

Portteus 1995 Zinfandel
Region: Washington, Yakima Valley $18
Golds/Awards: Gold (WWC-90 pts)

Did You Know . . . ?
Some people complain that red wine gives them a headache. Scientists hypothesize that this effect is caused by the amine compounds found in red wine, which cause blood vessels to expand or contract.

$Rabbit Ridge 1995 Zinfandel
Region: California, Sonoma County $13
Golds/Awards: Gold (OC)

Ravenswood 1995 Cooke Vineyard Zinfandel
Region: California, Sonoma Valley $21.50
Golds/Awards: Gold (WWC-91 pts); Cellar
Selection (WWC)

**Ravenswood 1995 Dickerson Vineyard
Zinfandel**
Region: California, Napa Valley $21.50
Golds/Awards: Gold (WWC-92 pts)

Ravenswood 1995 Monte Rosso Zinfandel
Region: California, Sonoma Valley $21.50
Golds/Awards: Gold (WWC-90 pts); Cellar
Selection (WWC)

Ravenswood 1995 Wood Road Zinfandel
Region: California, Russian River Valley $21.50
Golds/Awards: Gold (WWC-91 pts)

Renwood 1995 Grandpère Zinfandel
Region: California, Amador County $24
Golds/Awards: Gold (WWC-91 pts)

Renwood 1995 Jack Rabbit Flat Zinfandel
Region: California, Amador County $24
Golds/Awards: Gold (WWC-90 pts)

Ridge 1992 Geyserville Zinfandel
Region: California, Santa Cruz $27.50
Golds/Awards: Gold (IW); Best Spicy Red (IW)

Ridge 1995 Lytton Springs
Region: California, Dry Creek Valley $22.50
Golds/Awards: Gold (WWC-92pts)

Did You Know . . . ?
If Barbie drank wine, I'd like to think she's a Zin kind
of gal. In the last two decades Mattel has marketed
accessories for the popular doll that include a green
burgundy-style bottle with two glasses. Mattel's
spokeswoman insists it's just "sparkling water." Hmm.

Zinfandel   RED

Ridge 1995 Sonoma Station Zinfandel
Region: California, Sonoma County $16
Golds/Awards: Gold (WWC-91 pts)

Ridge 1995 Zinfandel
Region: California, Paso Robles $20
Golds/Awards: Gold (WWC-90 pts)

Robert Biale 1995 Old Vineyards Late Picked Zinfandel
Region: California, Napa Valley $22.99
Golds/Awards: Gold (WWC-90 pts)

$Robert Mondavi 1995 Coastal Zinfandel
Region: California, North Coast $10
Golds/Awards: Gold (SF)

Rodney Strong 1994 Old Vines Zinfandel
Region: California $16
Golds/Awards: Double Gold (TG, IV)

Rosenblum 1995 Brandlin Ranch Zinfandel
Region: California, Napa Valley $23
Golds/Awards: Gold (WWC-90 pts)

Rosenblum 1995 Continente Vineyard Old Vine Zinfandel
Region: California $18
Golds/Awards: Gold (WWC-90 pts)

Rosenblum 1995 Harris Kratka Vineyard Zinfandel
Region: California, Alexander Valley $20
Golds/Awards: Gold (WWC-90 pts, CA)

Rosenblum 1995 Old Vines Zinfandel
Region: California, Sonoma County $17.50
Golds/Awards: Gold (CA)

Rosenblum 1995 Pato Vineyard Reserve Zinfandel
Region: California $18
Golds/Awards: Gold (WWC-90 pts)

Did You Know . . . ?
There are an estimated 10,000 taste buds located on the human tongue.

Zinfandel   RED

Rosenblum 1995 Reserve Zinfandel
Region: California, Napa Valley $25
Golds/Awards: Gold (SF)

St. Francis 1995 Old Vines Zinfandel
Region: California, Sonoma County $22
Golds/Awards: Gold (WWC-91 pts); Cellar
Selection (WWC)

**St. Francis 1995 Pagani Vineyard Reserve
Zinfandel**
Region: California, Sonoma Valley $29
Golds/Awards: Gold (WWC-95 pts); Cellar
Selection (WWC)

Schuetz Oles 1994 Korte Ranch Zinfandel
Region: California, Napa Valley $16
Golds/Awards: Gold (WWC-90 pts)

**Sebastiani Vineyards 1995 Domenici Vineyard
Old Vines Zinfandel**
Region: California, Sonoma Valley $16
Golds/Awards: Gold (CA)

**$Sierra Vista 1995 Estate Bottled Vintner's Select
Zinfandel**
Region: California, El Dorado $8
Golds/Awards: Gold (NW); Tie for Best of Class
(NW)

$Sobon 1995 Vintner's Selection Zinfandel
Region: California, Amador County $15
Golds/Awards: Gold (WWC-91 pts)

**Sonora Winery 1995 Story Vineyard Old Vines
Zinfandel**
Region: California, Amador $16
Golds/Awards: Gold (NW)

Did You Know . . . ?
The Symposium, an ancient Greek all-male drinking
party, was, when properly observed, a strictly controlled
ritual of drinking combined with poetry, entertainment,
and debate. The aim was pleasant intoxication without
loss of reason.

Zinfandel   RED

Steele 1995 Du Pratt Vineyard Zinfandel
Region: California, Mendocino $18
Golds/Awards: Gold (WWC-90 pts)

Steele 1995 Pacini Vineyard Zinfandel
Region: California, Mendocino $16
Golds/Awards: Gold (WWC-90 pts)

Storrs 1995 Lion Oaks Vineyard Zinfandel
Region: California, Santa Clara County $25
Golds/Awards: Gold (CA); Best of Region
and Best of Class (CA)

**Storrs 1994 Beauregard Ranch Ben Lomond
Zinfandel**
Region: California $18
Golds/Awards: Gold (WWC-91 pts)

**Storybook Mountain Vineyards 1993 Reserve
Zinfandel**
Region: California, Napa Valley $25
Golds/Awards: Gold (WWC-90 pts); Cellar
Selection (WWC)

**$Sutter Home 1990 Amador County Reserve
Zinfandel**
Region: California, Napa Valley $9.95
Golds/Awards: Gold (IW)

$Talus 1995 Zinfandel
Region: California $7.99
Golds/Awards: Gold (NW); Tie for Best of Class (NW)

$Titus 1995 Zinfandel
Region California, Napa Valley $15
Golds/Awards: Gold (WWC-91 pts)

**Tobin James 1995 James Gang Reserve
Zinfandel**
Region: California, Paso Robles $20
Golds/Awards: Gold (OC)

Did You Know . . . ?
In the ancient Persian Archaemenid Dynasty, women
laborers who bore sons were rewarded with 10 quarts
of wine. Those who bore daughters received 5 quarts.

Zinfandel   RED

Topolos 1995 Pagani Ranch Zinfandel
Region: California, Sonoma Valley $40
Golds/Awards: Gold (WWC-91 pts)

Topolos 1995 Rossi Ranch Zinfandel
Region: California, Sonoma Valley $24.50
Golds/Awards: Gold (WWC-90 pts)

**$Turning Leaf 1993 Sonoma Reserve
Winemaker's Choice Zinfandel**
Region: California, Sonoma County $10
Golds/Awards: Gold (OC)

$Twin Hills 1993 Zinfandel
Region: California, Paso Robles $13.50
Golds/Awards: Gold (WWC-93 pts); Best Buy (WWC)

**Villa Mt. Eden 1994 Grand Reserve Monte
Rosso Vineyard Zinfandel**
Region: California, Napa Valley $16
Golds/Awards: Gold (WC); Best of Class (WC)

$Villa Mt. Eden 1994 Zinfandel
Region: California, Napa Valley $9.50
Golds/Awards: Gold (IW)

Wellington 1995 Casa Santinamaria Zinfandel
Region: California, Sonoma Valley $16
Golds/Awards: Gold (SD)

Wellington 1995 100 Year Old Vines Zinfandel
Region: California, Sonoma Valley $18
Golds/Awards: Gold (WWC-90 pts)

$Windsor 1994 Signature Series Zinfandel
Region: California, Alexander Valley $14.50
Golds/Awards: Gold (NW)
By mail order only: (800) 333-9987

$York Mountain 1994 Zinfandel
Region: California, San Luis Obispo $12
Golds/Awards: Gold (LA)

Did You Know . . . ?
The demand for wine to provision troops often provided a stimulus for wine regions not directly involved
in the fighting. Records show that when Edward I em-
barked on his Scottish campaign in 1300, he first
brought in vast quantities of wine from Bordeaux.

WHITE WINES

Chardonnay
Chenin Blanc
Gewurztraminer
Misc. Varietal Whites
Native & Hybrid Whites
Pinot Blanc
Riesling
Sauvignon Blanc
Semillon
Viognier
White Blends

Chardonnay

This is the white vinifera grape of France's white burgundy and champagne as well as American sparkling wine. Chardonnay is by far the most popular white wine produced in the New World. It's in such demand worldwide that it has the dubious distinction of being the variety of which the most cuttings are smuggled—in places like New Zealand, South Africa, and Australia, where rigid quarantine laws are enforced.

Chardonnay is easy to grow and adapts well to cool regions. That's why you see great Chardonnays from places like Canada and Washington State. This varietal ages well, and more than other whites, the interesting aromas and flavors derived from oak barrel fermentation and aging assume a key role in its personality.

There are two predominant Chardonnay styles. The first is fresh, fruity, and lightly oaked; the second is toasty, spicy, buttery, and big. Either way, most Chardonnay is fairly fruity, with plenty of balancing acidity, and has a flavor and bouquet that may include apple, pineapple, peaches, tangerine, and lime; cinnamon and clove spices; and buttery, vanilla, smoky, nutty, or grassy hints.

Most Chardonnay has so much personality that it tends to compete with complex foods. Serve this wine with unassuming dishes such as raw vegetable dippers before a main meal, seafood and shellfish (without fancy sauces); pasta with cream sauce; and roasted turkey or chicken. Lighter Chardonnays can complement mild cheeses.

Chardonnay WHITE

Adelaida 1994 Chardonnay
Region: California $19
Golds/Awards: Gold (WWC-94 pts)

Alderbrook 1994 Dorothy's Vineyard Chardonnay
Region: California, Dry Creek Valley $18.50
Golds/Awards: Gold (AT)

$Anapamu 1995 Barrel Fermented Chardonnay
Region: California, Central Coast $12
Golds/Awards: Gold (DA, AT, OC)

$Armida 1994 Chardonnay
Region: California, Russian River Valley $14
Golds/Awards: Gold (NW); Best of Class (NW)

$Armida 1995 Chardonnay
Region: Califonia, Russian River Valley $15
Golds/Awards: Gold (WC, NW, CA); Best of Class (NW)

Au Bon Climat 1994 Le Bouge D'à Côté Chardonnay
Region: California, Santa Barbara County $24.99
Golds/Awards: Gold (WWC-91 pts)

Au Bon Climat 1994 Reserve Talley Chardonnay
Region: California $24.99
Golds/Awards: Gold (WWC-92 pts)

Babcock 1994 Mt. Carmel Vineyard Chardonnay
Region: California, Santa Barbara County $23.99
Golds/Awards: Gold (WWC-90 pts); Cellar Selection (WWC)

Bargetto 1995 Chardonnay
Region: California, Santa Cruz Mountains $19
Golds/Awards: Gold (NW)

Did You Know . . . ?
In France's managed oak forests, rangers don't practice reforestation, as they do in America. Instead, "mother trees" are left standing. Acorns that fall from those trees are left to grow naturally; all other tree varieties are pulled out, leaving only the young oaks to grow.

Chardonnay WHITE

Beaucanon 1995 Jacques de Coninck Chardonnay
Region: California, Napa Valley $28
Golds/Awards: Gold (WWC-90 pts)

🏵**Basedow 1995 Chardonnay**
Region: Australia, Barossa Valley $16
Golds/Awards: Gold (IW)

Beaulieu 1995 Reserve Chardonnay
Region: California, Los Carneros (Napa) $20
Golds/Awards: Gold (CA)

$Belvedere 1995 Jimtown Ranch Vineyard Chardonnay
Region: California, Alexander Valley $12
Golds/Awards: Gold (CA)

Benziger 1995 Chardonnay
Region: Califonia, Carneros $23
Golds/Awards: Gold (WC)

Beringer 1994 Private Reserve Chardonnay
Region: California, Napa Valley $25
Golds/Awards: Gold (AT, WS)

Beringer 1995 Private Reserve Chardonnay
Region: California, Napa Valley $25
Golds/Awards: Gold (NW, CA); Best of Class (CA)

$Bernardus 1994 Chardonnay
Region: California, Monterey $14.50
Golds/Awards: Gold (WWC-90 pts); Cellar Selection and Best Buy (WWC)

$Blossom Hill 1995 Chardonnay
Region: California $5
Golds/Awards: Gold (NW)

Did You Know . . . ?
A 1630s law in post-Roman Britain made it illegal to sell wine in glass bottles. Unscrupulous wine merchants had been profiting unfairly from the fact that no two bottles held the same amount. For the next 230 years, people bought wine by measure, then poured it into their own personally stamped bottles.

Chardonnay   WHITE

$Bridgeview 1995 Blue Moon Chardonnay
Region: Oregon $7.99
Golds/Awards: Gold (OR)

$Buehler Vineyards 1995 Chardonnay
Region: California, Russian River Valley $13
Golds/Awards: Gold (SD)

Buena Vista 1994 Grand Reserve Chardonnay
Region: California, Carneros $22
Golds/Awards: Gold (NW)

Byron 1994 Estate Chardonnay
Region: California, Santa Maria Valley $30
Golds/Awards: Gold (WWC-90 pts)

Byron 1995 Reserve Chardonnay
Region: California, Santa Barbara County $24
Golds/Awards: Gold (OC)

Cakebread Cellars 1993 Reserve Chardonnay
Region: California, Carneros $30
Golds/Awards: Gold (WWC-90 pts)

Cakebread Cellars 1994 Reserve Chardonnay
Region: California, Napa Valley $33
Golds/Awards: Gold (SF)

Calera 1994 Chardonnay
Region: California $30
Golds/Awards: Gold (WWC-93 pts)

Calera 1995 Chardonnay
Region: California, Central Coast $16
Golds/Awards: Gold (WWC-90 pts)

$Callaway 1994 Calla Lees Chardonnay
Region: California, Temecula $10
Golds/Awards: Gold (AT)

Did You Know . . . ?
Roses are often planted alongside grapevines to act as
"canaries in a cave." Susceptible to powdery mildew,
they alert the grower when it's time to spray.

Chardonnay WHITE

$Callaway 1995 Calla-Lees Chardonnay
Region: California, Temecula $10
Golds/Awards: Gold (NW); Best of Class (NW)

Cambria 1994 Chardonnay
Region: California, Santa Barbara County $16
Golds/Awards: Gold (WWC-90 pts)

Cambria 1994 Reserve Chardonnay
Region: California, Santa Maria Valley $30
Golds/Awards: Gold (WWC-91 pts)

**Cambria 1995 Katherine's Vineyard Estate
Bottled Chardonnay**
Region: California, Santa Maria Valley $20
Golds/Awards: Gold (SD, WC, AT); Best of
Class (SD)

Cambria 1995 Reserve Chardonnay
Region: California, Santa Maria Valley $30
Golds/Awards: Gold (CA)

Camelot 1995 Chardonnay
Region: California, Santa Barbara County $18
Golds/Awards: Gold (LA); Double Gold (CA);
Best of Class (LA, CA); Best of Region (CA)

$Canyon Road 1996 Chardonnay
Region: Califonia $7.99
Golds/Awards: Gold (WC, FF); Best of Class (WC)

**$ ⌂ Casa Lapostolle 1995 Cuvée Alexandre
Chardonnay**
Region: Chile $15
Golds/Awards: Gold (WWC-90 pts)

Did You Know . . . ?
It was Chile's good fortune that Frenchman Claudio Gay
persuaded the Chilean government in the 1800s to set
up an experimental nursery for exotic botanical speci-
mens, including European grapevines. Chile had its own
collection of vinifera cuttings safely protected in viticultural isolation before the onset of the world's late-nine-
teenth-century epidemic of powdery mildew and
phylloxera, which wiped out most of the world's vines.

Chardonnay   WHITE

$Castoro Cellars 1995 Reserve Chardonnay
Region: California, Paso Robles $12.95
Golds/Awards: Gold (NW)

Chalone 1994 Estate Reserve Chardonnay
Region: California $45
Golds/Awards: Gold (WWC-90 pts)

$Chandelle of Sonoma 1995 Spirit of Flight Chard.
Region: California, Sonoma County $12
Golds/Awards: Gold (NW)

⌘Chateau des Charmes 1994 St. David's Bench Chardonnay
Region: Canada, Niagara Penin.   (Can $) 19.75
Golds/Awards: Gold (WS)

$Chateau Julien 1995 Private Reserve Chardonnay
Region: Califonia, Monterey County $15
Golds/Awards: Gold (WC)

⌘Chateau Reynella 1995 Chardonnay
Region: Australia, McLaren Vale $21.25
Golds/Awards: Gold (SY)

Chateau St. Jean 1993 Robert Young Vineyards Reserve Chardonnay
Region: California, Alexander Valley $57.50/1.5L
Golds/Awards: Gold (WWC-90 pts)

$Chateau Ste. Michelle 1994 Chardonnay
Region: Washington, Columbia Valley $13.99
Golds/Awards: Gold (AT)

Chateau Ste. Michelle 1994 Reserve Chardonnay
Region: Washington, Columbia Valley $31
Golds/Awards: Gold (AT, WWC-90 pts)

Did You Know . . . ?
In wine snob circles, the term *jug wine* is a dirty word, connoting a cheap, low-quality product. But as wine consciousness goes up, so do sales of "jug wine." If you want a large bottle of Cabernet or Chardonnay, be sure to ask for a "1.5L," short for 1.5-liter bottle, the new "in" term being promoted by the wine industry.

Chardonnay   WHITE

Chateau Ste. Michelle 1994 Canoe Ridge Estate Vineyard Chardonnay
Region: Washington, Columbia Valley $28
Golds/Awards: Gold (AT, WWC-91 pts); Best U.S. White (AT)

Chateau Ste. Michelle 1995 Canoe Ridge Estate Vineyard Chardonnay
Region: Washington, Columbia Valley $28
Golds/Awards: Gold (PR)

Chateau Ste. Michelle 1995 Cold Creek Vineyard Chardonnay
Region: Washington, Columbia Valley $26
Golds/Awards: Gold (PR, NW); Double Gold (SF); Best of Class (NW); Best Chardonnay (SF)

$Chateau Souverain 1995 Chardonnay
Region: California, Sonoma County $13.50
Golds/Awards: Gold (LA)

Chateau Souverain 1995 Winemaker's Reserve Chardonnay
Region: California, Russian River Valley $20
Golds/Awards: Gold (PR, NW); Tie for Best of Class (NW)

Cinnabar 1995 Estate Grown Chardonnay
Region: California, Santa Cruz Mountains $23
Golds/Awards: Gold (PR)

CJ Pask 1994 Gimblett Road Chardonnay
Region: New Zealand, Hawkes Bay $15.99
Golds/Awards: Gold (IW)

CJ Pask 1995 Reserve Chardonnay
Region: New Zealand, Hawkes Bay $24.99
Golds/Awards: Gold (IW)

Did You Know . . . ?

The wood in which a wine is fermented and/or ages has a profound and complex effect on its characteristics and flavor. For example, wine's alcohol acts as a solvent to dissolve and extract the vanillin molecule present in oak, thus creating those "hints of vanilla" you read about in tasting notes.

Chardonnay WHITE

Clos du Bois 1995 Calcaire Chardonnay
Region: California $18
Golds/Awards: Gold (IV, LA, FF)

Clos du Bois 1995 Flintwood Chardonnay
Region: California $17
Golds/Awards: Gold (IV)

Clos Du Val 1995 Carneros Chardonnay
Region: California, Napa Valley $16
Golds/Awards: Gold (OC)

Cobblestone 1995 Chardonnay
Region California, Monterey $17
Golds/Awards: Gold (WWC-90 pts)

⚘**Coldstream Hills 1995 Reserve Chardonnay**
Region: Australia, Yarra Valley $32
Golds/Awards: Gold (SY)

**Columbia Winery 1995 Wyckoff Vineyard
Chardonnay**
Region: Washington, Yakima Valley $18.99
Golds/Awards: Gold (PR)

\$⚘**Concha y Toro 1995 Trio Chardonnay**
Region: Chile, Central Valley $9.60
Golds/Awards: Gold (IW)

\$**Concannon 1995 Select Vineyard
Chardonnay**
Region: California, Mendocino County $9.95
Golds/Awards: Gold (SD); Best of Class (SD)

Cooper-Garrod 1994 Chardonnay
Region: California, Santa Cruz Mountains $18
Golds/Awards: Gold (WWC-91 pts)

Did You Know . . . ?

Some of the world's best-known winemakers are setting their sights on Chile. For example, Baroness Philippine de Rothschild, of France's Château Mouton-Rothschild, is pumping millions into a new winery, along with partner Concha y Toro, to produce a Chilean wine in 1998 that may be the most expensive wine to ever come from that country.

Cooper Mountain 1994 Reserve Chardonnay
Region: Oregon, Willamette Valley $17.95
Golds/Awards: Gold (WWC-91 pts)

$Cooper Mountain 1995 Barrel Fermented Estate Chardonnay
Region: Oregon, Willamette Valley $12
Golds/Awards: Double Gold (SF)

Cristom 1994 Chardonnay
Region: Oregon $20
Golds/Awards: Gold (WWC-92 pts)

Cronin 1994 Chardonnay
Region California, Santa Cruz Mountains $20
Golds/Awards: Gold (WWC-93 pts); Cellar Selection (WWC)

Curtis 1994 Reserve Chardonnay
Region California, Santa Barbara County $22.50
Golds/Awards: Gold (WWC-92 pts); Cellar Selection (WWC)

Curtis 1995 Premier Winemaker Chardonnay
Region: California, Santa Barbara $18
Golds/Awards: Gold (SD)

$ ⌂D'Arenberg 1995 The Olive Grove Chardonnay
Region: Australia, South Australia $15
Golds/Awards: Gold (IW)

Davis Bynum 1995 Limited Edition Chardonnay
Region: California, Russian River Valley $17
Golds/Awards: Gold (OC)

Delaney Vineyards 1995 Barrel Fermented Sur Lie Chardonnay
Region: Texas $18.95
Golds/Awards: Gold (AW)

> ### *Did You Know . . . ?*
> A wine's pH is an indication of its acidity expressed by the number of hydrogen ions it contains. Or put another way, pH indicates the *intensity* of the wine's acidity. The lower the pH number, the more intense its acid.

Chardonnay   WHITE

De Loach 1995 Chardonnay
Region: California, Russian River Valley $16
Golds/Awards: Gold (CA)

$De Loach 1995 Cuvée Chardonnay
Region: California, Russian River Valley $12
Golds/Awards: Gold (CA)

**De Loach 1995 O.F.S. Estate Bottled
Chardonnay**
Region: California, Russian River Valley $27.50
Golds/Awards: Gold (PR, OC, WWC-91 pts);
Double Gold (CA); Best of Class (CA)

**Domain Hill & Mayes 1994 Bighorn Ranch
Reserve Chardonnay**
Region California, Carneros $18
Golds/Awards: Gold (WWC-90 pts)

Dry Creek Vineyard 1994 Reserve Chardonnay
Region: California, Dry Creek $17
Golds/Awards: Gold (AT)

**$Duck Pond 1996 Barrel Fermented
Chardonnay**
Region: Oregon, Willamette Valley $8
Golds/Awards: Gold (OR, NE)

**Edna Valley Vineyard 1995 Paragon
Chardonnay**
Region: California, Edna Valley $16.50
Golds/Awards: Gold (OC)

$⌂Eikendal 1996 Chardonnay
Region: South Africa $12.99
Golds/Awards: Gold (VL)

Estancia 1994 Reserve Chardonnay
Region: California, Monterey $20
Golds/Awards: Gold (WWC-92 pts)

$Fallbrook 1995 Chardonnay
Region: California $6.99
Golds/Awards: Gold (NW)

Did You Know . . . ?
The approximate price of a French oak barrel is $600.

$Ferrante 1996 Barrel Fermented Chardonnay
Region: Ohio $9.99
Golds/Awards: Gold (LA)

Ferrari-Carano 1993 Reserve Chardonnay
Region: California, North Coast $30
Golds/Awards: Platinum (WWC-96 pts)

Ferrari-Carano 1994 Chardonnay
Region: California, Alexander Valley $20
Golds/Awards: Gold (WWC-90 pts)

Ferrari-Carano 1994 Tre Terre Chardonnay
Region: : California, Alexander Valley $26
Golds/Awards: Gold (WWC-92 pts)

Fess Parker 1994 Reserve Chardonnay
Region: California, Santa Barbara $22
Golds/Awards: Gold (AT)

Fess Parker 1995 Chardonnay
Region: California, Santa Barbara County $16
Golds/Awards: Gold (NW); Best of Class (NW)

Fetzer 1994 Sangiacomo Vineyard Chardonnay
Region: California, Sonoma County $16.99
Golds/Awards: Gold (NW)

$Fetzer 1995 Barrel Select Chardonnay
Region: California, Mendocino County $10.99
Golds/Awards: Gold (SD); Best of Class (SD)

$Fetzer 1996 Sundial Chardonnay
Region: California $6.99
Golds/Awards: Gold (SD, WC)

$Fisher 1994 Coach Insignia Chardonnay
Region: California, Sonoma County $12.99
Golds/Awards: Gold (WWC-92 pts); Cellar
Selection and Best Buy (WWC)

Did You Know . . . ?
Industry marketers are going nuts trying to figure out
how to get Generation X guzzlers to replace beer with
wine. The number of American wine consumers aged
thirty or under is only 5 percent.

Chardonnay   WHITE

Fisher 1994 Whitney's Vineyard Chardonnay
Region: California, Sonoma County $24.99
Golds/Awards: Platinum (WWC-97 pts)

Flora Springs 1994 Chardonnay
Region: California, Carneros $24
Golds/Awards: Gold (WWC-93 pts)

Flora Springs 1995 Carneros Chardonnay
Region: California, Napa Valley $24
Golds/Awards: Double Gold (SF)

Franciscan 1994 Cuvée Sauvage Chardonnay
Region: California, Napa Valley $30
Golds/Awards: Gold (WWC-92 pts)

Gallo Sonoma 1994 Estate Chardonnay
Region: California, Northern Sonoma $30
Golds/Awards: Gold (AT, AW, WWC-91 pts)

Gary Farrell 1994 Chardonnay
Region: California, Russian River Valley $20
Golds/Awards: Gold (WWC-90 pts)

Gary Farrell 1995 Allen Vineyard Chardonnay
Region: California, Russian River Valley $21.50
Golds/Awards: Gold (PR)

Geyser Peak 1995 Reserve Chardonnay
Region: California $23
Golds/Awards: Gold (VL)

$Geyser Peak 1996 Chardonnay
Region: California, Sonoma $14
Golds/Awards: Double Gold (SF)

♫ **Giesen 1995 Burnham School Road Reserve Chardonnay**
Region: New Zealand, Canterbury $24
Golds/Awards: Gold (SY)

Did You Know . . . ?
Who does not love wine, women, and song,
Remains a fool his whole life long.
   —Johann Heinrich Voss (1752–1832)

Chardonnay WHITE

Godwin 1995 Chardonnay
Region: California, Alexander Valley $20
Golds/Awards: Gold (CA)

Grgich Hills 1994 Chardonnay
Region: California, Napa Valley $28
Golds/Awards: Gold (PR)

**Guenoc 1994 Genevieve Magoon Reserve
Chardonnay**
Region: California, Guenoc Valley $25
Golds/Awards: Gold (AT)

**Guenoc 1994 Genevieve Magoon Unfiltered
Reserve Chardonnay**
Region: California, Guenoc Valley $30
Golds/Awards: Gold (AT, AW)

**Guenoc 1995 Genevieve Magoon Reserve
Chardonnay**
Region: California, Guenoc Valley $25
Golds/Awards: Gold (AT, AW, IV, WWC-90 pts);
Cellar Selection (WWC)

$Guenoc 1995 Estate Bottled Chardonnay
Region: California, Guenoc Valley $14.50
Golds/Awards: Gold (IV)

Guenoc 1995 Reserve Chardonnay
Region: California, Guenoc Valley $22.50
Golds/Awards: Gold (IV)

$Habersham 1994 Estate Chardonnay
Region: Georgia $10
Golds/Awards: Gold (AT)

$Hahn 1995 Chardonnay
Region: California, Monterey $10
Golds/Awards: Gold (NW)

Did You Know . . . ?
British stage actress Lillie Langtry, on Guenoc and Langtry labels, fled to the Wild West in the mid-1880s for a
divorce, bought a California ranch named Guenoc, re-
married a 28-year-old (she was 47—way to go, Lil!),
and vowed to make "the greatest claret in the country."
Her Victorian mansion has been restored at the present-
day winery.

---

208   The Gold Medal Winners

Chardonnay WHITE

Handley Cellars 1993 Cellar Select Chardonnay
Region: California, Dry Creek Valley $20
Golds/Awards: Gold (LA); Best of Class (LA);
Division Sweepstakes (LA)

Handley Cellars 1995 Chardonnay
Region: California, Dry Creek Valley $16
Golds/Awards: Gold (DA)

Hanzell 1994 Chardonnay
Region California, Sonoma Valley $29
Golds/Awards: Gold (WWC-90 pts); Cellar
Selection (WWC)

$⌻**Hardy's 1995 Chardonnay**
Region: Australia, Padthaway $7
Golds/Awards: Gold (AT)

$⌻**Hardys Nottage Hill 1996 Chardonnay**
Region: Australia, Southeast Region $7
Golds/Awards: Gold (BR)

$**Henry Estate 1994 Chardonnay**
Region: Oregon, Umpqua Valley $15
Golds/Awards: Gold (NE)

$**Hess 1994 Hess Collection Chardonnay**
Region: California, Napa Valley $13.99
Golds/Awards: Gold (WWC-90 pts); Best Buy
(WWC)

$**Hogue Cellars 1995 Chardonnay**
Region: Washington, Columbia Valley $10
Golds/Awards: Gold (PR, AW)

Husch 1994 Estate Bottled Reserve Chardonnay
Region: California, Napa Valley $18
Golds/Awards: Gold (LA)

$**Husch 1995 Estate Bottled Chardonnay**
Region: California, Mendocino County $12.50
Golds/Awards: Gold (NW)

> ### *Did You Know . . . ?*
> The larger the oak container, the less wood flavoring it
> will impart to the wine.

Chardonnay   WHITE

$Indigo Hills 1995 Chardonnay
Region: California, Mendocino County $10
Golds/Awards: Gold (NW): Best of Class (NW);
Best New World Chardonnay (NW)

$J. Lohr 1995 Riverstone Chardonnay
Region: California, Monterey $14
Golds/Awards: Gold (WWC-90 pts); Best Buy (WWC)

**Jarvis 1994 Estate Grown Cave Fermented
Chardonnay**
Region: California, Napa Valley $36
Golds/Awards: Gold (LA); Best of Class (LA)

$Jepson Vineyards 1995 Estate Select Chardonnay
Region: California, Mendocino $14
Golds/Awards: Gold (PR)

Jordan 1994 Chardonnay
Region: California, Sonoma County $20.25
Golds/Awards· Gold (NW)

**Jory 1994 Lion Oaks Ranch Selected Clone
Chardonnay**
Region: California $20
Golds/Awards: Gold (WWC-90 pts)

**Jory 1995 Lion Oaks Ranch Selected Clone
Chardonnay**
Region: California $25
Golds/Awards: Gold (WWC-90 pts)

Joseph Phelps 1994 Ovation Chardonnay
Region: California, Napa Valley $35
Golds/Awards: Gold (WWC-95 pts)

**Kendall-Jackson 1994 Grand Reserve
Chardonnay**
Region: California $26
Golds/Awards: Gold (AW)

Kendall-Jackson 1995 Grand Reserve Chardonnay
Region: California $26
Golds/Awards: Double Gold (TG); Gold (WC)

Did You Know . . . ?
For many years wines were identified by branded corks,
rather than by paper labels, as they are today.

Chardonnay   WHITE

Kendall-Jackson 1995 Paradise Vineyard Chardonnay
Region: California, Arroyo Seco $20
Golds/Awards: Gold (LA)

$Kendall-Jackson 1995 Vintner's Reserve Chardonnay
Region: California $15
Golds/Awards: Gold (PR, NW); Best of Class (NW)

$King Estate 1993 Chardonnay
Region: Oregon $13
Golds/Awards: Gold (WS)

$Korbel 1994 Chardonnay
Region: Califonia, Russian River Valley $14.99
Golds/Awards: Gold (WC)

La Crema 1994 Reserve Chardonnay
Region: California, Sonoma County $23
Golds/Awards: Gold (WWC-92 pts)

La Crema 1995 Reserve Chardonnay
Region: California, Sonoma Coast $26.50
Golds/Awards: Gold (LA); Best of Class (LA)

Lamoreaux Landing 1994 Reserve Chardonnay
Region: New York, Finger Lakes $20
Golds/Awards: Gold (WWC-91 pts)

$Lamoreaux Landing 1995 Estate Bottled Chardonnay
Region: New York, Finger Lakes $12
Golds/Awards: Gold (NW); Tie for Best of Class (NW)

Las Vinas 1996 Chardonnay
Region: California, Monterey County $23
Golds/Awards: Gold (WC)

L'Ecole No. 41 1995 Chardonnay
Region: Washington $20
Golds/Awards: Gold (WWC-91 pts)

Did You Know . . . ?
The Finger Lakes district is enjoying a revolution. Since 1990 native cultivars such as Aurore are being replaced by vinifera such as Chardonnay and Cabernet Franc.

Chardonnay   WHITE

Lewis Cellars 1994 Reserve Chardonnay
Region: California, Napa Valley $28
Golds/Awards: Gold (WWC-90 pts)

$ ⌨**Lindemans 1995 Chardonnay**
Region: Australia $12.99
Golds/Awards: Gold (WWC-90 pts); Tie for
National Champion Chardonnay (WWC)

$ ⌨**Lindemans 1996 Bin 65 Chardonnay**
Region: Australia, South Eastern Region $7.50
Golds/Awards: Gold (FF)

Longoria 1994 Huber Vineyard Chardonnay
Region: California, Santa Barbara County $22.99
Golds/Awards: Gold (WWC-93 pts)

$**Louis M. Martini 1995 Chardonnay**
Region: California $10.50
Golds/Awards: Gold (PR)

⌨**Magnotta 1994 Gran Riserva White**
(Chardonnay)
Region: Canada, Ontario   (Can $) 11.95
Golds/Awards: Gold (IV)

Marcelina 1995 Chardonnay
Region: California, Napa Valley $18
Golds/Awards: Gold (SF)

$**Markham 1995 Barrel Fermented Chardonnay**
Region: California, Napa Valley $12.49
Golds/Awards: Gold (CA)

Marquam Hill 1994 Chardonnay
Region: Oregon, Willamette Valley $16
Golds/Awards: Gold (WWC-90 pts)

Matanzas Creek 1993 Chardonnay
Region: California $30
Golds/Awards: Gold (IW)

Did You Know . . . ?
At many large wineries a card is attached to the head of
the barrel so the winemaker can follow the life of the
individual oak barrels, which have finite useful lives. In
smaller cellars, the winemaker may know every barrel so
intimately that formal markings are unnecessary.

Chardonnay   WHITE

Matanzas Creek 1993 Journey Chardonnay
Region: California, Sonoma Valley $75
Golds/Awards: Gold (WWC-94 pts); Cellar
Selection (WWC)

$Mc Crea 1995 Chardonnay
Region: Washington, Yakima Valley $12.50
Golds/Awards: Gold (WWC-90 pts); Best Buy (WWC)

**McIlroy Wines 1995 Aquarius Ranch
Chardonnay**
Region: California, Russian River Valley $17.50
Golds/Awards: Gold (PR)

Mer et Soleil 1994 Chardonnay
Region: California, Central Coast $31.99
Golds/Awards: Gold (WWC-93 pts)

$Meridian 1995 Reserve Chardonnay
Region: California, Edna Valley $14
Golds/Awards: Gold (AT)

$Meridian 1995 Chardonnay
Region: California, Santa Barbara County $11
Golds/Awards: Gold (PR)

Merryvale 1995 Reserve Chardonnay
Region: California, Napa Valley $25
Golds/Awards: Gold (OC, SF)

**$Michael Pozzan 1995 Special Reserve
Chardonnay**
Region: California, Monterey County $10
Golds/Awards: Gold (PR)

$Mill Creek Vineyards 1995 Chardonnay
Region: California, Sonoma County $12
Golds/Awards: Gold (NW): Tie for Best of Class
(NW)

Mirassou 1990 Harvest Reserve Chardonnay
Region: Monterey $19
Golds/Awards: Gold (CA)

Did You Know . . . ?
The standard size of early glass bottles corresponded,
not so surprisingly, to one natural "lungful" of air.

Chardonnay WHITE

$Mirassou 1994 Harvest Reserve Chardonnay
Region: California, Monterey $14.95
Golds/Awards: Gold (WWC-90 pts); Cellar
Selection and Best Buy (WWC)

**Mirassou 1995 Showcase Selection-Fifth
Generation Harvest Reserve Chardonnay**
Region: California, Monterey County $28
Golds/Awards: Gold (OC)

⊠Mitchelton 1994 Reserve Chardonnay
Region: Australia $16
Golds/Awards: Gold (WWC-90 pts) ; Tie for
National Champion Chardonnay (WWC)

**⊠Morton Estate Winery 1995 Black Label
Chardonnay**
Region: New Zealand, Hawkes Bay $29
Golds/Awards: Gold (PR)

Mount Eden Vineyards 1994 Chardonnay
Region: California, Santa Cruz Mountains $34.99
Golds/Awards: Gold (WWC-90 pts)

Murphy-Goode 1995 Reserve Chardonnay
Region: California, Russian River Valley $24
Golds/Awards: Double Gold (SF); Gold (WWC-90 pts)

$Murphy-Goode 1996 Chardonnay
Region: Califonia, Sonoma County $15
Golds/Awards: Gold (WC)

Napa Ridge 1994 Frisinger Vineyard Chardonnay
Region: California, Napa Valley $16
Golds/Awards: Gold (WWC-91 pts); Best Buy (WWC)

$Napa Ridge 1995 Chardonnay Reserve
Region: Califonia, Napa Valley $15
Golds/Awards: Gold (WC)

Did You Know . . . ?
There are no legal requirements enabling U.S. wineries
to call a wine "reserve." Unlike their Old World counterparts, any U.S. wine may be called "reserve." However, reputable wineries reserve this label for their best
wines.

Chardonnay   WHITE

**Navarro 1995 Anderson Valley Premiere
Reserve Chardonnay**
Region: California, Mendocino $16
Golds/Awards: Gold (OC)

$Navarro 1995 Chardonnay
Region: California, Mendocino $12
Golds/Awards: Gold (CA); Best of Class (CA)

Newton 1994 Chardonnay
Region: California, Napa Valley $16.99
Golds/Awards: Gold (WWC-94 pts); Best Buy (WWC)

Neyers 1995 Chardonnay
Region: California, Carneros $24.99
Golds/Awards: Gold (WWC-91 pts)

Oakville Ranch 1994 ORV Chardonnay
Region: California, Napa Valley $28
Golds/Awards: Gold (WWC-90 pts)

$Paraiso Springs 1995 Chardonnay
Region: California, Monterey $13
Golds/Awards: Gold (WWC-90 pts); Best Buy (WWC)

Patz & Hall 1994 Chardonnay
Region: California, Napa Valley $28.99
Golds/Awards: Platinum (WWC-96 pts)

Patz & Hall 1995 Chardonnay
Region: California, Napa Valley $28.99
Golds/Awards: Gold (WWC-92 pts)

Peju Province 1995 Chardonnay
Region: California, Napa Valley $16
Golds/Awards: Gold (WWC-93 pts); Best Buy (WWC)

Petaluma 1994 Piccadilly Valley Chardonnay
Region: Australia, South Australia $28
Golds/Awards: Gold (IW, BR)

> ### *Did You Know . . . ?*
> Today's word: *organoleptic.* When applied to evaluat-
> ing wines, it means what can be determined or per-
> ceived by the senses—taste, smell, and sight—rather
> than by physical or chemical analysis, as in a laboratory.

Chardonnay   WHITE

Peter Michael 1994 Cuvée Indigéne Chardonnay
Region: California, Sonoma County $39.99
Golds/Awards: Gold (WWC-93 pts); Cellar Selection
(WWC)

Peter Michael 1994 Mon Plasir Chardonnay
Region: California, Sonoma County $34.99
Golds/Awards: Gold (WWC-95 pts); Cellar
Selection (WWC)

**Piedmont 1995 Native Yeast Unfiltered
Chardonnay**
Region: Virginia $24
Golds/Awards: Gold (WWC-90 pts)

Piedmont 1995 Special Reserve Chardonnay
Region: Virginia $16
Golds/Awards: Gold (AW)

Pindar 1995 Sunflower Chardonnay
Region: New York $16.99
Golds/Awards: Gold (AW)

Pine Ridge 1995 Chardonnay
Region: California, Napa Valley $30
Golds/Awards: Double Gold (TG)

$Ponzi 1994 Chardonnay
Region: Oregon, Willamette Valley $15
Golds/Awards: Gold (WWC-91 pts); Best Buy (WWC)

Prince Michel 1995 Barrel Select Chardonnay
Region: Virginia $17
Golds/Awards: Gold (FF)

**Rabbit Ridge 1995 Winemaker's Grand Reserve
Chardonnay**
*Region:*California, Sonoma County $28
Golds/Awards: Gold (NW)

$Raymond 1995 Reserve Chardonnay
Region: California, Napa Valley $14
Golds/Awards: Gold (LA)

Did You Know . . . ?
Australia is the largest exporter of wines to the U.S.,
behind first- and second-ranking France and Italy.

Chardonnay

Robert Mondavi 1994 Chardonnay
Region: California, Carneros $24
Golds/Awards: Gold (WWC-90 pts)

$Rodney Strong 1995 Chardonnay
Region: California, Sonoma County $11
Golds/Awards: Gold (AW)

Rombauer 1995 Chardonnay
Region: California, Carneros $20.99
Golds/Awards: Gold (WWC-93 pts)

🏵**Rosemount 1993 Roxburgh Chardonnay**
Region: Australia, Hunter Valley $30
Golds/Awards: Gold (IW)

🏵**Rosemount 1995 Show Reserve Chardonnay**
Region: Australia, Hunter Valley $18.50
Golds/Awards: Gold (AT)

$Round Hill 1995 Chardonnay
Region: California, Napa Valley $12
Golds/Awards: Gold (OC)

$Rutherford Vintners 1996 Chardonnay
Region: California, Lodi $8.99
Golds/Awards: Gold (LA)

$Rutherford Hill 1993 Chardonnay
Region: California, Napa Valley $12
Golds/Awards: Gold (IW)

St. Francis 1995 Reserve Chardonnay
Region: California, Sonoma Valley $20
Golds/Awards: Gold (WWC-93 pts)

Saintsbury 1993 Reserve Chardonnay
Region California, Carneros $21.99
Golds/Awards: Gold (WWC-92 pts); Cellar Selection
(WWC)

Did You Know . . . ?
France's Michel Chapoutier is adding Braille to his labels
that will indicate the appellation, wine name, color,
producer, and where the wine was made.

Chardonnay   WHITE

⌑ **Sandalford 1995 Chardonnay**
Region: Australia, Western Australia $18.99
Golds/Awards: Gold and Best of Category (SY)

Santa Barbara 1994 Reserve Chardonnay
Region: California, Santa Ynez $22
Golds/Awards: Gold (PR, AT)

$ ⌑ **Seaview 1994 Chardonnay**
Region: Australia $8.99
Golds/Awards: Double Gold (TG)

$ **Sebastiani 1995 Chardonnay**
Region: California, Sonoma County $11.99
Golds/Awards: Gold (SD)

Sebastiani 1995 Dutton Ranch Chardonnay
Region: California, Russian River Valley $25
Golds/Awards: Gold (NW): Tie for Best of Class (NW)

Selby 1995 Chardonnay
Region: California, Sonoma County $20
Golds/Awards: Gold (NW)

Shafer 1994 Red Shoulder Ranch Chardonnay
Region: California, Carneros $23
Golds/Awards: Gold (WWC-91 pts)

$ **Shale Ridge 1996 Estate Grown and Bottled Chardonnay**
Region: California, Monterey County $10.50
Golds/Awards: Gold (LA)

Sierra Vista 1996 Estate Bottled Chardonnay
Region: California, El Dorado $16
Golds/Awards: Gold (LA)

Signorello 1995 Chardonnay
Region: California, Napa Valley $27.50
Golds/Awards: Gold (WWC-92 pts)

Signorello 1995 Founder's Reserve Chardonnay
Region: California, Napa Valley $40
Golds/Awards: Gold (WWC-93 pts)

Did You Know . . . ?
Teetotalers may feel conflicted about the bible, which is filled with praises to wine. Take Christ's first miracle, for example, when he turned water into wine at the marriage of Cana.

Chardonnay   WHITE

Signorello 1995 Hope's Cuvée Chardonnay
Region: California, Napa Valley $60
Golds/Awards: Gold (WWC-94 pts)

$Silvan Ridge 1994 Chardonnay
Region: Oregon $15
Golds/Awards: Gold (SF)

Silverado 1994 Limited Reserve Chardonnay
Region: California, Napa Valley $32.99
Golds/Awards: Gold (WWC-90 pts)

Sokol Blosser 1993 Redland Chardonnay
Region: Oregon, Willamette Valley $17
Golds/Awards: Gold (WWC-90 pts)

Sonoma-Loeb 1993 Private Reserve Chardonnay
Region: California, Sonoma County $30
Golds/Awards: Gold (WWC-92 pts)

Sonoma-Loeb 1995 Private Reserve Chardonnay
Region: California, Sonoma County $30
Golds/Awards: Gold (WWC-90 pts)

Spencer Hill Estate 1996 Tasman Bay Chardonnay
Region: New Zealand, Marlborough $16
Golds/Awards: Gold (SF)

SSV 1995 San Saba Vineyard Chardonnay
Region: California, Monterey $20
Golds/Awards: Gold (WWC-93 pts)

Stag's Leap Wine Cellars 1994 Reserve Chardonnay
Region: California, Napa Valley $32
Golds/Awards: Gold (WWC-91 pts)

Stevenot 1995 Shaw Ranch Chardonnay
Region: California, Calaveras $16
Golds/Awards: Double Gold (SF)

Did You Know . . . ?
The average life span of a grapevine is twenty-five years.

Stonestreet 1995 Chardonnay
Region: California, Sonoma County $25
Golds/Awards: Gold (NW)

Swanson 1993 Chardonnay
Region: California, Carneroa $20
Golds/Awards: Gold (IW)

Swanson 1995 Estate Bottled Chardonnay
Region: California, Carneros Napa Valley $24
Golds/Awards: Gold (NW)

$Taft Street 1995 Chardonnay
Region: California, Sonoma County $10
Golds/Awards: Gold (AT)

Talbott 1994 Sleepy Hollow Vnyrd Chardonnay
Region: California, Monterey $28
Golds/Awards: Gold (WWC-92 pts); Cellar
Selection (WWC)

Te Kairanga 1995 Reserve Chardonnay
Region: New Zealand, Martinborough $49.99
Golds/Awards: Gold (SY)

$Tessera 1995 Chardonnay
Region: California $9.99
Golds/Awards: Gold (PR)

Thomas Fogarty 1995 Chardonnay
Region: California, Santa Cruz Mountains $16.50
Golds/Awards: Gold (WWC-90 pts); Cellar
Selection (WWC)

Thomas Fogarty 1995 Estate Reserve Chardonnay
Region: California, Santa Cruz Mountains $22
Golds/Awards: Gold (WWC-92 pts)

**Trout Gulch 1995 Trout Gulch Vineyards
Chardonnay**
Region: California, Santa Cruz Mountain $16
Golds/Awards: Gold (CA); Best of California,
Best of Class (CA)

Did You Know . . . ?
A grapevine's reserves of carbohydrates act as a protective antifreeze in winter.

$Tulocay 1995 Oak Creek Vineyards Chardonnay
Region: California, Napa Valley $15
Golds/Awards: Gold (WWC-90 pts); Cellar
Selection and Best Buy (WWC)

Tyrrell's 1996 Moon Mountain Chardonnay
Region: Australia $19.95
Golds/Awards: Gold (IV, Hunter Valley Wine Show)

V. Sattui Winery 1995 Carsi Vineyard Chardonnay
Region: California $22
Golds/Awards: Gold (PR, Springfest, Wine Lovers'
Int'l); Best of Class (PR); Best Pacific Rim
Chardonnay (PR)
By mail-order only: (800) 799-2337

Van Duzer 1994 Reserve Chardonnay
Region: Oregon $18
Golds/Awards: Gold (WWC-90 pts)

Venezia 1995 Beaterra Vineyard Chardonnay
Region: Califonia, Napa Valley $20
Golds/Awards: Gold (WC, NW)

Venezia 1995 Regusci Vineyard Chardonnay
Region: Califonia, Napa Valley $20
Golds/Awards: Gold (WC); Best of Class (WC)

$Ventana 1996 Gold Stripe Estate Bottled Chardonnay
Region: California, Monterey County $12
Golds/Awards: Gold (SD, CA); Best of Class (CA)

$ Villa Maria 1996 Private Bin Chardonnay
Region: New Zealand, Gisbourne $13
Golds/Awards: Gold (SY)

$Villa Mt. Eden 1994 Chardonnay
Region: California $9.50
Golds/Awards: Gold (IW)

Did You Know . . . ?
The approximate ratio of beer advertising to wine advertising is 10 to 1.

$Wente Bros. 1994 Riva Ranch Reserve Arroyo Seco Chardonnay
Region: California, Monterey $14.99
Golds/Awards: Gold (PR)

Westport Rivers 1993 Gold Label Chardonnay
Region: Massachusetts $18.95
Golds/Awards: Gold (WWC-90 pts)

Westport Rivers 1994 Estate Grown Chardonnay
Region: Massachusetts $18.95
Golds/Awards: Gold (LA)

William Hill 1994 Reserve Chardonnay
Region: California, Napa Valley $18
Golds/Awards: Gold (WS)

Windemere 1995 MacGregor Vineyard Chardonnay
Region: California, Edna Valley $18
Golds/Awards: Gold (CA)

$ ⌂Wolf Blass 1996 Barrel Fermented Chardonnay
Region: Australia, South Australia $11
Golds/Awards: Gold (SY)

Woodward Canyon 1995 Chardonnay
Region: Washington, Walla Walla Valley $25
Golds/Awards: Gold (WWC-90 pts)

Zaca Mesa 1995 Chapel Vineyard Chardonnay
Region: California, Santa Barbara County $18
Golds/Awards: Gold (LA); Best of Class (LA)

ZD 1993 Library Selection Chardonnay
Region: California $30
Golds/Awards: Gold (WWC-90 pts)

Did You Know . . . ?

A few years ago a *Los Angeles Times* wine writer mocked Wente's pioneering marketing push in Moscow with the headline, WHAT WINE GOES WITH NO FOOD?— this at a time when Russian bread lines were the big story. Today, Wente has the last laugh as their Moscow office is incredibly successful.

Chenin Blanc

Here's a grape that's been largely ignored in the New World. However, that trend is changing as consumers are beginning to look for simple, appealing white wines at reasonable prices. Often blended with other whites, Chenin Blanc is a crowd pleaser and is coming into its own in places like California, Washington State, and Chile.

Chenin Blanc is made in two basic styles. The drier of the two is Chardonnay-like, taking on oak-barrel flavors and aromas (spicy, roasted, or vanilla). The second is sweeter, marked by delicate hints of flowers, melons, pears, and honey. Because this grape produces buds earlier and ripens later than most, either style will usually have lots of natural clean, crisp acidity and plenty of fruit, which means it can age well.

When you think of Chenin Blanc, think summer. August picnics with antipasti, raw clams or oysters, crudité, fresh fruit, pasta salad, and chicken. This wine also goes well with spicy Thai and Mexican dishes. Serve it cold and drink it up, or cellar it for a handful of years.

Chenin Blanc   WHITE

$Alexander Valley 1996 Estate Bottled Chenin Blanc
Region: California, Sonoma County $8.50
Golds/Awards: Gold (LA, OC)

$Baron Herzog 1996 Chenin Blanc
Region: California, Clarksburg $6.50
Golds/Awards: Gold (SD, OC); Best of Class (SD)

$Callaway 1996 Chenin Blanc
Region: California, Temecula $6
Golds/Awards: Gold (CA); Best of Class (CA)

Chalone 1994 Reserve Chenin Blanc
Region: California $16
Golds/Awards: Gold (WWC-91 pts)

$Chappellet 1995 Old Vine Cuvée Dry Chenin Blanc
Region: California $12
Golds/Awards: Gold (WWC-90 pts)

$Columbia Winery 1995 Chenin Blanc
Region: Washington $5.99
Golds/Awards: Gold (WWC-90 pts); Best Buy (WWC)

$Daniel Gehrs 1995 Carmel Vineyard Le Chenière Chenin Blanc
Region: California, Monterey County $8.67
Golds/Awards: Gold (AT)

$Fall Creek 1996 Chenin Blanc
Region: Texas $5
Golds/Awards: Gold (NW); Best of Class (NW);
Best New World Chenin Blanc (NW)

$Hogue Cellars 1996 Chenin Blanc
Region: Washington, Columbia Valley $6.99
Golds/Awards: Gold (WC)

Did You Know . . . ?
Some *broad generalizations* that characterize New World from Old World winegrowing/winemaking: New World vines are planted further apart; New World growers employ more mechanical harvesting and pruning; New World winemakers are more obsessed with hygiene.

Chenin Blanc   WHITE

⌂Stellenzicht 1996 Chenin Blanc
Region: South Africa $29.99
Golds/Awards: Gold (WWC-90 pts)

$Ventana 1996 Barrel Fermented Estate Chenin Blanc
Region: California, Monterey $8
Golds/Awards: Gold (CA); Best of Class (CA)

$Windsor Vineyards 1996 Chenin Blanc
Region: California $7.50
Golds/Awards: Gold (OC)
By mail order only: (800) 333-9987

Did You Know . . . ?

As odd as it sounds, one common way of controlling frost damage to fragile grapevines is by aspersion, or sprinkling water over the vines. As the water freezes, it releases latent heat, thus protecting the vine tissue from injury.

Gewurztraminer

The name is pronounced *guh-WERZ-truh-meener,* and in German *gewürz* means spicy. Words commonly used to describe this wine's flavors and bouquet include clove, nutmeg, lychee nut, carnations, and wildflowers. A great Gewurztraminer will indeed be spicy, with a heady perfume and slight sweetness. This pink-skinned grape makes whites that are exotic, deeply colored, and fuller bodied than almost any other white.

Australia has had a lot of success with this grape, where it's called Traminer. New Zealand is also producing fine examples, as well as the American Northwest and California.

Here's a bonus: Gewurztraminer is usually very reasonably priced. Serve it with pork sausages, foie gras, Oriental cuisine—especially mouth-searing Thai—crab, or trout.

Gewurztraminer   WHITE

$Adler Fels 1996 Gewurztraminer
Region: California, Sonoma County $11
Golds/Awards: Gold (SD, NW, WWC-90 pts, CA);
Best New World Gewurz. (NW); Best of Class (CA)

**$Alderbrook 1995 Dry Barrel Fermented
Gewurztraminer**
Region: California, Sonoma County $9.99
Golds/Awards: Gold (AT)

**$Alderbrook 1996 Saralee's Vineyard
Gewurztraminer**
Region: California, Russian River Valley $10
Golds/Awards: Gold (SD, OC, NW, SF)

**$Alderbrook 1996 McIlroy Vineyard
Gewurztraminer**
Region: California, Russian River Valley $12
Golds/Awards: Gold (FF)

$Bargetto 1995 Gewurztraminer
Region: California $10
Golds/Awards: Gold (WWC-90 pts); Best Buy
(WWC)

$Bargetto 1996 Gewurztraminer
Region: California, Monterey $10
Golds/Awards: Gold (PR)

$Beringer 1996 Gewurztraminer
Region: California $8
Golds/Awards: Gold (NW, CA)

$Concannon 1995 Arroyo Seco Gewurztraminer
Region: California, Monterey County $7.95
Golds/Awards: Gold (NW)

Cosentino 1996 Estate Bottled Gewurztraminer
Region: California, Napa Valley $16
Golds/Awards: Four-Star Gold (OC); Gold
(WWC-91 pts)

Did You Know . . . ?
Due to grape shortages and other factors, wine prices
have risen and threaten to keep doing so. Wines costing
$5 to $10 a bottle in 1996 rose an average of $1; $15
bottles went up an average of $2 in 1997.

Gewurztraminer   WHITE

$Covey Run 1995 Celilo Vineyard Gewurztraminer
Region: Washington $12
Golds/Awards: Gold (SD); Best of Class (SD)

Eola Hills 1996 Vin d'Epice Gewurztraminer
Region: Oregon $20
Golds/Awards: Gold (OR)

$Fetzer 1996 Gewurztraminer
Region: California $6
Golds/Awards: Gold (SD, LA); Double Gold (CA);
Best of Class (SD, CA)

French Lick Winery 1995 Gewurztraminer
Region: Indiana $18.95
Golds/Awards: Gold (AW)

$Geyser Peak 1996 Gewurztraminer
Region: California, North Coast $7.50
Golds/Awards: Gold (WC, NW); Best of Class (WC)

Gray Monk 1995 Broderson Vineyard Gewurztraminer
Region: Canada, Okanagan Valley   (Can $) 11.95
Golds/Awards: Gold (AT)

$Husch 1995 Gewurztraminer
Region: California, Anderson Valley $10
Golds/Awards: Gold (AT)

$Kendall-Jackson 1995 Vintner's Reserve Gewurztraminer
Region: California $10
Golds/Awards: Gold (NW; CA); Best of Region,
Best of Class (CA)

$McGregor Vineyard Winery 1995 Reserve Gewurztraminer
Region: New York, Finger Lakes $14.95
Golds/Awards: Gold (AW)

Did You Know . . . ?
Fine wine made in Indiana, you say? French Lick, the famous Indiana spa, buys Washington-grown grapes and then makes it into gold medal wine at their resort.

Gewurztraminer   WHITE

$M.G. Vallejo 1995 Gewurztraminer
Region: California $7
Golds/Awards: Gold (NW)

**$Navarro Vineyards 1995 Anderson Valley Estate
Bottled Dry Gewurztraminer**
Region: California, Mendocino $14
Golds/Awards: Gold (OC, WWC-90 pts)

**$Prejean Winery 1995 Semi Dry
Gewurztraminer**
Region: New York, Finger Lakes $12
Golds/Awards: Gold (PR)

$Sutter Home 1996 Gewurztraminer
Region: California $5.95
Golds/Awards: Gold (SD, CA); Best of Class (CA)

Did You Know . . . ?
Biodynamic viticulture, influenced by the teachings of
Rudolf Steiner, is an extreme and ideological alternative
approach to viticulture. Winegrowing and -making op-
erations are governed by the positions of the planets
and phases of the moon. One of the most famous do-
maines converted in the early 1990s to biodynamic
viticulture is Domaine Leroy of Vosne-Romanée, France.

Miscellaneous Varietal Whites

New World wine producers are beginning to take more chances with white varietals, knowing that consumers are ready to step away from the Chardonnay routine. In this section are some different, and in some cases unusual, varietal whites named "best" by the experts.

Malvasia Bianca   Widely planted in Italy, but rare in the New World, Malvasia is a grape with ancient origins. Malvasia Bianca is a white wine made from the Malvasia grape, and can be deeply colored, high in alcohol, and often slightly sweet.

Marsanne   Increasingly popular, Marsanne is a deeply colored white with full body and often heavy, almondlike aromas.

Pinot Gris   From beautiful pink-grey grapes, Pinot Gris is a white wine that's found widely in the New World, particularly Oregon and New Zealand. A typical Pinot Gris is full bodied yet soft with gentle perfumes.

Roussanne   This is an elegant Rhône varietal, often blended with Marsanne, that is known for its mysterious aroma of herb tea and its refreshing acidity.

Torrontés   This white grape indigenous to Spain is gaining popularity throughout South America, particularly Argentina. It produces whites with assertive acidity and wonderful aromas reminiscent of Muscat.

Trousseau Gris   Also known as Grey Riesling, Trousseau Gris is an uncommon white grape that produces light but pleasant whites.

Misc. Varietal Whites WHITE

Alban 1995 Alban Estate Vineyard Roussanne
Region: California $32
Golds/Awards: Gold (WWC-91 pts)

$Ca' Del Solo 1996 Malvasia Bianca
Region: California, Monterey $9
Golds/Awards: Gold (OC)

$Cooper Mountain 1996 Pinot Gris
Region: Oregon, Willamette Valley $12.99
Golds/Awards: Gold (WC); Best of Class (WC)

$Duck Pond 1995 Pinot Gris
Region: Oregon, Willamette Valley $12
Golds/Awards: Gold (AT)

$Duck Pond 1996 Estate Grown Pinot Gris
Region: Oregon, Willamette Valley $12
Golds/Awards: Gold (OR)

$Elk Cove 1996 Pinot Gris
Region: Oregon, Willamette Valley $12
Golds/Awards: Gold (LA)

$Erath Vineyards 1996 Pinot Gris
Region: Oregon, Willamette Valley $12
Golds/Awards: Gold (OR); Best of Show
White (OR)

$ ⌂Etchart 1996 Torrontés
Region: Argentina, Cafayate $5.99
Golds/Awards: Gold (VN)

**$Fanucchi 1996 Fanucchi Wood Road
Trousseau Gris**
Region: California, Russian River $12
Golds/Awards: Four-Star Gold (OC)

$Foris Vineyards 1996 Pinot Gris
Region: Oregon, Rogue Valley $11
Golds/Awards: Gold (OR)

$Good Harbor Vineyards 1995 Pinot Gris
Region: Michigan $15
Golds/Awards: Double Gold (TG)

Did You Know . . . ?
The religious significance of wine in Christianity ensured
the survival of viticulture after the fall of the Roman
Empire, and brought winemaking to the New World.

Misc. Varietal Whites   WHITE

$Hinman 1994 Pinot Gris
Region: Oregon $11
Golds/Awards: Gold (WWC-91 pts); Best Buy and
National Champion Pinot Gris (WWC)

$Ivan Tamas 1995 Pinot Grigio
Region: California, Monterey County $8.95
Golds/Awards: Gold (SD)

$ ⌂ Mitchelton 1993 Reserve Marsanne
Region: Australia $15
Golds/Awards: Gold (WWC-91 pts); National
Champion White (WWC)

Morgan 1995 Marsanne
Region: California $17
Golds/Awards: Gold (WWC-90 pts); National
Champion Marsanne (WWC)

Rey Sol 1996 Le Mediterrané Estate Marsanne
Region: California, Temecula $16
Golds/Awards: Gold (CA); Best of Class (CA)

$Silvan Ridge 1994 Pinot Gris
Region: Oregon $15
Golds/Awards: Gold (WWC-90 pts)

$Silvan Ridge 1995 Unfiltered Pinot Gris
Region: Oregon $15
Golds/Awards: Gold (SD)

$Tualatin 1996 Muller Thurgau
Region: Oregon, Willamette Valley $7
Golds/Awards: Gold (WC); Best of Class (WC)

$Twin Brook 1995 Pinot Gris
Region: Pennsylvania $13.89
Golds/Awards: Gold (WWC-90 pts)

$Willamette Valley Vineyards 1996 Pinot Gris
Region: Oregon $12.50
Golds/Awards: Gold (OR)

Zaca Mesa 1995 Zaca Vineyard Rousanne
Region: California, Santa Barbara County $17
Golds/Awards: Double Gold (SF)

Did You Know . . . ?
There are 31 Master Sommeliers in the U.S., and only
81 in the world. Of the Americans, only 3 are women.

Native & Hybrid Whites

In the cooler winemaking regions with shorter growing seasons, such as Canada and upstate New York, winemakers needed to find grapes that would withstand the harsh winters yet ones that wouldn't produce wines with the "foxy" flavor characteristics associated with native American species.

Ingenious scientists beginning in the late 1900s and continuing to the present have been developing French-American hybrids in order to find vines that combine the hardiness and disease resistance of American varieties with the flavor and elegance of French varieties. Some particularly successful results are Seyval and Vidal, both widely grown in New York and Canada.

The purely native wines in this section are the result of the efforts of tireless winemakers from unconventional regions such as the Midwest, determined to produce delicious examples of all-American wines.

$Blumenhof 1995 Vidal Blanc $8.47
Region: Missouri
Golds/Awards: Gold (NW); Best New World
Vidal (NW)

$Botham Vineyards NV Vidal Blanc $7.99
Region: Wisconsin
Golds/Awards: Double Gold (TG)

$Cedar Creek 1995 American Vidal $7
Region: Wisconsin
Golds/Awards: Gold (AT)

$Ferrante Wine Farm NV Niagara Bianco $5.99
Region: Ohio, Lake Erie
Golds/Awards: Gold (SD)

$Hermannhof 1995 Seyval Blanc $13.19
Region: Missouri
Golds/Awards: Gold (NW); Best of Class (NW);
Best New World Seyval Blanc (NW)

$Hermannhof 1995 Vignoles $13.75
Region: Missouri
Golds/Awards: Gold (NW); Best of Class (NW);
Best New World Vignoles (NW); Sweepstakes
White (NW)

$Horton 1994 Vidal Blanc $8
Region: Virginia
Golds/Awards: Gold (AT)

⌂Magnotta 1994 Limited Edition Vidal
Region: Canada   (Can $) 24.95
Golds/Awards: Double Gold (TG)

$Post Familie 1996 White Muscadine $5.50
Region: Arkansas
Golds/Awards: Gold (LA)

$St. James 1995 Vintner's Reserve Seyval $9.99
Region: Missouri
Golds/Awards: Gold (DA, SD)

> ### *Did You Know . . . ?*
> Vidal is often used to make rare Canadian icewines.

\$St. James 1996 School House White (Seyval/
Vignoles/Cayuga)
Region; Missouri $7.89
Golds/Awards: Gold (FF)

\$Standing Stone 1995 Semi-Dry Vidal Blanc
Region: New York, Finger Lakes $5.99
Golds/Awards: Gold (AT)

\$Stone Hill NV Golden Rhine
Region: Missouri $6.79
Golds/Awards: Gold (PR)

\$Stone Hill 1995 Barrel-Fermented Seyval
Region: Missouri $11.29
Golds/Awards: Gold (AT, SD, Florida State Fair);
Best of Class (SD)

\$Stone Hill 1995 Hermann Vignoles
Region: Missouri $11.29
Golds/Awards: Gold (AT, Long Beach Grand Cru)

\$Stone Hill 1996 Hermann Vignoles
Region: Missouri $10.99
Golds/Awards: Gold (FF); Chairman's Award (FF)

\$Tartan Hill Winery 1995 Tartan Mist (Cayuga/
Seyval/ Alden)
Region: Michigan $5
Golds/Awards: Gold (AW)

\$Winery at Wolf Creek 1995 Seyval Blanc
Region: Ohio $8
Golds/Awards: Gold (LA)

\$Wollersheim 1995 Prairie Fumé
Region: Wisconsin $7.50
Golds/Awards: Gold (AT)

Did You Know . . . ?
During Prohibition, Missouri produced 43 percent of
the wine consumed in America (used only for sacred
and medicinal purposes, of course).

Pinot Blanc

Pinot Blanc, widely planted in France, is a mutation of Pinot Gris, and bears some resemblance to Chardonnay. In fact, in California some wineries use the same winemaking techniques on Pinot Blanc that they use for Chardonnay, and end up with a wine that's similar in some respects, although without as much fruit concentration. Other Pinot Blancs are subtly fruity and light, with crisp acidity. Pinot Blanc is also used to make California sparkling wines.

It turns out that older vines of New World Pinot Blanc may actually be Melon, a white wine of Burgundian origins, and sometimes the two names are used interchangeably.

Pinot Blanc   WHITE

Benziger 1994 Imagery Series Pinot Blanc
Region: California $16
Golds/Awards: Gold (WWC-91 pts); Tie for
National Champion Pinot Blanc (WWC)

**Benziger 1995 Imagery Series Skinner Yount
Mill Pinot Blanc**
Region: California, North Coast $17.99
Golds/Awards: Gold (PR, NW); Best of Class (NW);
Best New World Pinot Blanc (NW)

**$Chateau St. Jean 1993 Robert Young Vineyards
Pinot Blanc**
Region: California $12
Golds/Awards: Gold (WWC-90 pts)

Laetitia 1995 La Colline Vineyard Pinot Blanc
Region: California, San Luis Obispo $24.99
Golds/Awards: Gold (OC); Four-Star Gold (OC)

Laetitia 1995 Reserve Pinot Blanc
Region: California, San Luis Obispo $16.99
Golds/Awards: Gold (LA)

$Lockwood 1994 Pinot Blanc
Region: California $9
Golds/Awards: Gold (WWC-91 pts); Best Buy and
Tie or National Champion Pinot Blanc (WWC)

Mirassou 1995 Harvest Reserve Pinot Blanc
Region: California, Monterey County $15.95
Golds/Awards: Gold (PR, OC); Best of Class (PR)

Did You Know . . . ?
The Mirassous claim to be America's oldest winemaking
family. Great, great, great-grandfather Pierre Pellier
came to California in the 1850s in search of gold. Instead he found his fortune in the fertile Santa Clara
Valley where he planted fine varietal cuttings he'd
brought from France. His eldest daughter married a
neighboring vintner, Mr. Mirassou, and today, to make
a long story short, the fifth generation owns and manages the family winery.

Mirassou 1996 Pinot Blanc
Region: California, Monterey County $16
Golds/Awards: Gold (OC); Four-Star Gold (OC)

$Mirassou 1996 White Burgundy Pinot Blanc
Region: California, Monterey County $10.95
Golds/Awards: Gold (AT, WC, LA); Best of
Class (WC)

**Paraiso Springs 1996 Santa Lucia Highlands
Reserve Barrel Fermented Pinot Blanc**
Region: California, Monterey County $22.50
Golds/Awards: Gold (OC)

$⌂ Sumac Ridge 1995 Private Reserve Pinot Blanc
Region: Canada, British Columbia $10.95
Golds/Awards: Gold (AW)

**Villa Mt. Eden 1995 Bien Nacido Vineyard
Grand Reserve Pinot Blanc**
Region: California, Santa Maria Valley $16
Golds/Awards: Gold (AT, OC)

Did You Know . . . ?
A home winemaking family in Alabama was making
berry and fruit wine from the produce on their own
farm. Unfortunately, a 1940 law says making more than
5 gallons for home consumption is punishable by a fine
of $50 to $500 and/or three months of hard labor. If
the Nilsson family wants to avoid legal sanction, they
can become bonded and produce up to 100,000 gallons of wine in their dry county. *That's* allowed.

Riesling

In Oregon it's White Riesling. In Australia it's Rhine Riesling. In California it's Johannisberg Riesling, or sometimes just Riesling. Regardless, they're all one and the same.

Riesling is a grape variety of German origin that makes wines in two basic styles: dry to off-dry, and lusciously sweet. The reason for the latter is that it is often harvested late and allowed to be infected with the "noble rot," also known as *Botrytis cinerea,* which produces juice that's highly concentrated and sweet, fragrant, with apricot and peach overtones. (Late-harvest Rieslings are listed in Chapter 13.) The drier versions are fresh, flowery, and delicate, with hints of apples and pears. What they both have in common is their surprisingly inexpensive price.

What you eat with your Riesling depends on the style of the wine. The medium-dry versions go well with cold meats, oysters, pasta salads, chicken, Thai cuisine, and even sushi. The sweeter ones can accompany hard cheeses, prosciutto, and fresh fruit.

Riesling   WHITE

$Amity 1995 Dry Riesling
Region: Oregon $9
Golds/Awards: Gold (WWC-90 pts)

$Argyle 1995 Dry Reserve Riesling
Region: Oregon $12
Golds/Awards: Gold (WWC-90 pts)

$Beringer 1996 Johannisberg Riesling
Region: California $8
Golds/Awards: Gold (SD)

$Cedar Creek 1996 Waterfall Mist Dry White Riesling
Region: Wisconsin $8
Golds/Awards: Gold (SD)

$Chateau St. Jean 1995 Johannisberg Riesling
Region: California, Sonoma County $8.99
Golds/Awards: Gold (AT)

$Concannon 1995 Select Vineyard Limited Bottling Johannisberg Riesling
Region: California, Arroyo Seco $7.95
Golds/Awards: Gold (SD)

$Concannon 1996 Johannisberg Riesling
Region: California, Monterey/Arroyo Seco $7.95
Golds/Awards: Gold (WC, CA); Best of Class (WC)

$Dr. Konstantin Frank NV Salmon Run Johannisberg Riesling
Region: New York $8.95
Golds/Awards: Gold (LA)

$Dr. Konstantin Frank 1996 Semi Dry Johannisberg Riesling
Region: New York, Finger Lakes $10
Golds/Awards: Gold (SF)

Did You Know . . . ?
Dr. Konstantin Frank, a German scientist born in the Ukraine, arrived in the U.S. in the 1950s and was the first winemaker to convince doubters that vinfera (or fine-wine) grapes could be grown in New York State.

Riesling   WHITE

$Fetzer 1996 Johannisberg Riesling
Region: California $6.99
Golds/Awards: Gold (PR, CA); Best of Class (CA)

$Gainey Vineyards 1996 Johannisberg Riesling
Region: California, Santa Ynez Valley $10
Golds/Awards: Gold (FF); Chairman's Award (FF)

$Geyser Peak 1996 Trione Cellars Johannisberg Riesling
Region: California $7.50
Golds/Awards: Gold (DA, NW)

$Hagafen 1996 Johannisberg Riesling
Region: California, Napa Valley $10
Golds/Awards: Gold (PR)

$Hogue Cellars 1995 Johannisberg Riesling
Region: Washington, Columbia Valley $6
Golds/Awards: Gold (AT)

$Hogue Cellars 1996 Johannisberg Riesling
Region: Washington, Columbia Valley $6
Golds/Awards: Gold (FF)

$Hoodsport 1995 Riesling
Region: Washington, Yakima Valley $7.99
Golds/Awards: Gold (NW)

$J. Lohr 1996 Bay Mist Riesling
Region: California, Monterey $7.50
Golds/Awards: Gold (NW); Best of Class (NW)

⌂Jost 1995 Dry Riesling Gold
Region: Canada, Nova Scotia   (Can) $8.75
Golds/Awards: Gold (AT)

Did You Know . . . ?
Hagafen Cellars is one of the few kosher wineries in the United States making fine wines, ones that win gold medals year after year. If you wish to order some kosher wines for your next holiday gathering, call the winery directly at (800) 456-VINO.

Riesling   WHITE

**$Kendall-Jackson 1995 Vintner's Reserve
Johannisberg Riesling**
Region: California $10
Golds/Awards: Gold (CA); Best of Class (CA)

**$Kendall-Jackson 1996 Vintner's Reserve
Johannisberg Riesling**
Region: California $11
Golds/Awards: Gold (IV, NW)

$ 🏠Lakeview Cellars 1995 Riesling
Region: Canada, Ontario $10.95
Golds/Awards: Gold (AW)

$Lamoreaux Landing 1996 Semi-Dry Riesling
Region: New York, Finger Lakes $10
Golds/Awards: Gold (FF)

$Maddalena 1995 Johannisberg Riesling
Region: California, Monterey/Santa Barbara $7
Golds/Awards: Gold (SD, WC, LA); Double Gold
(CA); Best of Class (SD, LA, CA)

$Maurice Car'rie 1996 Johannisberg Riesling
Region: California, Temecula $4.99
Golds/Awards: Gold (SD)

**McGregor Vineyard Winery 1994 Reserve
Riesling**
Region: New York, Finger Lakes $17.99
Golds/Awards: Gold (AW); Double Gold (AW)

**$Mirassou 1996 Fifth Generation Family
Selection** Johannisberg Riesling
Region: California $7.50
Golds/Awards: Gold (WWC-90 pts); Best Buy
(WWC)

$Paraiso Springs 1995 Johannisberg Riesling
Region: California $9
Golds/Awards: Gold (WWC-92 pts); Best Buy
(WWC)

Did You Know . . . ?
In the New Testament, Paul tells Timothy, "Use a little
wine for thy stomach's sake, and for thine infirmities."

Riesling WHITE

$Secret House 1996 White Riesling
Region: Oregon $8
Golds/Awards: Gold (OR)

$Springhill Cellars 1996 White Riesling
Region: Oregon, Willamette Valley $7.50
Golds/Awards: Gold (OR)

$Standing Stone 1995 Riesling
Region: New York, Finger Lakes $8.99
Golds/Awards: Gold (SD)

$V. Sattui 1996 Johannisberg Dry Riesling
Region: California, Napa Valley $11.25
Golds/Awards: Gold (WC); Double Gold (CA);
Best of Class (CA)
By mail-order only: (800) 799-2337

$Willamette Valley Vineyards 1996 Riesling
Region: Oregon $7.75
Golds/Awards: Double Gold (TG); Gold (Newport
Wine Festival and McMinnville Wine Classic)

Did You Know . . . ?

Here's a classic food and wine matchup, according to
Charlie Trotter's Seafood: a racy Riesling with a smoked
sturgeon terrine.

Sauvignon Blanc

This variety is responsible for some of the most distinctive and popular white wines of the world. It is grown virtually everywhere, with New Zealand, Australia, California, and South Africa the New World leaders, Washington and South America following.

What is most distinctive about wines made from Sauvignon Blanc is their crispness and their uniquely sharp aromas. Terms commonly used to describe this wine are grassy, musky, herbaceous, green fruits, nettles, and gooseberries.

The wine has lively acidity, making it a great match with Semillon, with which it is frequently blended and called White Meritage (a Bordeaux-style white blend).

Dry versions of Sauvignon Blanc are sometimes called Fumé Blanc, a term coined in the sixties by Robert Mondavi, who wanted to distinguish his dry Sauvignon Blanc from the popular jug wines of the time.

Serve this wine chilled, of course, with all sorts of seafood and shellfish dinners, Thai food, tomato dishes, or rich sauces such as hollandaise.

Sauvignon/Fumé Blanc   WHITE

$Adler Fels 1995 Fumé Blanc
Region: California, Sonoma County $10.50
Golds/Awards: Gold (NW); Double Gold (SF);
Best Sauvignon Blanc (SF)

$Alderbrook 1995 Sauvignon Blanc
Region: California, Dry Creek Valley $9.99
Golds/Awards: Gold (AT, LA)

$Alderbrook 1996 Sauvignon Blanc
Region: California, Dry Creek $11
Golds/Awards: Double Gold (TG); Gold (LA)

$Arbor Crest 1996 Sauvignon Blanc
Region: Washington, Columbia Valley $6.50
Golds/Awards: Gold (NE)

$Benziger 1995 Fumé Blanc
Region: California, Sonoma County $10
Golds/Awards: Gold (LA, FF); Best of Class (LA);
Chairman's Award (FF)

$Biltmore Estate 1995 Sauvignon Blanc
Region: North Carolina $9
Golds/Awards: Double Gold (SF)

**Cain 1995 Musque Ventana Vineyard
Sauvignon Blanc**
Region: California $16
Golds/Awards: Gold (WWC-90 pts)

Callaghan Vineyards 1996 Fumé Blanc
Region: Arizona $18
Golds/Awards: Gold (WWC-90 pts)

$Canyon Road 1996 Sauvignon Blanc
Region: California $6.99
Golds/Awards: Gold (WC); Best of Class (WC)

Did You Know . . . ?
Winemakers will take drastic measures to shoo pesky
birds out of a vineyard: pyrotechnics. Bird bombs and
whistlers are hand-held pistols that shoot a projectile
40 to 70 feet (aimed skyward) where they then explode.
The boom or whistling sound deters approaching birds
from landing in the vineyard. Then they fly into your
neighbor's vineyard instead!

Sauvignon/Fumé Blanc   WHITE

$Chateau St. Jean 1995 La Petite Etoile Fumé Blanc
Region: California, Russian River Valley $13
Golds/Awards: Double Gold (SF); Gold (WWC-90 pts)

$Chateau Ste. Michelle 1995 Barrel Fermented Sauvignon Blanc
Region: Washington, Columbia Valley $9.99
Golds/Awards: Gold (SD)

$Chateau Ste. Michelle 1995 Horse Heaven Vineyard Sauvignon Blanc
Region: Washington $12
Golds/Awards: Gold (WWC-91 pts)

$Chateau Souverain 1996 Sauvignon Blanc
Region: California, Alexander Valley $8.50
Golds/Awards: Gold (SD)

$Clos Du Bois 1996 Sauvignon Blanc
Region: California, Sonoma County $8
Golds/Awards: Gold (FF, CA); Chairman's Award (FF); Best of Class (CA)

$Concannon 1995 Sauvignon Blanc
Region: California, Livermore Valley $7.95
Golds/Awards: Gold (CA); Best of Class (CA)

$Corbett Canyon 1995 Coastal Classic Sauvignon Blanc
Region: California $4.99
Golds/Awards: Gold (AT)

$Davis Bynum 1996 Shone Farm Sauvignon Blanc
Region: California, Russian River Valley $10.50
Golds/Awards: Gold (NW); Best of Class (NW); Best New World Sauvignon Blanc (NW)

$De Lorimier 1996 Sauvignon Blanc
Region: California, Alexander Valley $10
Golds/Awards: Gold (WC)

Did You Know . . . ?
Wine drinkers are the least involved in drunk driving accidents (beer is a factor in 61%, wine in 10%).

Sauvignon/Fumé Blanc   WHITE

Dos Cabezas Wine Works 1996 Sauvignon Blanc
Region: Arizona $16
Golds/Awards: Gold (WWC-90 pts)

Dry Creek Vineyard 1995 Reserve Fumé Blanc
Region: California, Dry Creek Valley $15.75
Golds/Awards: Gold (PR, LA, AT)

$Dry Creek Vineyard 1996 Fumé Blanc
Region: California, Sonoma County $11.50
Golds/Awards: Gold (CA)

Ferrari Carano 1995 Reserve Fumé Blanc
Region: California $18
Golds/Awards: Gold (WWC-93 pts); National
Champion Sauvignon Blanc (WWC)

$Geyser Peak 1995 Sauvignon Blanc
Region: California, Sonoma County $8.50
Golds/Awards: Gold (WS); Best Sauvignon
Blanc (WS)

$Geyser Peak 1996 Sauvignon Blanc
Region: California, Sonoma County $8.50
Golds/Awards: Gold (SD, WC, VL, OC); Double
Gold (TG)

$Greenwood Ridge 1996 Sauvignon Blanc
Region: Mendocino County $9.50
Golds/Awards: Double Gold (CA); Best of Class
and Tie for Best of Region (CA)

Grove Mill 1996 Sauvignon Blanc
Region: New Zealand, Marlborough $17
Golds/Awards: Gold (SY)

$Grgich Hills 1995 Fumé Blanc
Region: California, Napa Valley $14
Golds/Awards: Gold (SD)

Did You Know . . . ?

Some trace the world's interest in New Zealand's wines
to a single tasting in London in 1983, when judges'
mouths dropped open upon sampling a New Zealand
Sauvignon Blanc. The country became world famous for
this varietal, and eventually, others.

Sauvignon/Fumé Blanc   WHITE

$Guenoc 1995 Estate Sauvignon Blanc
Region: California, Guenoc Valley $12.50
Golds/Awards: Gold (AT)

$Handley Cellars 1996 Sauvignon Blanc
Region: California, Dry Creek Valley $12
Golds/Awards: Gold (WC)

♪Hunter's 1996 Sauvignon Blanc
Region: New Zealand, Marlborough $18
Golds/Awards: Gold (SY)

$Husch Vineyards 1995 Estate Bottled Sauvignon Blanc
Region: California, Mendocino County $9.50
Golds/Awards: Gold (DA)

$Jory 1995 Sauvignon Blanc
Region: New Mexico $15
Golds/Awards: Gold (LA)

$Kendall-Jackson 1995 Grand Reserve Sauvignon Blanc
Region: California $11
Golds/Awards: Gold (NW)

$Kendall-Jackson 1995 Vintner's Reserve Sauvignon Blanc
Region: California $10.50
Golds/Awards: Gold (NW)

$Kenwood 1995 Sauvignon Blanc
Region: California, Sonoma County $9.50
Golds/Awards: Gold (AT)

$Kenwood 1996 Sauvignon Blanc
Region: California, Sonoma County $10
Golds/Awards: Gold (SF)

Did You Know . . . ?
Sauvignon Blanc, with its sassy citrus and herbal varietal character, matches well with a variety of foods, including spicy Szechuan noodles, chèvre soufflé, and squash risotto.

Sauvignon/Fumé Blanc   WHITE

$Lakewood 1995 Sauvignon Blanc
Region: California, Clear Lake $11
Golds/Awards: Gold (AT)

$Lava Cap 1996 Fumé Blanc
Region: California, El Dorado $8.50
Golds/Awards: Gold (CA); Best of Class (CA)

⌂Magnotta 1995 Sauvignon Blanc Reserve
Region: Canada   (Can $) 7.35
Golds/Awards: Gold (AW)

$Maurice Car'rie 1994 Sauvignon Blanc
Region: California $4.99
Golds/Awards: Gold (AW)

$Montevina 1996 Fumé Blanc
Region: California $7
Golds/Awards: Gold (OC)

Murphy-Goode 1995 The Deuce Fumé II
Region: California $24
Golds/Awards: Gold (WWC-92 pts)

Murphy-Goode 1995 Reserve Fumé
Region: California $16
Golds/Awards: Gold (WWC-90 pts)

$Napa Ridge 1995 Sauvignon Blanc
Region: California, North Coast $6
Golds/Awards: Gold (PR)

⌂Neudorf 1996 Sauvignon Blanc
Region: Australia, Nelson/Marlborough $16.99
Golds/Awards: Gold (SY)

$⌂Oxford Landing 1994 Sauvignon Blanc
Region: Australia $7
Golds/Awards: Gold (WWC-90 pts); Best Buy (WWC)

Did You Know . . . ?
If you want to put on a wine tasting, according to the experts, choose a theme, say, 1995 Sauvignon Blancs. That way the tasters' experience will be broad and deep. They'll really understand the concept of *varietal character.* Never plan to sample more than 15 bottles.

Sauvignon/Fumé Blanc　　WHITE

$Renaissance 1996 Estate Bottled Sauvignon Blanc
Region: California, North Yuba　　　　$11
Golds/Awards: Gold (LA)

$Rochioli 1996 Sauvignon Blanc
Region: California　　　　$14.99
Golds/Awards: Gold (WWC-90 pts)

$Ste. Genevieve NV Sauvignon Blanc
Region: Texas　　　　$7.99
Golds/Awards: Gold (AW); Gold, Best of Class,
Star of Texas (Lone Star Wine Competition)

$St. Supéry 1995 Sauvignon Blanc
Region: California　　　　$9.90
Golds/Awards: Gold (AW)

$St. Supéry 1996 Dollarhide Ranch Sauvignon Blanc
Region: California, Napa Valley　　　　$9.90
Golds/Awards: Four-Star Gold (OC); Gold (CA);
Best of California, Best of Region, Best of Class (CA)

$Sanford 1995 Sauvignon Blanc
Region: California, Santa Barbara　　　　$10
Golds/Awards: Gold (AT)

$Sierra Vista 1996 Estate Bottled Fumé Blanc
Region: California, El Dorado　　　　$8.50
Golds/Awards: Gold (OC)

$ ⌂ Stellenzicht 1996 Sauvignon Blanc
Region: South Africa　　　　$13.50
Golds/Awards: Gold (WWC-90 pts)

$Sterling 1995 Sauvignon Blanc
Region: California, Napa Valley　　　　$8
Golds/Awards: Double Gold (CA); Best of Class (CA)

Did You Know . . . ?
Georg Riedel, famous inventor of Riedel stemware, changed the wine world by demonstrating how the same wine will vary when sampled from different-shaped glasses. His taste-sensitive designs guide the wine to specific areas of your tongue, greatly enhancing the experience, according to experts.

Sauvignon/Fumé Blanc   WHITE

$ ⚑Taltarni 1996 Estate Grown Sauvignon Blanc
Region: Australia, Victoria $12
Golds/Awards: Gold (PR); Best of Class (PR); Best
Pacific Rim White Wine (PR)

$V. Sattui 1996 Sauvignon Blanc
Region: California, Napa Valley $15
Golds/Awards: Gold (WC); Best of Class (WC)
By mail-order only: (800) 799-2337

$Vichon 1995 Sauvignon Blanc
Region: Calif., Mediterranean grapes $7.99
Golds/Awards: Gold (LA)

$Voss 1996 Sauvignon Blanc
Region: California $12
Golds/Awards: Gold (WWC-90 pts)

$Windsor 1995 Fumé Blanc
Region: California, North Coast $9.50
Golds/Awards: Gold (FF)
By mail-order only: (800) 333-9987

Did You Know . . . ?
Owned by Robert Mondavi Winery, Vichon is made in
California from French grapes. Plans are to move the
whole operation to southern France over the next few
years. A shortage of premium grapes is one of the
reasons for the move, and illustrates an increasing (and
controversial) trend on the part of California winemakers to produce "global wine"—California-made wine
sourced from international grapes.

Semillon

This is an excellent, high-yielding grape that produces classy and distinctive white wines that are low in acidity. Because of its wieght and plentifulness, Semillon is frequently used as a blending wine, to add background to Chardonnay (called Semchard), or to add weight and fruit to Sauvignon Blanc in white Meritage, or Bordeaux-style blends.

Susceptible to botrytis, Semillon is often made into rich, sweet dessert wines (listed in Chapter 13).

California, Washington, and Australia are making wonderful (and often inexpensive) Semillon, as are Chile and Argentina.

Semillon   WHITE

$ ☙ Basedow 1996 Semillon (White Burgundy)
Region: Australia, Barossa Valley $10
Golds/Awards: Gold (SY)

$ Hogue Cellars 1996 Semillon
Region: Washington, Columbia Valley $8.99
Golds/Awards: Gold (WC); Best of Class (WC)

**$ Kendall-Jackson 1995 Vintner's
Reserve Semillon**
Region: California $12
Golds/Awards: Gold (FF, CA); Chairman's Award
(FF); Best of Class (CA)

$ Rosenblum 1996 Semillon
Region: California $14
Golds/Awards: Gold (WWC-90 pts); National
Champion Semillon (WWC)

☙ Stellenzicht 1996 Reserve Semillon
Region: South Africa $19.50
Golds/Awards: Gold (WWC-91 pts)

☙ Tyrrell's 1992 Aged Release Vat 1 Semillon
Region: Australia, Lower Hunter Valley $39.95
Golds/Awards: Gold (SY)

☙ Vasse Felix 1995 Semillon
Region: Australia, Margaret River $21
Golds/Awards: Gold (SY)

Did You Know . . . ?
What do you do with a bunch of supertalented Aussie
winemakers during harvest season in the Western
Hemisphere, which is their off-season? You fly them to
vineyards in Europe and America, where they can do
their magic, share their expertise, and stay out of trouble! This trend started in 1987 in France, and gave birth
to the term "Flying Winemakers."

Viognier

There's nothing quite so humbling as bumbling through French words with a leftover midwestern accent. So for your enlightenment, the pronunciation is *vee-on-YAY*.

This Rhône white wine grape is rather rare and difficult to grow. In recent years it's captured the imagination of California as well as Australian winemakers, who love its unusual spicy flavors and its aromas of violets, peaches, and apricots. It makes an excellent Riesling-like white wine, but it can also be vinified in the style of an oaky Chardonnay. With American consumers looking for Chardonnay alternatives, Viognier's fortunes will no doubt steadily rise.

Viognier   WHITE

Alban 1995 Alban Estate Vineyard Viognier
Region: California $29
Golds/Awards: Gold (WWC-90 pts)

Beringer 1994 Hudson Ranch Vineyard Viognier
Region: California $25
Golds/Awards: Gold (WWC-92 pts); National
Champion (WWC)

**Bonterra 1995 Organically Grown Grapes
Viognier**
Region: California, Mendocino County $22
Golds/Awards: Gold (PR)

Callaway 1995 Viognier
Region: California, Temecula $16
Golds/Awards: Gold (NW); Best of Class, Best Viog. (NW)

Callaway 1996 Estate Bottled Viognier
Region: California, Temecula $16
Golds/Awards: Gold (LA, CA); Best of Region, Best
of Class (CA)

Eberle 1996 Fralich Vineyard Viognier
Region: California, Paso Robles $20
Golds/Awards: Gold (WC); Best of Class (WC)

Horton 1995 Viognier
Region: Virginia $20
Golds/Awards: Gold (AT)

Ojai Vineyard 1996 Roll Ranch Vineyard Viognier
Region: California, Paso Robles $20
Golds/Awards: Gold (OC)

$R.H. Phillips 1996 EXP Viognier
Region: California, Dunnigan Hills $12
Golds/Awards: Gold (CA); Best of Region, Best of Class (CA)

$Sobon 1996 Viognier
Region: California, Shenandoah Valley $15
Golds/Awards: Gold (WC, OC)

Zaca Mesa 1996 Misty Ridge Vineyard Viognier
Region: California, Santa Barbara County $18
Golds/Awards: Gold (LA); Best of Class (LA)

Did You Know . . . ?
The recommended minimum number of years a cork
tree must grow before it can yield corks is forty.

White Blends

Most wines are blends. After all, it's the wine-maker's way of balancing out and enhancing certain characteristics in the varietal that's used as a base. But in the U.S., if the base wine, red or white, is made of less than 75 percent of that grape, the resulting wine cannot take the varietal name.

Some wineries give these blended wines fancy proprietary names; other simply give them a hyphenated name, the result of a balanced and happy marriage.

Either way, you're likely to find high-quality, delicious, but sometimes expensive wines in this section. To me, at least, Semillon-Chardonnay seems more interesting than either of these varietals alone. It so happens that I'm not the only one in the wine world who likes this trend, which is prevalent throughout the New World. The Australians, in particular, love blended wines—and love giving them unpretentious names derived from their constituent parts.

Meritage, or Bordeaux-style blends   To use the trademarked name *Meritage,* an American wine must be composed only of specific grape varieties that grow in the Bordeaux region of France. For white wines these include Sauvignon Blanc, Semillon, and Muscadelle. Meritage wines can be white or red.

Semchard   A classic combination of Semillon and Chardonnay.

White Blends   WHITE

$Baily 1996 Montage (Bordeaux-style blend)
Region: California, Temecula $11
Golds/Awards: Gold (CA); Best of Class (CA)

$Beringer 1995 Alluvium Blanc (Mixed white blend)
Region: California, Napa Valley $15
Golds/Awards: Gold (VN)

$Carmenet 1995 Paragon Vineyard White Meritage
Region: California $15
Golds/Awards: Gold (WWC-92 pts)

Cosentino 1996 The Novelist (Bordeaux-style
blend)
Region: California $16
Golds/Awards: Gold (OC, NW)

$De Lorimier 1995 Estate Bottled Spectrum
(Bordeaux-style blend)
Region: California, Alexander Valley $12
Golds/Awards: Gold (OC, CA); Best of Class (CA)

$Folie à Deux NV Menage à Trois (Mixed white blend)
Region: California $8
Golds/Awards: Gold (CA); Best of Class (CA)

$℗Jacob's Creek 1995 Semillon-Chardonnay
Region: Australia, Southeast Australia $7
Golds/Awards: Gold (AT)

$℗Jacob's Creek 1996 Semillon-Chardonnay
Region: Australia, Southeast Australia $6.99
Golds/Awards: Gold (VL)

**Kendall-Jackson 1995 Grand Reserve White
Meritage**
Region: California $25
Golds/Awards: Gold (PR, FF, NW); Best of Class
(NW); Best New World Meritage-Type White (NW)

$℗Rosemount 1996 Semillon Chardonnay
Region: Australia, Southeast Region $7.95
Golds/Awards: Gold (PR)

Did You Know . . . ?
To legally call one's wine *Meritage,* a winery may not
produce more than 25,000 cases of it.

White Blends   WHITE

$ ⌂ Rosemount Estates 1996 Traminer Riesling
(Gewurztraminer/Riesling blend)
Region: Australia, Southeast Region $7.95
Golds/Awards: Gold (PR, AT)

$ ⌂ Santa Ana 1996 Chardonnay-Chenin Blanc
Region: Argentina, Mendoza $3.99
Golds/Awards: Gold (AT)

$ ⌂ Selaks 1995 Sauvignon Blanc/Semillon
Region: New Zealand $12.99
Golds/Awards: Gold (WWC-90 pts); Cellar
Selection (WWC)

$ Sutter Home 1996 White Soleo (Chen. Blanc/ Muscat)
Region: California $4.45
Golds/Awards: Gold (LA)

Venezia 1995 Bianca Nuovo Mondo (Bordeaux-
style blend)
Region: California; Northern Sonoma $20
Golds/Awards: Gold (AT, FF, SF)

Venezia 1995 Stella Bianco White Table Wine
(Semchard)
Region: California; Sonoma County $20
Golds/Awards: Gold (PR, AT, AW, NW,); Best of
Class (PR, NW); Best New World Semchard (NW)

$ ⌂ Wyndham Estate 1995 Bin TR2 (Gewurztraminer/
Riesling)
Region: Australia, Southeast Region $6.99
Golds/Awards: Gold (PR)

**Yorkville Cellars 1995 Eleanor of Aquitaine,
Randle Hill Vineyard** (Bordeaux-style blend)
Region: California $16
Golds/Awards: Gold (WWC-93 pts); National White
Meritage Champion and Cellar Selection (WWC)

Did You Know . . . ?

Three companies, Aromascan, Alpha M.O.S., and Neo-
tronics, currently sell electronic "noses" to the wine
industry. These noses are programmed with silicon
chips to accurately detect 100 times more aromas than
humans can.

🍷 11 🍷
BLUSH WINES

White Zinfandel
&
Miscellaneous Rosés

White Zinfandel & Misc. Rosés

Don't listen to wine bullies. There's no reason to blush, and nothing politically incorrect, naïve, or unsophisticated about pink wines. There are plenty of terrific examples of blush wines, especially the ones on this section, which were stupendous enough to win gold medals from some of the greatest world wine experts.

White Zinfandel Despite its name, White Zinfandel is actually pink. Made from Zinfandel grapes, the juice is left in contact with the skins just long enough to tint the juice. (Wine gets its color from the pigment in the grape skins.)

White Zinfandel became wildly popular in the last few years, and California is the biggest New World producer. The wines are fresh and fruity, on the sweet side, but with enough acidity to balance out the sugar. Some White Zins have a bit of spritziness. Others have some Riesling or Muscat blended in to add more balance and character.

Wine snobs don't take this wine seriously. However, the fact that it's light, fruit-filled, and lively—and made to be drunk young—gives it a lot of popular appeal, especially for people who wouldn't otherwise drink wine. Another great feature: its reasonable price.

Drink it chilled with equally light foods such as vegetable hors d'oeuvres, shrimp cocktail, or picnic fare.

$Augusta Winery NV River Valley Blush
Region: Missouri $7
Golds/Awards: Gold (SD)

$Barefoot Cellars NV White Zinfandel
Region: California $4.99
Golds/Awards: Gold (SD, FF, CA); Chairman's
Award (FF)

**$Bel Arbor 1995 Vintner's Selection White
Zinfandel**
Region: California $4.99
Golds/Awards: Gold (SD, NW); Best of Class (SD)

$Beringer 1996 White Zinfandel
Region: California $7.50
Golds/Awards: Double Gold (CA); Best of
California and Best of Class (CA)

$Blossom Hill 1995 White Zinfandel
Region: California $4
Golds/Awards: Gold (NW); Best of Class (NW)

$Concannon 1996 Righteously Rosé
Region: California $8.95
Golds/Awards: Gold (CA); Best of Class (CA)

$Cosentino 1996 Tenero Rosa
Region: California $10.50
Golds/Awards: Gold (FF); Chairman's Award (FF)

$De Loach Vineyards 1996 White Zinfandel
Region: California, Sonoma County $8
Golds/Awards: Gold (PR); Best of Class (PR)

$Ferrante Wine Farm NV Pink Catawba
Region: Ohio, Lake Erie $5.99
Golds/Awards: Gold (SD)

Did You Know . . . ?
White Zinfandel is the second most ordered wine in
restaurants. (Don't ask me what the first is.)

$Grand Cru Vineyards 1996 Premium Selection White Zinfandel
Region: California $7.99
Golds/Awards: Gold (CA)

$Hart Winery 1996 Grenache Rosé
Region: California, Cucamonga Valley $7.50
Golds/Awards: Gold (SD, FF, NW); Chairman's Award (FF); Best of Class (NW); Best New World Rosé (NW)

$Les Vieux Cepages 1995 Ronfleur
Region: California $6.99
Golds/Awards: Gold (WWC-90 pts); Best Buy (WWC)

$Montpellier Vineyards 1996 White Zinfandel
Region: California $6.99
Golds/Awards: Gold (CA)

$Paraiso Springs 1995 Baby Blush
Region: California $12.50
Golds/Awards: Gold (WWC-93 pts)

$Pedroncelli 1996 Vintage Selection Rosé of Zinfandel
Region: California, Sonoma County $7
Golds/Awards: Gold (OC)

$Stone Hill Winery NV Pink Catawba
Region: Missouri $6.79
Golds/Awards: Double Gold (TG); Gold (NW)

$Van Roekel Vineyards 1996 Rosé of Syrah
Region: California, Temecula $12.95
Golds/Awards: Gold (OC)

$Wollersheim 1996 Prairie Blush White Foch
Region: Wisconsin $7
Golds/Awards: Gold (FF); Best of Category (FF)

Did You Know . . . ?
Some (supersensitve? neurotic?) experts claim that wine tastes different at the high altitudes and under the dry conditions of airplane flight.

⚘ 12 ⚘
SPARKLING WINES

Blanc de Blancs
Blanc de Noirs
Brut
Misc. Sparklers

Sparkling Wines

Open up any wine and food magazine around holiday time and you're bound to read about sparkling wines. And they'll also tell you that sparkling wines shouldn't be reserved for special occasions. I couldn't agree more. There are delicious sparkling wines in this chapter that, once you've tried them, you'll want to keep on hand for spontaneous gleeful moments.

There are lots of sparkling wines being made outside of France's Champagne district. California, the Pacific Northwest, and Australia are the New World leaders. Sparkling wine may be made from Chardonnay, Pinot Noir, Pinot Blanc, Pinot Gris, Riesling, Muscat, Symphony, and others, including native American grapes such as Catawba.

The main difference between traditional champagne-style wines and other sparkling wines has to do with the vinification method used. See Appendix 2 for an explanation of *méthode champenoise,* or the champagne style.

Blanc de Blancs (also written Blanc de Blanc) In French this means, literally, "white from whites," and refers to wines that are made exclusively from white grapes. Many Blanc de Blancs sparklers are blends of different varieties, with Chardonnay the key component.

Blanc de Noirs (also written Blanc de Noir) These are light-colored sparkling wines (the translation is "white from blacks") made from black-skinned (red wine) grapes by fermenting the crushed grapes or grape juice, known as the must, without the skins, and therefore without the pigment that gives wine its ruby hues.

Brut France has laws that govern the maximum amount of residual sugar a champagne may have and still be labeled Brut. In America and elsewhere a Brut is merely a very dry sparkling wine.

Blanc de Blancs SPARKLING

Adelaida 1984 Blanc de Blancs
Region: California $24.50
Golds/Awards: Gold (WWC-91 pts)

$Buena Vista Carneros 1990 Blanc de Blanc
Region: California, Carneros $14
Golds/Awards: Gold (AT)

Equinox 1991 Blanc de Blanc Reserve
Region; California $40
Golds/Awards: Gold (WWC-91 pts); Cellar
Selection (WWC)

Equinox NV Blanc de Blanc
Region; California $23
Golds/Awards: Gold (WWC-90 pts)

Gruet 1992 Blanc de Blanc
Region: New Mexico $20
Golds/Awards: Gold (NW, WWC-90 pts)

Iron Horse 1990 Blanc de Blancs
Region: California $24.50
Golds/Awards: Gold (WWC-90 pts)

$Korbel NV Sparkling Champagne Chardonnay
Region: California $12.99
Golds/Awards: Gold (LA)

**Paradise Ridge NV Private Reserve Blanc
de Blanc**
Region: California $17
Golds/Awards: Gold (WWC-92 pts)

Westport Rivers 1991 Blanc de Blancs
Region: Massachusetts $34.95
Golds/Awards: Gold (LA)

Did You Know . . . ?
New technology to deter birds in vineyards, one of
winegrowers' most troubling pests, is a device made by
Brain Corp. It keeps birds away by disturbing the earth's
geomagnetic field, which birds use to navigate. So if
you see a flock of birds heading north for the winter—
or east or west—you'll understand why.

Blanc de Noirs   SPARKLING

Adelaida 1985 Blanc de Noirs
Region: California $24.50
Golds/Awards: Gold (WWC-92 pts)

$Chandon NV Cuvée 391 Blanc de Noirs
Region: California $12
Golds/Awards: Gold (WWC-91 pts)

$Gloria Ferrer Champagne Caves NV Blanc de Noirs
Region: California, Carneros $15
Golds/Awards: Double Gold (TG); Gold (FF, OC, NW, CA); Best of Category (FF); 4-Star Gold (OC); Sweepstakes White (Sonoma County Fair)

Iron Horse 1993 Wedding Cuvée
Region: California $23.50
Golds/Awards: Gold (WWC-90 pts); Cellar Selection (WWC)

$Korbel 1991 Master's Reserve Blanc de Noirs
Region: California $13.99
Golds/Awards: Gold (LA, NW, CA); Best of Class (CA)

Mirassou 1992 Fifth Generation Cuvée, Méthode Champenoise Blanc de Noir
Region: California, Monterey County $16.75
Golds/Awards: Gold (OC)

Mumm Cuvée Napa NV Blanc de Noirs
Region: California, Napa Valley $16
Golds/Awards: Gold (DA)

Robert Hunter 1992 Brut de Noirs Sparkling Wine
Region: Califonia, Sonoma Valley $25
Golds/Awards: Gold (WC, OC)

Did You Know . . . ?
Increasingly, champagne is being paired with food rather than saved for ultraspecial affairs: lobster ravioi in saffron sauce; venison with mascarpone polenta; Ahi tuna and wasabi; Moroccan spiced duck—these were some of the recent sparkler/food pairings at Xavier's in Piedmont, NY.

Blanc de Noirs   SPARKLING

S. Anderson 1992 Blanc de Noirs
Region: California, Napa Valley $22
Golds/Awards: Gold (DA, PR); Best of Class (PR);
Best Pacific Rim Sparkling Wine (PR)

Schramsberg 1989 Blanc de Noirs
Region: California, Napa Valley $24.50
Golds/Awards: Gold (WWC-90 pts)

Schramsberg 1990 Blanc de Noirs
Region: California, Napa Valley $23.75
Golds/Awards: Gold (LA); Best of Class (LA)

$Windsor 1994 Blanc De Noirs
Region: California, Sonoma County $14
Golds/Awards: Gold (FF, CA)
By mail order only: (800) 333-9987

Did You Know . . . ?
The diminishing concentration of carbon dioxide with
altitude has a direct effect on grapevines, as it does on
other plants. Almost all of the world's best wines have
come historically fom vineyards below 500 meters. Current and future rises in carbon dioxide levels in the at-
mosphere may override such differences. Could global
warming have its advantages?

Argyle 1991 Brut
Region: Oregon $18.50
Golds/Awards: Gold (WWC-92 pts)

Briceland NV Méthode Champenoise Brut
Region: California, Humboldt County $19
Golds/Awards: Gold (OC)

Chandon NV Reserve Cuvée 490
Region: California $18
Golds/Awards: Gold (WWC-90 pts)

$Culbertson NV Brut
Region: California $10
Golds/Awards: Gold (NW)

Domaine Carneros 1992 Taittinger Brut
Region: California, Napa Valley $21
Golds/Awards: Gold (SF)

Edna Valley Vineyard 1989 Brut
Region: California $25
Golds/Awards: Gold (WWC-91 pts)

$Glenora 1992 Brut
Region: New York $12.99
Golds/Awards: Gold (WWC-90 pts); Best Buy
(WWC)

$Gloria Ferrer NV Brut
Region: California, Sonoma County $15
Golds/Awards: Gold (LA, NW)

**$Gloria Ferrer 1988 Royal Cuvée Late Disgorged
Brut**
Region: California, Carneros $14
Golds/Awards: Gold (AT, WC, LA, NW, WWC-90
pts); Best of Class (LA); Grand Champion (NW);
Best New World Sparkling Wine (NW)

Did You Know . . . ?
Sixty-three percent of U.S. wine consumers today are
currently married. (Maybe someone should find these
statisticians a more useful job.) Thought you'd want to
know.

Gloria Ferrer 1989 Royal Cuvée Brut
Region: California, Sonoma County $19
Golds/Awards: Gold (LA, SF)

$Gruet NV Brut
Region: New Mexico $13
Golds/Awards: Gold (NW)

Handley Cellars 1992 Méthode Champenoise Brut
Region: California, Alexander Valley $19
Golds/Awards: Gold (OC)

Iron Horse 1989 Brut LD
Region: California $45
Golds/Awards: Gold (WWC-92 pts); Cellar Selection (WWC)

Iron Horse 1990 Vrais Amis
Region: California $23.50
Golds/Awards: Gold (WWC-93 pts); National Sparkling Wine Champ. and Cellar Selection (WWC)

Jordan J 1991 Brut
Region: California, Russian River Valley $25
Golds/Awards: Gold (DA, NW)

Jordan J 1993 Brut
Region: California, Russian River Valley $25
Golds/Awards: Double Gold (TG, CA); Gold (OC); Four-Star Gold (OC); Best of Class (CA)

Lamoreaux Landing 1990 Brut
Region: New York $16
Golds/Awards: Gold (WWC-90 pts); Cellar Selection (WWC)

$Maison Deutz NV Brut Cuvée
Region: Cal., Santa Barbara/San Luis Obispo $12.75
Golds/Awards: Gold (PR, NW)

Maison Deutz 1992 Brut Reserve
Region: California $20
Golds/Awards: Double Gold (TG); Gold (NW)

Did You Know . . . ?
In France it's legal for fifteen-year-olds to purchase wine. It's even sold at fast-food joints.

Palmer 1992 Méthode Champenoise Special Reserve Brut
Region: New York, Long Island $20
Golds/Awards: Double Gold (SF); Best Sparkling Wine (SF)

Robert Hunter 1992 Brut
Region: California, Sonoma Valley $25
Golds/Awards: Gold (FF)

Roederer Estate 1991 L'Ermitage Brut
Region: California $35
Golds/Awards: Gold (WWC-90 pts)

S. Anderson 1992 Brut
Region: California, Napa Valley $24
Golds/Awards: Gold (SD, NW)

Scharffenberger 1991 Prestige Cuvée Allure Brut
Region: California, Mendocino County $18
Golds/Awards: Four-Star Gold (OC)

Schramsberg 1990 J. Schram
Region: California $50
Golds/Awards: Gold (WWC-92 pts)

Van der Kamp 1993 English Cuvée Méthode Champenoise Brut
Region: California, Sonoma Valley $20
Golds/Awards: Four-Star Gold (OC)

$Wente NV Reserve Brut
*Region:*California, Arroyo Seco/Monterey $12
Golds/Awards: Gold (FF, WWC-91 pts)

Westport Rivers 1992 RJR Cuvée Brut
Region: Massachusetts $20.95
Golds/Awards: Gold (AT)

$Windsor 1994 Brut
Region: California, Sonoma County $13
Golds/Awards: Gold (FF); Chairman's Award (FF)
By mail order only: (800) 333-9987

Did You Know . . . ?
Physician Galen (2nd century AD) of ancient Rome
disinfected the wounds of injured gladiators with wine.

Misc. Sparklers   SPARKLING

$Ballatore NV Gran Spumante
Region: California $6.49
Golds/Awards: Gold (DA, NW)

Bricout 1989 Premier Cru Champagne
Region: California $26
Golds/Awards: Gold (AW)

$Cook's Wine Cellars NV Sweet Spumante Cook's
Wine Cellars NV Sweet Spumante
Region: California $3.99
Golds/Awards: Gold (CA); Best of Class (CA)

$Firelands Winery NV Sparkling Riesling
Region: Ohio $9.95
Golds/Awards: Double Gold (TG)

$Korbel NV Rouge Champagne
Region: California $11.99
Golds/Awards: Gold (LA); Best of Class (LA)

$Korbel NV Extra Dry Champagne
Region: California $9.99
Golds/Awards: Gold (LA)

⏦Magnotta NV Rossana Rosé (Brut Rosé)
Region: Canada   (Can $) 11.95
Golds/Awards: Gold (LA)

Maison Deutz NV Brut Rosé
Region: Cal., San Luis Obispo County $20
Golds/Awards: Gold (PR, NW)

$Meier's Wine Cellars Sparkling Pink Catawba
Region: Ohio $2.29
Golds/Awards: Gold (PR); Best of Class (PR)

> ### *Did You Know . . . ?*
> It was in Cincinnati, Ohio, where the first commercially
> successful American wine was born, Nicholas Long-
> worth's famous Sparkling Catawba. The "foxiness,"
> which the American colonists so disliked in native
> grapes, was not unpleasant in sparkling wines. By 1850
> Longworth had 1,200 acres of Catawba and had made
> a fortune.

Misc. Sparklers   SPARKLING

Schramsberg 1992 Brut Rosé
Region: California $22.75
Golds/Awards: Gold (WWC-90 pts)

Schramsberg 1992 Champagne
Region: California $22.75
Golds/Awards: Gold (WWC-90 pts)

$Silvan Ridge 1995 Semi-Sparkling Early Muscat
Region: Oregon $12
Golds/Awards: Gold (FF, WWC-90 pts); Double
Gold (SF); Best of Category (FF)

$Stone Hill NV Golden Spumante
Region: Missouri $8.29
Golds/Awards: Gold (LA)

$Swedish Hill NV Spumante
Region: New York, Finger Lakes $8.99
Golds/Awards: Gold (LA); Best of Class (LA)

Thornton NV Artist Series Cuvée de Frontignan
Region: California $20
Golds/Awards: Gold (LA, NW)

Thornton NV Cuvée Rouge
Region: California $18
Golds/Awards: Gold (AT)

**Westport Rivers 1993 Imperial Sec Sparkling
Riesling**
Region: Massachusetts $24.95
Golds/Awards: Gold (LA)

Did You Know . . . ?
When Russian soldiers occupied Europe in 1914 they
did what most soldiers do: pillage and plunder. The
Russians helped themselves to bottles of bubbly in
Champagne's most famous cellars. After the war, however, Russians became France's most loyal peacetime
consumers of champagne.

✒ 13 ✒
SWEET/DESSERT
& FORTIFIED WINES

Icewine
Misc. Sweet Wines
Muscat
Port
Sherry

Sweet/Dessert/Fortified Wines

If you haven't discovered the incredible world of sweet and/or fortified wines, now's your chance. Try some wines you wouldn't ordinarily buy. They add intrigue to a dinner party with friends, and many aren't too expensive, since a small glass is all one usually drinks.

For an explanation of late harvest and botrytized wines, see the glossary, Appendix 2.

Icewine (also known as Eiswein) One of the best things about researching and writing this book was discovering icewine. Now I tell all my friends about it. It's surprising how many Americans have never heard of icewine, especially given that our northern neighbor, Canada, has surpassed Germany in world recognition of this exotic wine. New York isn't far behind. This is a very sweet dessert wine made from an interesting process. The grapes are allowed to freeze right on the vine, producing a high concentration of sugar in the juice when pressed. A handful of North American wineries make this treasured wine. Try it as dessert, or with sweets such as cakes, fruit tarts or pies, and flan.

Muscat Muscat is a family of grapes that's been around for centuries. There are at least four varieties of Muscat, ranging in hues, thus producing wines that vary from pale golden to dark, dark brown. Some Muscats have nicknames that reflect their hue, hence Orange Muscat, Black Muscat, and so on. Muscat Alexandria and Muscat Canelli are but two Muscat varieties. Muscat grapes are known for their incredibly perfumed berries. New World varieties include off-dry sipping wines and sweet late harvest styles that often have a distinctive spicy aroma. Depending on the wine, of course, Muscat is ideal as an aperitif. Try it with hard cheese, foie gras, or with prosciutto and melon. For dessert it complements fruit pies and puddings.

Port Port is a fortified wine that can be made from any grape variety. Portugal is where the world's most famous ports hail from, but South

Africa, California, and Australia are the New World leaders in producing outstanding ports as well.

Here's the process: red wine grapes are crushed and begin to ferment in the usual way. After two to four days, the partially fermented grape juice has about 6 percent alcohol and about 10 percent residual sugar, which is quite sweet. At this point, the grape juice is run off into containers holding 154-proof neutral wine spirits. The spirits act immediately to stop the fermenting process, and what's left is very flavorful, very sweet wine with a whopping 20 percent alcohol.

There are two main types of port: wood-aged and vintage ports. Wood-aged ports are ready to drink when bottled, and are made from many different vintages, added during the aging process to achieve a continuity of style. Ruby port is one type of wood-aged port that's dark red, young, fruity, and flavorful, and aged for three to four years on average before it's bottled. Tawny port is the other wood-aged port, and it's aged for eight to ten years. As a result, it's lighter in color, and more mellow and subdued.

Vintage ports, on the other hand, are made from a single vintage, and they're bottled after about two years, but it takes from ten to twenty years or more of bottle age before they reach maturity. Therefore, vintage ports may be produced only two or three times in a decade.

Port are wonderful after dinner or before bed (as Jackie O used to have it).

Sherry Australia, South Africa, and California are the New World regions producing sherry, a fortified wine made from white grapes, that, when made in that traditional way, gets its distinctive flavors from a yeast called *flor* that forms on the top of the wine as it's fermenting. California "sherry" often refers to fortified wines, usually sweet ones, that have been baked, aged, or artificially infused with yeast to create a product similar in flavor to Spanish sherry.

Casa Larga 1995 Fiore delle Stelle Vidal Icewine
Region: New York $25
Golds/Awards: Gold (AW, IV)

⌘**Cedar Creek 1994 Riesling Icewine**
Region: Canada (Can $) 49.95
Golds/Awards: Gold (WWC-90 pts)

⌘**Cedar Creek 1995 Ice Wine**
Region: Canada, Okanagan Valley (Can $) 49.95
Golds/Awards: Gold (LA)

Chateau Grand Traverse 1995 Johannisberg Riesling Icewine
Region: Michigan $65
Golds/Awards: Gold (WWC-90 pts)

Chateau Ste. Michelle 1995 Chateau Reserve White Riesling Ice Wine
Region: Washington $30
Golds/Awards: Gold (WWC-92 pts, NE)

⌘**Cilento Wines 1995 Riesling Icewine**
Region: Canada $64.95
Golds/Awards: Gold (AW)

Dr. Konstantin Frank 1995 Riesling Icewine
Region: New York $29.95
Golds/Awards: Double Gold (TG); Gold (NW, WWC-90 pts); Best New World Riesling (NW)

⌘**Inniskillin Wines 1995 Petronio Vineyards Chenin Blanc Ice Wine**
Region: Canada $36
Golds/Awards: Gold (PR)

Did You Know . . . ?

Come harvest time in Ontario, when icewine grapes have to be picked frozen solid on a specific night, volunteers flock to the vineyards to participate in what's becoming a national tradition: snowy harvest parties. Many have to be awakened in the middle of the night, and some travel hundreds of miles to be part of the icewine experience.

Joseph Phelps 1995 Eisrebe
Region: California $40
Golds/Awards: Gold (WWC-91 pts)

℣**Kittling Ridge 1995 Vidal Icewine**
Region: Canada $45.95
Golds/Awards: Double Gold (TG); Grand Gold
(VinItaly 1996); Gold (IV 1996)

℣**Konzelmann 1994 Vidal Icewine**
Region: Canada, Niagara Peninsula (Can $) 45.55
Golds/Awards: Gold (WS)

℣**Konzelmann 1995 Vidal Icewine**
Region: Canada, Niagara Peninsula (Can $) 45.55
Golds/Awards: Gold (IV)

$Lakewood 1995 Borealis (Concord) Ice Wine
Region: New York, Finger Lakes $8.99
Golds/Awards: Gold (AT)

$Lakewood 1995 Glaciovinum Ice Wine
Region: New York, Finger Lakes $8.99
Golds/Awards: Gold (AW)

℣**Magnotta 1995 Limited Edition Vidal Icewine**
Region: Canada $45
Golds/Awards: Gold (VL, WWC-92 pts)

℣**Magnotta 1996 Limited Edition Vidal Icewine**
Region: Canada $45
Golds/Awards: Gold (IV)

℣**Pillitteri Estates 1994 Icewine**
Region: Canada, Niagara Penin. (Can $) 29.95
Golds/Awards: Gold (WS)

Did You Know . . . ?
Ontario, the world's largest producer of icewine, is also
the only winemaking region in the world whose winters
are cold enough to ensure a crop every year.

⌐**Stonechurch 1994 Vidal Icewine**
Region: Canada   **$32**
Golds/Awards: Gold (WWC-90 pts)

⌐**Stoney Ridge 1996 Riesling Traminer Ice Wine**
Region: Canada, Ontario   (Can $) 49.95
Golds/Awards: Gold (IV)

$Wagner Vineyards 1995 Ice Wine
Region: New York   **$9.99**
Golds/Awards: Double Gold (TG)

$Anthony Road 1995 Late Harvest Vignoles
Region: New York, Finger Lakes $13.99
Golds/Awards: Gold (FF, SF); Best of Category (FF)

$Baron Herzog 1995 Late Harvest Johannisberg Riesling
Region: California, Monterey County $14
Golds/Awards: Gold (SY, FF, CA); Best of California, Best of Class, Best of Region (CA)

$Beringer 1994 Special Select Late Harvest Johannisberg Riesling
Region: California $15
Golds/Awards: Gold (WWC-94 pts)

$Breitenbach Wine Cellars 1996 Late Harvest Johannisberg Riesling
Region: Ohio $10
Golds/Awards: Gold (PR)

Callaway NV Sweet Nancy Chenin Blanc
Region: California, Temecula $25
Golds/Awards: Gold (FF)

Chalk Hill 1994 Botrytised Semillon
Region: California $35
Golds/Awards: Gold (WWC-90 pts)

Chappellet 1994 Moelleux Chenin Blanc
Region: California $40
Golds/Awards: Gold (WWC-95 pts)

Chateau St. Jean 1992 Special Select Late Harvest Johannisberg Riesling
Region: California, Alexander Valley $25
Golds/Awards: Gold (FF, WWC-94 pts)

Did You Know . . . ?
More than sixty brands have independently announced that they'll stop selling their wine in Kentucky since the state government made direct shipping of wine to Kentucky citizens a felony.

Chateau Ste. Michelle 1995 Horse Heaven Vineyard Late Harvest Chateau Reserve White Riesling
Region: Washington $19
Golds/Awards: Gold (WWC-91 pts)

$Concannon 1995 Late Harvest Zinfandel
Region: California, Livermore Valley $12.95
Golds/Awards: Gold (WC); Best of Class (WC)

De Loach 1996 Estate Bottled Late Harvest Gewurztraminer
Region: California, Russian River Valley $16
Golds/Awards: Gold (PR, WWC-93); Best of Class (PR)

Dolce 1993
Region: California $50
Golds/Awards: Gold (WWC-92 pts); National Sauternes Style Champion (WWC)

$Duck Walk Vineyards 1995 Aphrodite (Late Harvest Gewurztraminer)
Region: New York $14.95
Golds/Awards: Gold (LA)

Elk Run 1995 Vin de Jus Glacé Riesling
Region: Maryland $16
Golds/Awards: Gold (WWC-90 pts)

$Gan Eden 1996 Late Harvest Gewurztraminer
Region: California $12
Golds/Awards: Double Gold (TG)

Geyser Peak 1996 Late Harvest Riesling
Region: California, Sonoma County $16
Golds/Awards: Gold (WC)

$⌂Giesen 1995 Botrytised Riesling
Region: New Zealand, Canterbury $14.99
Golds/Awards: Gold (SY)

Did You Know . . . ?
Bronze is the mirror of the form; wine, of the heart.
—Aeschylus, 525–456 BC

Grgich Hills 1994 Violetta (Late Harvest Chardonnay/ Riesling)
Region: California $50
Golds/Awards: Gold (WWC-94 pts)

$Hogue Cellars 1996 Late Harvest Johannisberg Riesling
Region: Washington, Columbia Valley $6.45
Golds/Awards: Gold (LA)

$Husch 1996 Estate Bottled Late Harvest Gewurztaminer
Region: California, Anderson Valley $14
Golds/Awards: Gold (OC); Double Gold (CA); Best of California, Best of Class (CA)

Joseph Fillipi NV Fondante Ciello (Portlike fortified wine)
Region: California $18
Golds/Awards: Gold (NW)

$Kent Rasmussen 1993 Late Harvest Sauvignon Blanc
Region: California, North Coast $11
Golds/Awards: Gold (AT); Best U.S. Unfortified Dessert Wine (AT); Runner-up for Best of Show (AT)

$King's Road 1995 Late Harvest Riesling
Region: New Jersey $8.85
Golds/Awards: Gold (AW)

$Kiona 1995 Late Harvest Gewurztraminer
Region: Washington, Yakima Valley $7
Golds/Awards: Gold (DA)

Kittling Ridge Icewine and Brandy
Region: Canada, Ontario $19.95
Golds/Awards: Gold (WS); Double Gold (TG)

Did You Know . . . ?
90.1% of those who consume wine in the United States today are white.

Misc. Sweet Wines

♫**Konzelmann 1994 Select Late Harvest Vidal**
Region: Canada, Niagara Peninsula   (Can $) 17.95
Golds/Awards: Gold (WS)

♫**Martinborough 1996 Late Harvest Riesling**
Region: Australia, Martinborough $19.99
Golds/Awards: Gold (BR)

$Montevina 1994 Aleatico
Region: California, Amador County $7.50
Golds/Awards: Gold (DA)

**Navarro 1994 Late Harvest Cluster Select White
Riesling**
Region: California, Anderson Valley $19.50
Golds/Awards: Gold (PR, WWC-93 pts, Mendocino
Wine Competition)

♫**Neethlingshof 1996 Noble Late Harvest White
Riesling**
Region: South Africa   19.50
Golds/Awards: Gold (WWC-94 pts)

**Newlan 1994/1995 Late Harvest Johannisberg
Riesling**
Region: California, Napa Valley $25
Golds/Awards: Gold (SF, WWC-92 pts)

$Palmer 1994 Select Harvest Gewurztraminer
Region: New York $15
Golds/Awards: Gold (AW)

**Paraiso Springs 1995 Late Harvest
Johannisberg Riesling**
Region: California $25
Golds/Awards: Gold (WWC-90 pts)

$Prejean Winery 1995 Late Harvest Vignoles
Region: New York, Finger Lakes $12
Golds/Awards: Gold (PR, AT)

Did You Know . . . ?
U.S. wine exports to 164 countries soared 35 percent
last year, or $327 million.

⌐Quail's Gate 1994 Late Harvest Botrytis
Affected Optima
Region: Canada, Okanagan Vall.   (Can $) 24.95
Golds/Awards: Gold (WS)

$ ⌐Reif Estate 1996 Select Late Harvest Vidal
Region: Canada, Ontario $12.50
Golds/Awards: Gold (IV)

Renaissance 1994 Late Harvest
Estate White
Region: California, North Yuba $18
Golds/Awards: Gold (CA); Best of Class (CA)

$St. James 1995 Late Harvest Seyval Blanc
Region: Missouri $12.99
Golds/Awards: Gold (NW); Best of Class (NW)

$Stone Hill 1994 Late Harvest Vignoles
Region: Missouri, Hermann $14.99
Golds/Awards: Gold (FF)

⌐Stoney Ridge 1996 Late Harvest Riesling
Traminer
Region: Canada, Ontario   (Can $) 19.95
Golds/Awards: Gold (IV)

$Swedish Hill 1995 Late Harvest Vignoles
Region: New York, Cayuga Lake $11.99
Golds/Awards: Double Gold (TG, SF); Gold (NW)

Thornton 1995 Aleatico
Region: California $18
Golds/Awards: Gold (NW)

Did You Know . . . ?
A trend among wealthy Europeans in the mid-19th
century was to have elaborate gardens, greenhouses,
and conservatories. In 1865 alone 460 tons of plants
worth 230,000 francs had been imported into France
from the "exotic" United States. Unfortunately, deadly
vine diseases were also brought in that nearly wiped
out all of Europe's fine wine production.

Muscat

**Alderbrook 1995 Late Harvest Kunde Vineyard
Muscat de Frontignan**
Region: California, Sonoma Valley $20
Golds/Awards: Gold (AT, FF, NW, six other '96
golds); Double Gold (TG, SF); Best of Category (FF)

$Arciero 1996 Estate Bottled Muscat Canelli
Region: California, Paso Robles $6.75
Golds/Awards: Gold (PR); Best of Class (PR)

$Bonny Doon 1995 Vin de Glaciere Muscat
Region: California $15
Golds/Awards: Gold (WWC-90 pts)

$Eberle 1996 Estate Muscat Canelli
Region: California, Paso Robles $10
Golds/Awards: Gold (NW)

**$Kendall-Jackson 1995 Vinter's Reserve Muscat
Canelli**
Region: California $11
Golds/Awards: Gold (PR)

KWV Red Muscadel
Region: South Africa, Breede River $19.50
Golds/Awards: Gold (WS)

$Martin Brothers 1996 Allegro Moscato
Region: California $10
Golds/Awards: Gold (WWC-90 pts); Best Buy
(WWC)

$Maurice Car'rie 1996 Muscat Canelli
Region: California, Temecula $7.95
Golds/Awards: Gold (NW)

Merryvale NV Antigua Muscat de Frontignan
Region: California $16
Golds/Awards: Gold (WWC-90 pts)

Did You Know . . . ?
The percentage of urban-dwelling U.S. wine consumers
today: 87.55 percent. So what do farmers drink?

$Perry Creek 1996 Muscat Canelli
Region: California, El Dorado $9.50
Golds/Awards: Gold (NW)

$Quady 1996 Electra (Orange Muscat)
Region: California $7.50
Golds/Awards: Gold (PR, NW); Double Gold
(CA); Best of Class (NW)

$Quady 1995 Elysium (Black Muscat)
Region: California $14
Golds/Awards: Gold (WWC 91 pts)

$Quady 1996 Elysium (Black Muscat)
Region: California $14
Golds/Awards: Gold (SD, LA, FF); Double Gold
(CA); Best of Class (CA)

$Quady 1995 Essensia (Orange Muscat)
Region: California $14
Golds/Awards: Double Gold (TG); Gold (OC,
WWC-91 pts)

$Sutter Home 1996 Moscato (Muscat Alexandria)
Region: California, Napa Valley $5.95
Golds/Awards: Gold (LA, NW); Best of Class (NW)

$V. Sattui 1996 Muscat
Region: California $12.25
Golds/Awards: Gold (LA, CA); Best of Class (CA)
By mail-order only: (800) 799-2337

Did You Know . . . ?
Reference to a professional wine taster is found in a
document of the 3rd century AD, from Roman Egypt:
"The wine taster has declared the Euboean wine to be
unsuitable."

$Beringer 1991 Port of Cabernet Sauvignon
Region: California $13
Golds/Awards: Gold (WWC-92 pts); National Champion Fortified Wine, Cellar Selection, and Best Buy (WWC)

Cedar Mountain 1995 Cabernet Royale Cabernet Port
Region: California, Livermore Valley $21.50
Golds/Awards: Gold (OC)

$Christian Brothers NV Tawny Port
Region: California $5.99
Golds/Awards: Gold (NW); Best of Class (NW); Best New World Traditional Dessert Wine (NW)

$Ficklin NV Tinta Port
Region: California, Madera $12
Golds/Awards: Gold (NW)

Ficklin NV Aged 10 Years Estate Bottled Tawny Port
Region: California, Madera $22
Golds/Awards: Gold (DA, WWC-90 pts); Double Gold (CA); Best of Class (CA)

Fox Run 1995 Cabernet Port
Region: New York $19.99
Golds/Awards: Gold (PR)

$Geyser Peak 1994 Henry's Reserve Shiraz Vintage Port
Region: California $15
Golds/Awards: Gold (WWC-90 pts)

Geyser Peak 1995 Henry's Reserve Port
Region: California, Alexander Valley $30
Golds/Awards: Gold (NW)

> ### Did You Know . . . ?
> Thomas Jefferson is probably chuckling in his grave at the $23,000 a buyer paid at a Sotheby's auction for a bottle of port that belonged to the former president.

Guenoc 1994 Vintage Port
Region: California $25
Golds/Awards: Gold (DA, OC, WWC-91 pts);
Double Gold (TG); Four-Star Gold (OC)

$ ℍ**Hardys NV Whiskers Blake Tawny Port**
Region: Australia $14
Golds/Awards: Gold (AT, IV)

$**Heitz 1993 Grignolino Port**
Region: California $12.75
Golds/Awards: Gold (AW)

$**Kalyra 1986 Tawny Port**
Region: California $11
Golds/Awards: Four-Star Gold (OC)

$**La Quinta NV Rare Souzao Port**
Region: California $10
Golds/Awards: Gold (OC)

$ ℍ**Penfolds Club Port Reserve**
Region: Australia $15
Golds/Awards: Gold (WWC-90 pts)

ℍ**Penfolds Grandfather Fine Old Liqueur Port**
Region: Australia, Barossa Valley $58.99
Golds/Awards: Gold (SY)

$**Pindar 1994 Port**
Region: New York, Long Island $12.99
Golds/Awards: Gold (LA)

Prager 1993 Aria White Port
Region: California, Napa Valley $32.50
Golds/Awards: Gold (OC, NW)

> ### *Did You Know . . . ?*
> On luxury liners such as the QE2, the most well-to-do passengers are subjected to greater movement than the wine they drink. They're in the penthouses, while their wines are thirteen decks below in warehouselike rooms, probably the stillest place in the ship.

$Quady NV Batch 88 Starboard Port
Region: California, $14
Golds/Awards: Gold (CA); Best of Class (CA)

Quady 1986 Frank's Vineyard Vintage Port
Region: California, Amador County $15.50
Golds/Awards: Gold (CA)

Quady 1989 Vintage Starboard
Region: California $19
Golds/Awards: Gold (WWC-90 pts)

$Quady 1990 Vintage Starboard
Region: California $14
Golds/Awards: Double Gold (TG, CA); Gold (OC);
Best of Class (CA)

$Quady 1993 Late Bottled Vintage Port
Region: California, Amador $12
Golds/Awards: Double Gold (SF)

Sonora Winery 1992 Port
Region: California, Sierra Foothills $16
Golds/Awards: Gold (NW)

Trentadue Winery 1994 Petite Sirah Port
Region: California, Alexander Valley $20
Golds/Awards: Gold (PR, FF); Best of Class (PR)

Vignoble Le Cep D'Argent 1995 Archer
Region: Canada, Quebec   (Can $) 18.95
Golds/Awards: Gold (AW)

$Whidbey 1990 Port
Region: Washington $12.99
Golds/Awards: Gold (WWC-90 pts); Cellar
Selection and Best Buy (WWC)

Did You Know . . . ?
A 10-year French study has concluded that elderly persons who were also moderate drinkers showed a 75% decrease in Alzheimer's disease and an 80% decrease in the rate of dementia compared with nondrinkers.

Sherry

$E. & J. Gallo NV Sheffield Cellars Cream Sherry
Region: California, Livingston $3.99
Golds/Awards: Gold (OC)

Galleano NV Nino's Solera Sherry
Region: California $19.14
Golds/Awards: Gold (AT)

Galleano NV Cellar Reserve Triple Cream Sherry
Region: California, Cucamonga Valley $16.95
Golds/Awards: Gold (PR, LA); Best of Class (LA);
Division Sweepstakes (LA)

$Galleano NV Pale Dry Sherry
Region: California, Cucamonga Valley $8.25
Golds/Awards: Gold (NW); Best of Class (NW);
Best New World Sherry (NW)

$Meier's Wine Cellars NV No. 44 Cream Sherry
Region: Ohio $7.49
Golds/Awards: Gold (AW)

$St. Julian NV Solera Cream Sherry
Region: Michigan, Lake Michigan Shore $12
Golds/Awards: Gold (AW)

$Three Islands Lonz Winery NV Madeira
Region: Ohio $5.95
Golds/Awards: Gold (DA, PR)

Did You Know . . . ?

Sherry and olives make a great duet. Sherry also goes great with other salty foods such as grilled sardines, salty cheeses, and cured meats. Or try it with fresh seafood at the dinner table.

APPENDIX 1

The World Wine Championships: Mother of all Wine Judgings

The World Wine Championships is unlike the other wine competitions in this book, which are annual events that take place over a short period of time. Any book that features the gold medal wines from the world's best competitions would be sorely lacking if it didn't include the gold and platinum wines from World Wine Championships.

The wineries I spoke with all agreed: a 90-plus rating from this judging brings loads of prestige, so revered are its judges and impeccable its standards. One of the real advantages of including this judging is that it allows for greater diversity in the book, mainly because many of the top wineries who don't enter conventional wine competitions *do* enter The World Wine Championships.

The World Wine Championships is conducted by the Beverage Testing Institute, an independent professional tasting body that reviews more than 5,000 wines from more than twenty different countries, throughout their year-round tasting program. Tasters consist of highly trained institute staff members and selected beverage industry professionals. The World Wine Championships has gained international recognition for its impartiality and professionalism. All wines are tasted strictly on premise at the Chicago facility, using procedures that minimize palate fatigue and psychological biases.

The results of the World Wine Championships, i.e., the scores and reviews, are published electronically every month on the Food and Drink Network on America Online (keyword FDN) and on the World Wide Web at http://www.fdn.com. In print, they're published monthly as the Buying Guide of *Wine Enthusiast* magazine, one of the nation's leading nationally distributed wine publications. Condensed portions of the reviews also appear in monthly features for *Restaurant Hospitality*, the leading trade magazine for restaurants. And now the complete New World gold and platinum wines are in Best Wines!, which is a wonderful addition for wine lovers and fans of this book.

The tastings are conducted weekdays from 9 a.m. to early afternoon, with a panel of five people tasting no more than thirty-five wines a day. This year-round schedule addresses wines from different regions and countries each month. Panelists typically face five flights of seven wines. The following factors are considered when determining the flighting: grape variety, style, vintage, residual sugar, and specific area of origin (i.e., appellation). The wines are served in Riedel stemware and only identified by a three-digit code on the base of the stem. Great care is taken to ensure that flawed samples are not served to the panel. The director of The World Wine Championships tastes, inspects, and scores each sample before serving it to the panel.

Scoring Panelists score on a fourteen-point scale, chosen for its ability to accurately represent the precision of the average trained taster. Average scores are then converted to the industry standard of the 100-point scale. Further awards are issued within a specified rating range. Bronze medals are given for 80–85 points, silver for 85–89, gold for 90–95 points, and platinum for exceptional scores of 95–100 points.

Best Buy "Best Buy" awards, which factor price to score, are made by the staff when scoring is complete.

Cellar Selection "Cellar Selection" designations are given when the panel feels a wine has the structure to improve significantly with age.

APPENDIX 2

A Glossary of Winespeak

If you're not an avid reader and fan of wine magazines and wine guides, you may feel that wine writers belong to a secret society, one that excludes you with its enigmatic language. I used to shrug my shoulders, roll my eyes, and ask, "Who writes this stuff?"

The problem stems from the very thing that makes wine so special. As people have known since the dawning of Greek civilization and before, wine isn't merely a beverage. It's been embued in people's hearts and minds with nearly divine qualities. It's been used and is still used in religious ceremonies; it's associated with love, happiness, passages, status, sin, decadence—you name it. So to describe its flavors and aromas, the effect it has in your mouth, the sensations it imparts beyond taste, and the other subtle, almost imperceptible feelings it evokes requires a special language.

Believe it or not, once you have the rosetta stone that unlocks the mysteries of *winespeak*, you'll find much of this once-boggling (and often goofy) set of terms quite useful. As with any other jargon, the better you can navigate in and around the terminology, the more you'll come to understand the subject itself.

Really grasping the most common terms will enhance your wine-tasting experience. For example, once I realized that *vanilla* refers to a subtle aroma imparted by *oak barrel aging,* I was able to train my nose to detect it, and then to pick up, for example, *toasty* scents too, also associated with oak.

The good news is that wine descriptions generally follow a simple—and, yes, logical!—six-part formulaic structure that exactly corresponds to how one experiences and tastes one's first sip of wine (see Chapter 1). Each wine term in tasting notes will fall into one of six categories, as illustrated by the following chart:

TASTING TERM	TASTING STEP
Color	Look at the wine
Nose/aroma/bouquet	Swirl and sniff
Flavors	Sip and "whistle" in air
Body/texture	"Chew" the wine
Structure and balance (oak/tannins/acidity/ sugar/alcohol)	Consciously gather impressions while wine is in your mouth
Finish	Swallow the wine (or spit)

The following glossary will help to untangle some of the more common terms of winespeak.

acid/acidity Acid is to wine what a good zing of lime juice is to food: it adds zest and liveliness. Terms such as *crisp, tart, lively,* and *refreshing* refer to wines that have a good balance of acidity. Acidity is what keeps sweet and semisweet wines from being too cloying, and it's what helps deliver the flavor in sparkling wines, since the mousse (foamy bubbles) can sometimes disperse the fruity elements. Acidity makes white wines a good dinner guest, since acid stimulates the appetite, cleanses the palate, and cuts through rich foods. Acidity is especially important in white wines, which lack the tannin levels of reds, because it contributes to white wine's ability to age well in your cellar.

aroma How a wine smells after you pour it into a glass will tell much of the story, at least in terms of the kinds of flavors you can expect. A wine's aroma is often referred to as its *nose, bouquet,* or *scent.* Aromas in winespeak may include everything from saddle leather to flint, tropical fruits to common garden vegetables.

backbone Here's a term that can be taken rather literally. It generally refers to either tannin or acid levels that "hold up" or "support" the wine. A wine without adequate backbone might be too soft, too light bodied, too fruity, or too sweet. Wines with firm tannic or acidic backbones are *full bodied.*

balance This is a term of praise that describes that magic moment in a wine's development when its components—chiefly acid, sugar, alcohol and fruit—work together to achieve harmony. Acid is what balances sweetness; the concentration of fruit is what balances tannin and oakiness; and the overall flavor and acidity of the wine balance out the alcohol. It's reasonable to assume that all balanced wines won't have the same intensity. For example, a balanced light wine should be delicate, while a balanced full-bodied wine might inspire such adjectives as blockbuster or powerhouse.

barrel aging Most wines spend only a brief period of time in large vats or tanks to rid them of impurities and to prepare them for bottling. But the fuller-flavored reds and some whites, such as drier-style Chardonnays, Sauvignon Blancs, Chenin Blancs, and Pinot Blancs, are aged in large or small oak barrels or larger casks, which matures them, adds *structure,* and improves their taste, if done correctly.

Barrel aging requires time, money, knowledge, and considerable effort, so winemakers like to brag about what nationality of oak they used, how old their barrels were, how long their wine spent in the precious barrels, and so on. But there's another reason they mention it, especially in the case of white wines, which has to do with identifying a certain style of wine. Barrel-aged wines have specific flavor characteristics that nonbarrel-aged wines lack. Some terms that derive from oak barrel aging include *oak, vanilla, clove, nutmeg, cinnamon, toast, smoke,* and sometimes *chocolate.*

Oak barrel aging imparts all-important tannin necessary for longer shelf life to whites, but, oddly, mellows the sharp tannin levels in robust red wines.

big See *body.*

blend Blending is not too different in winemaking than it is in cooking up the perfect curry—a dash of this, a pinch of that, all to accomplish the perfect balance of flavors, bite, and piquancy. A wine might be a blend of the same varietal grown in different vineyards, a blend of the same wine aged in different casks, a blend of wines from different vintages, or a blend of two or more varieties.

The winemaker's goal in blending might be to produce a wine that consumers can depend on for flavor and quality consistency year after year. Often, though, blending is the art of maximizing the assets of each lot for the good of the whole. Certain varieties, such as Cabernet Sauvignon, simply become "friendlier" after marrying with, say, Merlot or Cabernet Franc in a Bordeaux-style blend. Most wines are blends of one type or another, and it is a perfectly legitimate practice for which every wine-producing country and region has laws that dictate how a blended wine can be labeled.

body This is a term for a sensation that's simple to identify if you pay attention. "Body" describes how a wine feels in your mouth—its texture, weight, and fullness—and refers to a combination of the wine's alcohol, sugar, and glycerin content (glycerin, a by-product of fermentation, is a colorless, sweet, slippery liquid that adds *smoothness* to wine). Body is substance; think of body as being the opposite of thin and watery. A light- and medium-bodied wine might be described as *soft, attractive, simple,* or *delicate.* A full-bodied wine might be called *brawny, mouth filling, chewy, big,* or *weighty.* Most wines are not full bodied, and there's no rule that says a medium-bodied wine is inferior to a full-bodied one. They are different, and will complement different foods. Remember that the key to a wine's greatness is its *balance,* not the measure of its body.

botrytis Its formal name is *Botrytis cinerea,* and it's also known as "noble rot." When wine grapes grow in just the right conditions—dry, sunny days alternating with damp, foggy mornings—they may become *botrytized,* or infected with the beneficial mold that transforms normal grape juice into a honeyed, aromatic, magical liquid. Since this condition is apt to happen after harvest season, as late as December in some places, the resultant wines are called *late harvest* wines, and they're prized the world over.

Here's how it works. The beneficial mold covers the grapes, sending little filaments into the skin that perforates the grapes and causes them to shrivel up. The mold doesn't rot the grapes, but 90 percent of the water evaporates, and the sugar and acids remain in the grape pulp. When this is pressed and fermented, you get very sweet wine (since all the sugar isn't fermented into alcohol) that has extremely concentrated flavors and aromas. Think, for example, of how intense a dried tomato or dried pear tastes compared to the fresh item, and you get the idea.

The most common grapes used to make late harvest wines are Semillon, Sauvignon Blanc, Riesling, Gewurztraminer, and Chenin Blanc, although there are others that are susceptible to the noble rot. These wines age extremely well in the bottle.

bouquet See *aroma*.

brawny See *powerful*.

breathing/airing To breathe or not to breathe seems to be the question, and the answer, as far as I'm concerned, doesn't seem all that unclear. Breathing refers to the act of pouring wine into another container, such as a decanter, in order to allow the wine to aerate and mix with oxygen. This permits the aroma components of the wine to oxidize, thus intensifying them. (Breathing does *not* refer to uncorking a wine. The narrow neck of the bottle prohibits an adequate supply of oxygen from making any discernible difference in the wine's bouquet.)

But much of the material I've read seems to lean on the side of the pour-wine-into-your-glass-and-just-drink-it side of the argument. Only the surface is getting oxidized anyway, and some of the fruitiness and flavor is at risk if a wine is exposed to oxygen too long. (This makes sense; otherwise, why would we bother to recork a half-consumed bottle?) If you're serving a young, tannic red wine, breathing may lessen some of the tannins. If you're serving a very old wine, careful decanting should be done to separate the wine from the sediments in the bottom of the bottle.

In general, though, serve your wine in a large, wide wine glass (for maximum surface contact with the air), swirl it around a bit before sipping it, and your wine will get enough air to achieve the desired results. (For more on tasting and smelling wine, see Chapter 1.)

brut This is a term that refers to the driest champagnes and other sparkling wine. In Europe, Common Market laws dictate that a sparkling wine labeled "brut" must have no more than 1.5 percent sugar. In America and elsewhere, the term is merely a descriptive one that means "very dry." There is no good way to tell if a non-European brut sparkling wine will be dry, very dry, or very, very dry without tasting it.

buttery See *creamy*.

chewy You'll know a chewy wine when you drink one. The term is used to describe red wines that have high levels of tannin and are rich, heavy, textured, and full of fruit extract. See also *body* and *mouth feel*.

cigarbox A term used to describe the aroma of cedar and/or tobacco in a wine. It's not an uncomplimentary adjective.

citrus Although citrus fruits include oranges, lemons, and limes, among others, in winespeak the term *citrus* most often refers to grapefruit. Chardonnays grown in cool climates will often display a grapefruitlike character.

closed It may sound insulting to a layperson, but to say that a wine is closed implies that it has great potential. In other words, the wine has a loads of fruit concentration and good character, but needs more time in the bottle to mature to full intensity.

complex In a complex wine, layers and layers of flavors and aromas reveal themselves, the wine has just the right *mouth feel*, a lovely *finish*, and all of the compenents are in *balance*. Complexity is elusive, but the best wines have it.

concentrated Concentrated wines are not watery and thin, but possess intense fruit flavor components that jump out at you and make a distinct impression on your palate. The aftereffects of a concentrated wine tend to linger. See also *finish*.

creamy Some wines are described as having a creamy or *buttery* texture, or creamy, buttery flavors. In sparkling wines, this is a result of contact with the *lees,* or yeast cells. In certain whites, this creaminess may be a result of malolactic fermentation, a process by which malic acid, the acid in apples and other fruit, is converted into lactic acid, the acid found in milk, to create wines that are softer and more *supple* in texure, less harsh and less *tart.* In wine terms, creamy is the opposite of *crisp,* which refers to a wine's *lively acidity.*

crisp *Crisp* is a code word that indicates a wine's acid content, in this case a pleasing level of acidity. It is synonymous with *refreshing, fresh,* and *tart.* See *acid/acidity.*

cuvée This word comes from the French *cuve,* meaning vat or tank, particularly a large one used for blending or fermenting wines. In places other than Europe, the term has come to mean a specific lot or batch of a particular wine or blend.

delicate See *body.*

demi-sec Is the glass half full or half empty? *Demi* is from the French meaning "half," and *sec* means "dry." But demi-sec wines are closer to being half sweet than they are to being half dry. This term is usually applied to sparkling wines that are sweet to medium sweet.

depth Some of these wine terms get tricky, and you have to use your imagination a bit. Where *weight* refers to a wine's body, or how a wine "feels" in your mouth, depth has more to do with how *much* of your mouth experiences the wine. It's a subtle distinction, but a wine that has good depth is one full of layers of flavors that seem to fill your mouth from front to back.

dry Quick: What's the opposite of dry? If you said wet, you haven't read enough of this book. The opposite of dry, in wine terms, is sweet. A still or sparkling wine in which an ordinary taster perceives no sweetness is dry, and that would fall somewhere between 0.5 and 0.7 percent *residual* *sugar,* which is the amount of sugar left after a wine has finished fermenting. Dry does not necessarily mean better; there are many wines that are supposed to be sweet. See *sweet.*

estate bottled   In the United States, "estate bottled" on a label means that the wine comes from the winery's own vineyards, or from vineyards leased on a long-term basis, only if the vineyards and winery are both located within the appellation shown on the label. In other words, the grape juice wasn't purchased from a winery a thousand miles away, and then made into wine. Or conversely, the wine wasn't grown in the vineyards, and then made into wine a thousand miles away. Estate bottling is supposed to connote superior quality.

extract   Elements that add flavor, aroma, and character to a wine are known as extract. A "highly extracted" wine, or one with "loads of extract," implies that the grapes used to make this wine had very concentrated juice, and this could be for any number of reasons, among them a great vintage; careful avoidance of overcropping; *old vines*; *late harvest*; or possibly because they were just great grapes.

fat   Fat is good when it describes dessert wines. It refers to the naturally occurring glycerin in sweet dessert wines, the oily richness that coats your mouth. The term is less complimentary when it refers to nondessert wines that are medium to full bodied, slightly low in acid, and leave a fat or full impression on your palate.

filtered   There's a lot of stuff floating around in wine after it's been fermented. After all, fermentation is caused by little living critters, and they don't just disappear, nor do their by-products. Therefore, the vast majority of winemakers fine and filter their wine at least a little. The reason is because most people expect a nice clear glass of wine in their wine glass. Explaining the types of filters and extent to which wines should be filtered could fill the rest of this book. Know, however, that even as you read this, someone, somewhere is getting hot under the collar debating how extensively wines should be filtered. Why? Because wine lovers complain that *fining* and overfiltering wine removes from it the very thing we love: its character.

Therefore, many winemakers are moving back to the traditional (European, Old World) practice of not overdoing it, figuring that New World wine lovers would rather put up with a little sediment than drink something with no personality. Some wineries put "Unfined, Unfiltered" on their labels to alert consumers to a purist approach, a more handcrafted winemaking method that, theoretically at least, leads to a higher-quality, more sensuous wine-drinking experience. See *fined*.

fined   Fining is similar to filtering, resultwise at least. As opposed to filtering, where the wine is poured through something that screens out the sediments and other junk, in fining something is *added* to the wine that captures the unwanted solid particles. It's the same process cooks use to clarify broth or to make jelly clear (by adding egg whites). In fact, winemakers also use egg whites sometimes, but more commonly gelatin or bentonite (a type of clay). Like filtering, it's a controversial practice if done to excess, because it's a bit like giving the wine a lobotomy: a lot of personality can get lost in the process. See *filtered*.

fine-grained tannins   When a winemaker refers to *tannins* as being fine-grained, he or she is saying that tannins are present, but they're smooth and refined, well behaved, and not overpowering.

finish   If only winespeakers would come up with some new ways to describe a great finish other than "long and lingering." After you swallow the wine, its finish is characterized both by how long the flavors linger in your mouth, and by what kind of qualities are still perceptible. So, a finish in a quality wine might be medium or long, but it could also be soft, creamy, slightly tannic, or just "good." A wine's *length* or "persistence" is a component of its finish.

firm   Used to describe a wine that hits your palate with an acidic or tannic bang, this is a complimentary term that implies your wine may be rather young, but will make a great accompaniment to strong-flavored foods.

fleshy/meaty These terms refer to *body* and texture, and often suggest a wine of great smoothness and richness, where suppleness and flavor are in harmony. See *chewy*.

fortified wine Sherry and port are the best-known examples of fortified wines in the New World. These are wines in which the alcoholic content has been increased to the tune of 17 to 21 percent in the finished product by the addition of brandy or neutral spirits. Because of their high alcohol, fortified wines are less likely to spoil after opening than table wines, and they also have long, long cellaring potential. In the United States, sweet fortified wines have to be labeled "Dessert Wine" because the federal authorities want to prevent street alcoholics from misunderstanding and then mistakenly buying up and glugging down all the expensive twenty-year-old rare port they can find.

fruity This is a term that often applies to young wines. A fruity wine is full of intense fruit flavors such as berries or apples, and possesses a quality of freshness.

glycerin A by-product of fermentation, glycerin is found in all wines, but is most obvious in higher-alcohol and late harvest wines. At high levels it feels slippery and smooth on the tongue, and adds fullness to the wine's body.

grassy You will often see this term when Sauvignon Blanc is being described because it is part of that wine's *varietal character*. Grassiness is a nice quality if you think of the light, fresh, green smell of a summer lawn being mowed. Sometimes "gooseberry" is used to describe a similar flavor/aroma. Too much grassiness is a negative.

grip When a wine, like a handshake, is forceful, it has grip. Grip is used to describe a red wine distinguished by rich texture and an assertive personality.

herbs/herbaceous   Certain wines (for instance, Cabernet Sauvignon, Sauvignon Blanc, and Merlot) are sometimes described as having herbal aromas and/or flavors. Which herbs depends on the wine's *varietal character*.

hybrid   When two or more grape varieties are genetically crossed by human intervention, you get a hybrid. The idea is to create a grape that's superior to the parents, or one that's better able to cope with such conditions as climatic extremes or proneness to disease. In the northern United States, French–native American hybrids have resulted in wines that are much better than those of native varieties in many cases. It may take thousands of crosses to come up with a commercially successful wine, and it takes about fifteen years to determine if that hybrid will produce consistently sound wine.

late harvest   If harvest time is autumn, then grapes picked later than that would be late harvest, right? Well, yes, but late harvest on a label really refers to how *ripe* the grapes were at harvest time. If grapes are picked at a stage where they're riper than normal (i.e., they have a higher-than-normal sugar content), then they will be made into a late harvest wine. Often, but not always, these later-picked grapes have been infected with noble rot, or *botrytis*. Either way, late harvest on a label means that the wine will be sweeter than normal—possibly very, very sweet—or with higher-than-normal alcohol levels. Most late harvest wines are after-dinner wines, sipped in place of dessert.

lees   You'll often read that a wine "sat on the lees" or that it was "left in contact with the lees" for several months. Lees means sediment, or more precisely, dead yeast cells that are a by-product of fermentation. When wine ferments, this sediment sinks to the bottom of the barrel or tank and is promptly removed so as not to contribute unwanted odors or flavors. But some wines, particularly some Chardonnays and Sauvignon Blancs, are left in contact with the lees (called *sur lie*) after fermentation. This adds complexity and a lovely toasty, roasted grain character. Sparkling wines get much of their character from aging on the lees, done during a second fermentation inside the bottle—sediment and all—before the lees are removed. This is why the best sparkling wines taste akin to freshly toasted homemade bread. The lees contact also contributes richness and creaminess to these sparkling wines.

length The amount of time the aftertaste lingers in your mouth after swallowing your wine is a wine's length. Ten seconds is good, fifteen is great, and twenty seconds is spectacular. See *finish*.

méthode champenoise All champagnes from France are produced by the *méthode champenoise*. For producers of sparkling wine in the New World (some of whom insist on calling their sparklers "champagne," which is punishable by law in France if not produced in that eponymous region!), this wine term has definite snooty connotations. In fact, wines made by this method take a lot more expertise, time, and money, so the resultant sparklers are generally of higher quality.

After the wine has fermented it is bottled, and a measured amount of sugar and yeast is added. When the bottle is corked, fermentation occurs, but the carbon dioxide that is produced gets trapped inside, thus creating those great bubbles. The sediment that is a by-product then must be expelled. These champagnes (go ahead: arrest me) are marketed in the very bottle in which the second fermentation took place.

mouth feel/mouth filling Wine writers love this term, which refers to wines with intense, round flavors, often in combination with glycerin or slightly low acidity. The idea here is that the wine's various characteristics seem to expand in the mouth, thus "filling" it up (as opposed, say, to an acidic wine that would have a distinct cutting or biting edge). Mouth feel is often used in conjuction with the modifiers *chewy* or *fleshy*. See *body*.

must The juice of grapes produced by pressing or crushing, before it is fermented.

natural In *méthode champenoise* sparkling wines, after the lees have been removed, a small amount of wine is lost. So winemakers commonly add a mixture of wine and sugar (known as the dosage) to fill up the bottle and to add some degree of sweetness, depending on how dry they want the final sparkler to be. Natural (sometimes spelled naturel) sparkling wines have no sweetener added. Thus, a natural champagne or sparkling wine is driest of all. Winemakers sometimes refer to these as "no dosage" wines.

noble rot See *botrytis.*

no dosage See *natural.*

nose See *aroma.*

NV These initials, commonly seen on labels, stand for nonvintage. The word means that the wine you're drinking is a blend of several different vintages, usually based mainly on the most recent one, with the products of some past vintages, sometimes called "reserve wines," blended in. Just because a wine has no vintage does not mean it is of lower quality. Indeed, some winemakers attempt to produce wines year after year that will be consistent and always excellent. NV is often seen on sparkling wines or champagnes.

oak/oaky Aging in oak barrels imparts certain flavors and aromas to wines, including, obviously, oakiness. Vanillin, which comes from the oak itself, and toasty or roasted qualities, derived from the charring that comes from the open flames used to heat the barrel staves during barrel making, are common ways to describe oaky wines. *Woody* is another word for oaky.

old vines Like classic, well-cared-for cars, old grapevines are considered valuable. The reason, oddly enough, is that the older a vineyard becomes, the lower its yield. But since each vine has to devote all of its energy into producing fewer grapes, those fewer grapes will have a higher level of *extract*. In the New World, Australia seems to have the most old vines, since many of the vineyards there were planted in the last century. Since conventional wisdom would state unabashedly that old vines make better wines, you'll often see "Old Vines" or "80 Year Old" or some such right on the label to announce to potential buyers that this wine should be jam-packed with flavor.

phylloxera If you're seeking revenge on a mean and nasty winemaker who has dis'd you, whisper "phylloxera" in his ear and walk away. He'll turn several shades of white, for this vine disease, brought about by tiny aphids or lice that attack the roots of most grapevines, was responsible for wiping out virtually all vineyards in France and America in the last century. Grape growers are deadly afraid of it, and for good reason. The little pests live on in the soil, and will attack *Vitis vinifera* vines (which includes all of the European varieties from which the finest wines in the world are made) like there's no tomorrow.

In the late nineteenth century, it was discovered that most native American varieties were immune to phylloxera, so grafting the European varieties onto American rootstock was done, both in America and throughout Europe. Unfortunately, that didn't solve the problem completely, since the little devils have found a way to show up again on the American rootstock that was widely used in the 1980s. (By the year 2000, for instance, 30 to 50 percent of all U.S. coastal vineyards will have to be systematically replanted because of phylloxera.) Some varieties are more resistant than others, and some regions—Chile, for example—have never had the problem at all.

powerful Powerful red wines are ones that are high in alcohol and tannin, also sometimes called *brawny* reds. A powerful white wine would be a dry wine with lots of body.

private reserve See *reserve*.

proprietary wine This is a name or brand dreamed up by a producer that's exclusive to that producer, and is used instead of the varietal name. So, for example, if a producer wants his 1993 Cabernet

Sauvignon to stand out from the pack, he might name it Midnight Red, and the next year's wine would be the 1994 Midnight Red. It's a bit like trademarking your wine. The problem for consumers, of course, is that it's impossible to determine from the proprietary name what kind of wine they're buying. On the other hand, this growing trend has added some sparkle, fun, and mystique to the formerly stuffy wine world.

proprietor's reserve See *reserve.*

reserve Although there's no official regulation governing how this term is used, a reserve wine usually represents a wine of higher quality than the regular bottling of that same variety. You'll see the term alone, or sometimes as Grand Reserve, Private Reserve, Proprietor's Reserve, Special Reserve, Vintner's Reserve, Winemaker's Reserve, and the like. A high-quality producer with a conscience won't abuse the term; it should be merited.

Reserve wines get their name because the wine has been separated out, or reserved, from the rest of the batch. It might be the same as the regular wine, but aged longer or differently. It might be from selected vineyards, or from selected lots of wine. Or sometimes reserve wines are merely chosen and bottled from the top 5 to 10 percent of the existing batches.

Regardless, expect to pay more for reserve wines. If both the reserve and the regular bottling have won gold medals, try both and see if the difference in quality warrants the difference in price.

residual sugar After a wine is done fermenting, there's usually at least a small amount of unfermented grape sugar, known as residual sugar. Winemakers put this statistic in their notes, and occasionally on their labels, especially for dessert wines, to let consumers know how sweet the wine is and how and with what foods to enjoy it. It's expressed as a percentage by volume or weight. See *sweet.*

roasted See *oaky.*

round A wine described as being round has enough residual sugar to balance out any rough edges such as tannin and acid, and may be rich and ripe, leaving a full sensation in your mouth. The key word here is *balance,* since round wines have a quality of fullness or completeness, without any one taste or tactile sensation dominating.

sec Applied to sparkling wines, *sec,* which in French means "dry," actually means sweet or very sweet. You figure it.

soft See *body.*

spicy Certain varietals are often, and appropriately, described as being spicy. Gewurztraminer's *varietal character* evokes such a description, as do Zinfandel, Shiraz, and red Rhône blends. Spicy generally refers to pungent, attractive aromas and flavors including black pepper, clove, cinnamon, anise, cardamom, and caraway, depending on the wine.

structure How body, acid, alcohol, glycerin, and tannin interact in a wine make up its structure. A good wine will have "firm" or "good" structure.

supple This is a complimentary term that's generally used to describe full-bodied reds that have achieved a kind of softness, in spite of high levels of *tannin* and *acidity,* and a fairly firm *structure.*

sur lie See *lees.*

sweet As I've mentioned, sweetness is not a fault. Sweet wines are *supposed* to be sweet. The key is to have enough *acid* present to maintain *balance.* Many wines will have the residual sugar levels right on their label. If you happen to love Riesling, but not supersweet Riesling, you'll need to know about residual sugar (RS):

Less than 0.5% RS	= dry
0.6% to 1.4% RS	= slightly sweet
1.5% to 2.9% RS	= medium sweet
3.0% to 5.9% RS	= sweet
More than 5.9% RS	= very sweet

tannin Tannin, or tannic acid, comes from the stems, seeds, and skins of grapes, as well as the wooden barrels in which the wines are stored and aged. Red wines have about five times more tannin than whites.

Tannins are detected not by taste but by *feel*. That puckery feeling in your mouth, also known as astringency, is from tannin. Brawny young reds will often have overpowering tannin, which means you should cellar them until the tannins soften and make room for the fruit. If the tasting notes say the wine is fairly tannic, that's winespeak for "don't touch this bottle for a year or two at least." Since tannin is a natural preservative, it's a necessary component of wines that are meant to have a very long life. However, in order to age gracefully, a tannic wine must have adequate acid, sugar, and alcohol to stay in *balance*.

tart See *acid/acidity*.

texture See *body*.

toasted Caramel and toffee are toasty aromas. See also *oaky* and *yeasty*.

vanilla/vanillin When you see vanilla or vanillin in tasting notes, think oak. The reason is because aromas of vanilla come from the vanillin that is contributed by oak barrel staves. Just as in food, a whiff of vanilla, however subtle, gives an impression of sweetness. See *oaky*.

varietal Varietal is a wine that takes its name from the grape variety of which it's primarily (at least 75 percent) composed.

varietal character Each variety of grape has a distinct set of flavor and aroma characteristics when picked at the optimum moment of ripeness. Occasionally a winemaker will say that a wine "displays typical varietal *characteristics*," (or *bouquet* or *flavors*), which means, in effect, that he or she feels the wine is a typical but brilliant example of its variety. Once you know, for example, that California Zinfandels are spicy and berrylike, the phrase is convenient shorthand for all the spicy/berry flavors you're already likely to encounter and expect.

vinifera Short for *Vitis vinifera,* this is the species of grape used for the world's finest and most acclaimed wines. Except for the native American species, all the wines in this book are made from vinifera grapes.

vintage Vintage basically means year, so a vintage 1993 bottle would contain wine that was grown and harvested in 1993. The rule is that at least 95 percent of that wine has to have come from 1993-grown grapes.

vintner's reserve See *reserve.*

weight See *body.*

yeast/yeasty Commonly used to describe sparkling wines, yeastiness comes from—you guessed it—the yeast that is part of the fermentation process. "Toastiness" and "fresh baked bread" express the same aromas.

young To say that a wine is "still young" means that it could benefit from more time in the bottle to reach its full potential. A young wine might be good, but will be better still if given time to mature.

APPENDIX 3

Mail-Order/Internet Wine-Buying Guide

In Woodstock there are three really excellent wine shops. Not only do they have remarkable selections, but they're always willing to go out of their way to order special wines I want, and to make any number of calls to locate the exact vintage I seek.

However, there are times when I just want be in the privacy of my own home or office and browse the net for gold medal wines. I can get the exact vintage I want delivered to my door, or that of a friend's if it's a gift, in a couple of days, or even overnight. It's a fun way to shop since many of the retailers below have excellent sites, with information about wine, wine clubs, wine-related events, newsletters, gift ideas, and more.

I've seen scores of articles on this subject, and it appears that Internet wine-buying is a trend that's catching on. After all, you can now choose a CD, book, car, and even a home through the Internet, so why not wine?

Well, it's not that simple. For one thing, Florida has now joined Tennessee, Georgia, and Kentucky as states that have made interstate shipments of wine a felony. (At press time, Maryland was threatening to join this group.) Other states have laws on the books that make direct shipments illegal, but the offence is usually a misdemeanor and rarely enforced. In the simplest terms possible, the reasoning behind the new prohibitions seems to be threefold: (1) State legislators don't want minors ordering alcohol by mail, since their age can't be verified; (2) Direct shipment of wine means that state taxes are being sidestepped; and (3) State and local wine distributors and retailers lose money along with their status as middlemen.

Never mind that every other mail-order business has managed to solve these problems, except for item number one, above. Open any current wine publication and you're bound to hear all the sides of this issue rehashed month after month. All I can say is, if you're unlucky enough to live in one of the neoprohibitionist states, either contact your legislators or take your chances.

Rather than going into long, legal explanations here, my advice is to log into the Wine Institute's website. Their address is http://wineinstitute.org, and they're at the forefront of issues related to wine and health, direct-mail wine buyng, and other breaking wine-related news. There you'll get an explanation of *reciprocal state,* a term used by some of the retailers in this section to determine whether shipping to you will be legal or not.

Don't despair, however. Some of the mail-order retailers below have found legal ways to jump through the tangle of wine-shipping loop-holes. Others don't care, as long as you're a loyal customer. If you're in doubt, just ask them.

Too, don't forget that if you become a fan of one of the gold medal wineries, you can always contact them directly, or find their website, which an increasing number of wineries are developing. You can then order the wines directly from the winery, sometimes at substantial savings.

A caveat: My research has shown that these are reputable places with good customer service people and policies. However, I can't make any guarantees. Be a smart shopper before you spend your hard-earned money. Find out if the retailer has a minimum order. Find out what the shipping costs are. Chat with the customer service person about how their company packs the wines, and when you can expect to get them. A reputable firm will guarantee safe delivery, and should allow you to return bottles that get broken or otherwise damaged in transit. Happy shopping!

Brown Derby
International Wine Center
2023 South Glenstone
Springfield, MO 65804
(417) 883-4066
http://www.brownderby.com

They've been around since 1937 and take pride in their in-depth selection of wines from all over, including some of the uncommon wines from their region. All wines are shipped in preapproved boxes and go second-day air. Also, if you're in the market for Riedel crystal from Austria, they're one of the top retailers. Check out their website for more about these top-of-the-line wine glasses. Call them up to get on their mailing list. You'll receive their annual catalog and monthly flyers. They'll ship anywhere except FL, MD, GA, KY, UT, and NC.

Cellar Masters of America
http://www.cellarmasters.com

Cellar Masters bill themselves as "The only *authorized* interstate shipper of wine on the Web." They say if you're an average consumer, you may not be aware of the laws regulating wine shipments in your home state. Some of the frustrations consumers face include not being able to order less than a case of any one type of wine or having to stay within an annual limit on how much wine you can receive. Cellar Masters is committed to bringing wineries and consumers together without these hassles. I liked their wine list and their site in general, which features Wine Regions of the World, a French pronunciation guide, and more.

City Wine
347 South Colorado Boulevard
Denver, CO 80222
303-393-7576 / fax (303) 393-1725
http://www.citywine.com

If City Wine is as good as their website, you need go no further. It's incredibly easy to look up wines in their wine portfolio, and if there's a wine you want that's not listed, contact them and they'll get it for you. The people at City Wine personally taste and select every wine they carry, and the selection changes constantly.

Duke of Bourbon
20908 Roscoe Boulevard
Canoga Park CA 91304
800-4FINE-WINE / fax 818-341-1234
http://www.dukeofbourbon.com

The Duke of Bourbon is an award-winning family-run retail wine and spirits enterprise established in 1967 in the West San Fernando Valley area of Los Angeles. They specialize in personalized service, and offer a hand-picked selection of unique and rare California wines as well as a fine selection of French, Italian and other world-class wines. Among their offerings: a newsletter, events, wine club, California wines matched with gourmet recipes, and custom gift baskets. They ship nationwide. To get on their mailing list, just give them a call.

Geerlings and Wade, Inc.
960 Turnpike Street
Canton MA 02021
800-782-WINE / fax 800-329-8466
http://www.geerwade.com

This is a big, reputable company with connections galore. If they can't get a wine, I doubt it can be got. At press time the website was still in development, but no doubt it will be up and running soon, with loads of helpful lists and hot links to make your shopping easier. Mix a 3-, 6-, or 12-bottle case. Ask for their full list of imported and domestic wines. Subscribe to their monthly newsletter and also get a free wine accessories catalog. Become a G&W member and save. Satisfaction guaranteed. They accept major credit cards and deliver wine to the following states: AZ, CA, CO, CT, FL, IA, ID, IL, MA, MN, MO, NE, NJ, NM, NY, OH, OR, VA, WA, WV.

K&L Wine Merchants
3005 El Camino Real
Redwood City, CA 94061
800-247-5987 / fax 415-364-4687
http://www.klwines.com

I loved this site, which was designed for readers who want an easy way to search their inventory. Besides having a great wine list, these people sell wine accessories, single malt scotch and other spirits, and have a wine club you can join as well as a monthly newsletter.

Mr. Liquor

250 Taraval Street
San Francisco, CA 94116
(800) 681-WINE / fax (415) 731-0155
http://www.mrliquor.com

I had a chance to visit Mr. Liquor this summer when I was on the West Coast. When you walk in it looks like an ordinary wine shop, except that there's a small wine-tasting bar by the door. But when you begin to look at the wines they stock, it's clear that this is no ordinary store. And the kind owner told me "not to be deceived" by appearances. A couple blocks away from the store is a giant high-tech wine-storing warehouse where they care for and keep the world's most astonishing wines. Mr. Liquor's philosophy is simple: "big enough to serve you, small enough to know you." They give personalized service to all of their customers, and ship anywhere. Call them to get on their mailing list. Or "introduce yourself" over the phone, and they'll definitely take car of all your wine needs. By the way, their website is also excellent, easy to use and understand, and very comprehensive.

Red Carpet Wines

400 East Glenoaks Boulevard
Glendale, CA 91207
(800) 339-0609
http://redcarpetwine.com

If you're looking for a California wine that's from a small producer, a so-called boutique winery, look no further than Red Carpet. They specialize in California wineries whose case productions are from 100 to 1,000. Log on to their exciting website for a listing of wines they stock. You can use their virtual shopping cart to make the order, or call them up to get on their mailing list. The site also features wonderful writers, wine events listings, and a Wine-O-Meter, which is a bit like a mini competition, with ratings of wines by a dozen well-respected tasters. All in all, an enjoyable Internet experience. Red Carpet ships anywhere in the world.

Sam's

1720 N. Marcey Street
Chicago, IL 60614
800-777-9137 / fax 312-664-7037
http://www.samw-wine.com

Sam's website is user-friendly, with easy-to-access lists of wines you can browse. They have it all: wines, spirits, cigars, accessories, gift baskets, books, gourmet cheese, coffee, olive oil, and more. You can also sign up to receive their electronic newsletter. Their motto is, no order too big, no destination too far—and they ship anywhere.

Schaefer's

(800) 933-WINE
http://www.schaefers.com

Shaefer's, one of America's finest wine retailers, is a giant department store that sounds like a lot of fun if you live in Chicago. The Wine Department is celebrated across the U.S. for its selection of classic and new-discovery wines. They also sell single malts, Cognacs, Armagnacs, and more in their Spirits Department. The Food Department has a huge array of imported cheeses and locally prepared specialty foods. They also have microbrews, including draft beers you can buy fresh by the jug, party planning, tastings, a newsletter, and gifts galore. Locally they deliver by truck twice a day. Over the net you can get most of these goodies too.

301 Wine Shop

800-404-1390 / fax 707-444-8067
http://www.301wines.com

These people offer a really enjoyable Internet shopping experience. Their wine list is excellent, and they have a wine club you can join for special values. I was lucky enough to speak to the very cordial owner, and he described the monthly newsletter (you can subscribe to it right on their website), which lists their top picks each month along with recipes, travel-related articles, winemaker profiles, chef profiles, and more. Here's a real thinking man's (and woman's) wine shop. Give them a call, or pay them a visit.

Virtual Vineyards
http://www.virtualvin.com

Here's a fun site. Virtual Vineyards tries to make wine shopping entertaining as well as easy. The site features an excellent wine list that's easy to use, and various food items as well as other gifts. While you're at it, go into their Q&A section, or learn about food pairings, recipes, travel information, and more.

Wally's
2107 Westwood Boulevard
Los Angeles, CA 90025
(889) WALLYS / fax (310) 474-1450

The people at Wally's are great. At press time, they were in the process of revamping their website, which should be up and running now. Call them for the address. It's bound to be a winner. This is a huge wine store rated number one wine store in LA by Zagat's guide. In addition to carrying a huge selection of wine, they sell books, Riedel glassware, gourmet food, cigars in Wally's Cigarbox, gift baskets, and more. They'll ship anywhere in the world. Call them up to receive their free newletter.

Wine Cask
813 Anacapa Street
Santa Barbara, CA 93101
((800) 436-9463 / (805) 568-0664
http://www.winecask.com

This wine store has an extensive wine list, which you can browse in their website that also features information on travel and wine-related events. They specialize in hard-to-get wines, and will ship anywhere except KY, TN, FL, GA, and MD. If you're in the Santa Barbara area, check out their store, which sells some gourmet food items and has a cafe/bar/tabac joint next door called Intermezzo, open until midnight every night. By the way, the wine site is great, and the store is recommended by wine guru Robert Parker.

Wine Country
2301 Redondo Avenue
Signal Hill, CA 90806
(800) 505-5564 / fax (562) 587-9493

This sounds like a great place to visit if you're in the area. They just added a 90-foot mural of the California wine region to their collection of other murals, Spanish tiles, and their 3-D replica of the Mondavi arch. The Wine Country folks aren't driven by reviews; in fact, they ignore them. Instead, they try to find wines from all regions that offer a "lot of goodness" for the value, according to the owner. You'll find discounted prices on many of their selections, which spans the 6,000-square-foot store. Call for a free monthly newletter. They also sell microbeers, imported beers, and some gourmet food items.

Wine Exchange
2368 N. Orangemall
Orange, CA, 92665
800-76-WINEX / fax 714-974-1792 1454
http://www.winex.com

Wine Exchange carries "the best, the most interesting, the most famous, and the rarest in wines and spirits." Their buying power enables them to get substantial discounts, which they pass on to you. One can browse their website for new arrivals, premium imported cigars, glassware, events, and more. They also have a great monthly newsletter. This company will ship to any state.

The Wine Shop
1215 Silverado Trail
Napa, CA 94558
888-CALWINE / fax 707-226-2086
http://www.calwine.com

I love sites like this one, which features a WineFinder, an easy way to look up the bottles you want, and an efficient way to just browse their selection. Their wine list is good, and the site features gift baskets and a food shop too. The Wine Shop has a nifty Wine Club you can join. If the wine's available, they say, they'll find it for you.

A WINESTORE on the Internet
800-533-0898
www.winestore.com

There's nothing pretentious about their name or their site. The website is user-friendly and informative. They have a nice feature called "Wine Library," which contains lots of illuminating stuff about wines and wine regions. They offer sampler packs, and say that if you have questions about receiving wine shipped from out of state, drop them an email (info@winestore.com) or give them a call.

APPENDIX 4

The Gold Medal Wineries by Region

ARGENTINA

Etchart
Santa Ana
Santa Julia

AUSTRALIA

Basedow
Chapel Hill
Charles Melton
Chateau Reynella
Coldstream Hills
Coriole
D' Arenberg
Eileen Hardy
Georgia's Paddock
Hamilton
Hardys
Henschke
Jacob's Creek
Lawson's
Leasingham
Lindemans
Marienberg
McGuigan Brothers
Mitchelton
Neudorf
Orlando

Oxford Landing
Parker
Penfolds
Penley
Petaluma
Peter Lehmann
Plantagenet
Rosemount
Rothbury Estate
St. Hallett
St. Hugo
Sandalford
Seaview
Taltarni
Tim Adams
Tyrrells
Vasse Felix
Wolf Blass
Wyndham
Yalumba

CANADA

Cedar Creek
Chateau des
   Charmes
Cilento Wines
Gray Monk
Hawthorne
   Mountain
Inniskillin Wines
Jost
Kittling Ridge
Konzelmann

Lakeview Cellars
Magnotta
Mission Hill
Pillitteri Estates
Quail's Gate
Reif Estate
Stonechurch
Stoney Ridge
Sumac Ridge
Vignoble Le Cep
   D'Argent

CHILE

Carmen
Casa Lapostolle
Chateau La Joya
Concha y Toro
Manso de Velasco
Santa Carolina

Santa Digna
Santa Rita
Vina Gracia
Vina Tarapaca
Viu Manent

NEW ZEALAND

CJ Pask
Giesen
Grove Mill
Hunters
Martinborough
Matua Valley

Morton Estate
  Winery
Selaks
Spencer Hill Estate
Te Kairanga
Villa Maria

SOUTH AFRICA

Boland
Cathedral Cellar
Clos Malverne
Eikendal
Fairview
Kanonkop
KWV

Meerlust
Neethlingshof
Neil Ellis
Rust en Verde
Stellenryck
Stellenzicht
Swartland

URUGUAY

Hector Stagnari

UNITED STATES

Arizona
Callaghan
Dos Cabezas Wine Works

Arkansas
Post Familie

California
Abundance
Adelaida
Adler Fels
Alban
Alderbrook
Alexander Valley
Altamura

Anapamu
Arciero
Armida
Arrowood
Atlas Peak
Au Bon Climat
Audubon

California (cont.)

Babcock
Baily
Ballatore
Barefoot Cellars
Bargetto
Baron Herzog
Bartholomew Park
Beaucanon
Beaulieu
Bel Arbor
Bella Vista
Bellerose
Belvedere
Benziger
Beringer
Bernardus
Bettinelli
Blossom Hill
Boeger
Bogle
Bonny Doon
Bonterra
Briceland
Bricout
Buehler Vineyards
Buena Vista
Buttonwood Farm
Byington
Byron
Ca' del Solo
Cafaro
Cain
Cakebread Cellars
Calera
Callaway
Cambria
Camelot
Canyon Road
Carmenet
Carneros Creek
Castle
Castoro Cellars
Caymus

Cecchetti-Sebastiani
Cellar
Cedar Brook
Cedar Mountain
Chalk Hill
Chalone
Chameleon Cellars
Chandelle of Sonoma
Chandon
Chappellet
Charles B. Mitchell
    Vineyards
Charles Krug
Chateau Julien
Chateau Montelena
Chateau Souverain
Chateau St. Jean
Chimere
Christian Brothers
Cinnabar
Claudia Springs
Cline
Cloninger
Clos du Bois
Clos du Val
Clos LaChance
Cobblestone
Concannon
Conn Creek
Cook's Wine Cellars
Cooper-Garrod
Corbett Canyon
Cosentino
Cottonwood Canyon
Coturri
Creston
Crichton Hall
Cronin
Culbertson
Curtis
Cypress
Daniel Gehrs
Dark Star Cellars

California (cont.)

Dave Nichol's Cellars
David Bruce
Davis Bynum
De Loach
De Lorimier
De Rose
Dickerson
Dolce
Domain Hill & Mayes
Domaine Carneros
Domaine Michel
Domaine St. George
Dry Creek Vineyard
Duckhorn
E. & J. Gallo
Eberle
Edgewood Estate
Edmeades
Edna Valley Vineyard
Ehlers Grove
Elkhorn Peak Cellars
Equinox
Estancia
Estate Baccala
Étude
Fallbrook
Famille Bonverre
Fanucchi
Farella-Park
Ferrari-Carano
Fess Parker
Ficklin
Fife
Firestone
Fisher
Flora Springs
Folie à Deux
Foppiano
Forest Glen
Fox Hollow
Foxen
Franciscan
Freemark Abbey

Gainey Vineyards
Galleano
Gallo Sonoma
Gan Eden
Gary Farrell
Geyser Peak
Glen Ellen
Gloria Ferrer
Godwin
Gold Hill
Grand Cru Vineyards
Granite Springs
Greenwood Ridge
Grey Wolf Cellars
Grgich Hills
Grove Street
Guenoc
Gundlach-Bundschu
Hagafen
Hahn
Handley Cellars
Hanzell
Hart Winery
Hartford Court
Havens
Haywood
Heitz
Helena View
Hendry
Hess
Hidden Cellars
Husch
Indian Springs
Indigo Hills
Iron Horse
Ivan Tamas
J. Lohr
Jade Mountain
Jarvis
Jekel
Jepson Vineyards
Jodar Wine Company
Jordan

California (cont.)

Jory
Joseph Fillipi
Joseph Phelps
Justin
Kalin
Kalyra
Kathryn Kennedy
Kendall-Jackson
Kent Rasmussen
Kenwood
Konrad Estate
Korbel
Kunde
La Crema
LaJota
La Quinta
Laetitia
Lake Sonoma Winery
Lambert Bridge
Lamborn Family
  Vineyards
Langtry
Las Viñas
Laurel Glen
Laurier
Lava Cap
Les Vieux Cepages
Lewis Cellars
Liparita
Lockwood
Lolonis
Longoria
Louis M. Martini
M.G. Vallejo
Maddalena
Madrona
Maison Deutz
Marcelina
Markham
Martin Brothers
Martin Ray
Matanzas Creek
Maurice Car'rie

McDowell Valley
  Vineyards
McHenry
McIlroy Wines
Meeker
Mer et Soleil
Meridian
Merryvale
Michael Pozzan
Michel Schlumberger
Mietz Cellars
Mill Creek Vineyards
Mirassou
Monterey Peninsula
Montevina
Monthaven
Montpellier
  Vineyards
Morgan
Mount Eden
  Vineyards
Mount Veeder
  Winery
Mumm
Murphy-Goode
Nalle
Napa Ridge
Navarro Vineyards
Neb
Nevada City
Newlan
Newton
Neyers
Oakville Ranch
Ojai Vineyard
Opus One
Orfila Vineyards
Page Mill
Pahlmeyer
Paradigm
Paradise Ridge
Paraiso Springs
Parducci

California (cont.)

Patz & Hall
Pedroncelli
Peju Province
Pepperwood Springs
Perry Creek
Peter Michael
Pezzi King
Pine Ridge
Plam
Prager
Pride Mountain
Quady
Quail Ridge
Quivera
R.H. Phillips
Rabbit Ridge
Ramsay
Ravenswood
Raymond
Renaissance
Renwood
Rey Sol
Richardson
Ridge
River Run
Robert Biale
Robert Hunter
Robert Keenan
Robert Mondavi
Robert Pecota
Robert Pepi
Rochioli
Rodney Strong
Roederer Estate
Rombauer
Rosenblum
Round Hill
Rutherford
Rutherford Hill
Rutherford Vintners
S. Anderson
Saintsbury
St. Clement

St. Francis
St. Supéry
Ste. Genevieve
Sanford
Santa Barbara
Scharffenberger
Schramsberg
Schuetz Oles
Schug
Sebastiani
Selby
Shafer
Shale Ridge
Sierra Vista
Signorello
Silver Oak
Silver Ridge
Silverado
Sobon
Solis
Sonoma-Loeb
Sonora Winery
Soquel
Spottswoode
SSV
Stag's Leap
Steele
Stephen Ross
Sterling
Stevenot
Stone Creek
Stonestreet
Storrs
Storybook Mountain
Sutter Home
Swanson
Taft Street
Talbott
Talus
Temecula Crest
Tessera
Thackrey
Thomas Fogarty

California (cont.)

Thornton
Titus
Tobin James
Topolos
Trefethen Vineyards
Trellis Vineyards
Trentadue
Troon Vineyards
Trout Gulch
Tulocay
Turning Leaf
Twin Hills
Tyee Wine Cellars
V. Sattui
Van der Kamp
Van Roekel Vineyards
Venezia
Venezio Vineyard
Ventana
Vichon

Vigil
Villa Mt.Eden
Vino Noceto
Voss
Weinstock
Wellington
Wente
Whitehall Lane
Whitford Cellars
Wild Horse
Wild Horse
Wildhurst
William Hill
Windemere
Windsor
York Mountain
Yorkville Cellars
Zabaco
Zaca Mesa
ZD Wines

Colorado
Plum Creek Cellars

Georgia
Habersham

Idaho
Indian Creek Winery

Indiana
French Lick Winery

Maryland
Elk Run

Massachusetts
Westport Rivers

Michigan
Chateau Grand
 Traverse
Good Harbor
St. Julian
Tartan Hill

Missouri

Augusta Winery
Blumenhof
Hermannhof
Mount Pleasant
St. James
Stone Hill

New Jersey

King's Road

New Mexico

Gruet

New York

Anthony Road
Casa Larga Vineyards
Dr. Konstantin Frank
Duck Walk Vineyards
Fox Run
Glenora
Lakewood
Lamoreaux Landing
McGregor Vineyard
  Winery
Palmer
Pindar
Prejean
Standing Stone
Swedish Hill
Wagner

North Carolina

Biltmore Estate

Ohio

Breitenbach Wine
  Cellars
Ferrante Wine Farm
Firelands Winery
Meier's Wine Cellars
3 Islands Lonz Winery
Winery at Wolf Creek

Oregon

Adelsheim
Amity
Argyle
Autumn Wind
Benton Lane
Bridgeview
Chateau Benoit
Chateau Lorane
Cooper Mountain
Cristom
Cuneo
Domaine Drouhin
Domaine Serene
Duck Pond
Elk Cove
Eola Hills
Erath
Evesham Wood
Firesteed
Foris
Henry Estate
Hinman
King Estate
La Garza Cellars
Lange
Marquam
Oak Knoll
Panther Creek

Oregon (cont.)

Ponzi
Redhawk
Secret House
Siduri
Seven Hills
Silvan Ridge
Sokol Blosser

Springhill Cellars
St. Innocent
Torii Mor
Tualatin
Van Duzer
Willamette Valley
Yamhill Valley

Pennsylvania

Twin Brook

Texas

Delaney Vineyards
Lorval Wines

Virginia

Horton
Piedmont
Prince Michel
White Hall Vineyards

Washington

Andrew Will
Apex
Arbor Crest
Barnard Griffin
Bookwalter
Canoe Ridge
Vineyard
Chateau Ste.
Michelle
Columbia Crest
Columbia Winery
Covey Run
Glen Fiona
Gordon Brothers
Hedges
Hogue
Hoodsport
Hyatt

Kiona
L'Ecole No. 41
Mc Crea
Patrick M. Paul
Paul Thomas
Portteus
Powers
Preston
Seven Hills
Silver Lake Winery
Staton Hills
Tefft Cellars
W.B. Bridgman
Waterbrook
Whidbey
Woodward Canyon
Worden
Yakima River

Wisconsin

Botham Vineyards
Wollersheim

INDEX/SHOPPING GUIDE

Arrowood 1993 Merlot, CA, $35.99, **125**
Atlas Peak 1993 Consenso (Cabernet Sauvignon/Sangiovese), CA, $22, **164**
Atlas Peak 1994 Cabernet Sauvignon, CA, $18, **92**
Atlas Peak 1994 Reserve Sangiovese, CA, $24, **120**
Atlas Peak 1995 Sangiovese, CA, $16, **120**
Au Bon Climat 1994 Le Bouge D'à Côté Chardonnay, CA, $24.99, **197**
Au Bon Climat 1994 Pinot Noir, CA, $18, **149**
Au Bon Climat 1994 Reserve Talley Chardonnay, CA, $24.99, **197**
$Audubon Collection 1993 Graeser Vineyards Cabernet Sauvignon, CA, $15, **60, 92**
$Augusta Winery NV River Valley Blush, MO, $7, 261
Autumn Wind 1994 Reserve Pinot Noir, OR, $30, **149**

–B–

Babcock 1994 Mt. Carmel Vineyard Chardonnay, CA, $23.99, **197**
$Baily 1996 Montage (Bordeaux-style white blend), CA, $11, **82, 257**
$Ballatore NV Gran Spumante, CA, $6.49, **77, 271**
$Barefoot Cellars NV White Zinfandel, CA, $4.99, **33, 261**
Bargetto 1995 Chardonnay, CA, $19, **197**
$Bargetto 1995 Gewurztraminer, CA, $10, **227**
Bargetto 1995 Merlot, CA, $18, **125**
$Bargetto 1996 Dolcetto, CA, $15, **67, 120**
$Bargetto 1996 Gewurztraminer, CA, $10, **227**
Barnard Griffin 1994 Reserve Merlot, WA, $24, **125**
$Baron Herzog 1995 Late Harvest Johannisberg Riesling, CA, $14, **33, 279**
$Baron Herzog 1996 Chenin Blanc, CA, $6.50, **224**
$Baron Herzog 1996 Gamay, CA, $6.99, **139**
Bartholomew Park Winery 1994 Desnudos Vineyard Cabernet Sauvignon, CA, $20, **33, 92**
Bartholomew Park Winery 1995 Desnudos Vineyard Merlot, CA, $22, **125**
⚐Basedow 1995 Chardonnay, AUS, $16, **199**
$⚐Basedow 1996 Semillon (White Burgundy), AUS, $10, **253**
Beaucanon 1995 Jacques de Coninck Chardonnay, CA, $28, 198
Beaulieu 1992 Georges de Latour Private Reserve Cabernet Sauvignon, CA, $40, **92**
Beaulieu 1993 Georges de Latour Private Reserve Cabernet Sauvignon, CA, $40, **33, 92**
Beaulieu 1993 Tapestry Reserve (Bordeaux-style red blend), CA, $20, **164**
$Beaulieu 1994 Cabernet Sauvignon, CA, $15, **61, 93**
Beaulieu 1994 Georges de Latour Private Reserve Cabernet Sauvignon, CA, $50, **93**
Beaulieu 1994 Tapestry Reserve (Bordeaux-style red blend), CA, $20, **164**
Beaulieu 1995 Reserve Chardonnay, CA, $20, 198

Beaulieu 1995 Signet Collection Sangiovese, CA, $16, **120**

$Bel Arbor 1995 Vintner's Selection White Zinfandel, CA, $4.99, **261**

$Bel Arbor 1996 Vintner's Selection Merlot, CA/CHI, $6.99, **68, 125**

Bella Vista 1995 Estate Merlot, CA, $18, **126**

Bella Vista 1995 Estate Syrah, CA, $18, **176**

Bella Vista 1995 Sangiovese, CA, $20, **120**

$Bellerose 1995 Pinot Noir, CA, $10.25, **149**

$Belvedere 1994 Cabernet Sauvignon, CA, $13.50, **61, 93**

$Belvedere 1995 Jimtown Ranch Vineyard Chardonnay, CA, $12, **198**

Benton Lane 1994 Reserve Pinot Noir, OR, $28.50, **149**

Benziger 1993 Tribute Red Estate (Bordeaux-style blend), CA, $23, **33, 164**

$Benziger 1994 Cabernet Sauvignon, CA, $15, **35, 61, 93**

Benziger 1994 Estate Tribute Merlot, CA, $25, 126

Benziger 1994 Imagery Series Larga Vista Vineyards Sangiovese, CA, $17.99, **35, 120**

Benziger 1994 Imagery Series Petite Sirah, CA, $17.99, **146**

Benziger 1994 Imagery Series Pinot Blanc, CA, $16, **237**

Benziger 1994 Old Vines Zinfandel, CA, $16, **183**

Benziger 1994 Syrah, CA, $17, **176**

Benziger 1994 Tribute Red (Bordeaux-style red blend), CA, $25, **164**

Benziger 1995 Chardonnay, CA, $23, **198**

$Benziger 1995 Fumé Blanc, CA, $10, **245**

Benziger 1995 Imagery Series Skinner Yount Mill Pinot Blanc, CA, $17.99, **237**

Benziger 1995 Merlot, CA, $16, 126

Benziger 1995 Old Vines Zinfandel, CA, $17, **183**

Benziger 1995 Pinot Noir, CA, $16, **149**

$Beringer 1991 Port of Cabernet Sauvignon, CA, $13, **286**

$Beringer 1992 Meritage (Bordeaux-style red blend), CA, $14, **73, 164**

Beringer 1992 Napa Valley Private Reserve Cabernet Sauvignon, CA, $60, **93**

Beringer 1993 Bancroft Ranch Estate Bottled Merlot, CA, $40, **126**

Beringer 1993 Knights Valley Alluvium (Bordeaux-style red blend), CA, $25, **164**

$Beringer 1993 Knights Valley Cabernet Sauvignon, CA, $15, **61, 93**

$Beringer 1993 Zinfandel, CA, $12, **84, 183**

Beringer 1994 Hudson Ranch Vineyard Viognier, CA, $25, **255**

Beringer 1994 Knights Valley Cabernet Sauvignon, CA, $17.50, **35, 93**

Beringer 1994 Private Reserve Chardonnay, CA, $25, 198

$Beringer 1994 Special Select Late Harvest Johannisberg Riesling, CA, $15, **279**

Beringer 1994 Stanly Ranch Pinot Noir, CA, $30, **150**

Byington 1994 Special Reserve Vineyards Pinot Noir, CA, $20, **150**

Byron 1993 Reserve Pinot Noir, CA, $22.50, **150**

Byron 1994 Estate Chardonnay, CA, $30, **199**

Byron 1994 Pinot Noir, CA, $17, **150**

Byron 1994 Reserve Pinot Noir, CA, $24, **150**

Byron 1995 Reserve Chardonnay, CA, $24, **199**

–C–

$Ca' del Solo 1994 Big House Red (Rhône-style red blend), CA, $8.50, **72, 165**

$Ca' del Solo 1996 Malvasia Bianca, CA, $9, **231**

Cafaro 1993 Merlot, CA, 28, **126**

Cain 1995 Musque Ventana Vineyard Sauvignon Blanc, CA, $16, **245**

Cakebread Cellars 1993 Cabernet Sauvignon, CA, $22, **94**

Cakebread Cellars 1993 Reserve Chardonnay, CA, $30, **199**

Cakebread Cellars 1994 Reserve Chardonnay, CA, $33, **199**

Calera 1992 Jensen Pinot Noir, CA, $35, **150**

Calera 1992 Mills Pinot Noir, CA, $35, **150**

Calera 1993 Selleck Pinot Noir, CA, $38, **151**

Calera 1994 Chardonnay, CA, $30, **199**

Calera 1994 Pinot Noir, CA, $16, **151**

Calera 1995 Chardonnay, CA, $16, **199**

Callaghan Vineyards 1996 Fumé Blanc, AZ, $18, **245**

$Callaway 1994 Calla Lees Chardonnay, CA, $10, **65, 199**

$Callaway 1995 Calla-Lees Chardonnay, CA, $10, **64, 200**

Callaway 1995 Viognier, CA, $16, **255**

$Callaway 1996 Chenin Blanc, CA, $6, **224**

Callaway 1996 Estate Bottled Viognier, CA, $16, **255**

Callaway NV Sweet Nancy Chenin Blanc, CA, $25, **279**

Cambria 1994 Chardonnay, CA, $16, **200**

Cambria 1994 Julia's Vineyard Pinot Noir, CA, $27, **151**

Cambria 1994 Reserve Chardonnay, CA, $30, **200**

Cambria 1994 Reserve Pinot Noir, CA, $42, **151**

Cambria 1994 Tepusquet Sangiovese, CA, $25, **121**

Cambria 1995 Katherine's Vineyard Estate Bottled Chardonnay, CA, $20, **200**

Cambria 1995 Reserve Chardonnay, CA, $30, **200**

Camelot 1995 Chardonnay, CA, $18, **200**

Canoe Ridge Vineyard 1994 Merlot, WA, $18, **126**

Canyon Road 1994 Reserve Cabernet Sauvignon, CA, $18, **94**

$Canyon Road 1995 Cabernet Sauvignon, CA, $8, **61, 94**

$Canyon Road 1996 Chardonnay, CA, $7.99, **65, 200**

$Canyon Road 1996 Sauvignon Blanc, CA, $6.99, **76, 245**

$ ⌂Carmen 1995 Reserve Grande Vidure Cabernet, CHI, $9.99, **61, 94**

Carmenet 1993 Moon Mountain Vineyard Cabernet Franc, CA, $20, **89**

$Carmenet 1995 Paragon Vineyard White Meritage (Bordeaux-style blend), CA, $15, **81, 257**

$Carneros Creek 1994 Fleur de Carneros Pinot Noir, CA, $12, **151**

Carneros Creek 1994 Signature Reserve Pinot Noir, CA, $35, **151**

$ ⏛Casa Lapostolle 1995 Cuvée Alexandre Chardonnay, CHI, $15, **200**

$ ⏛Casa Lapostolle 1995 Cuvée Alexandre Estate Merlot, CHI, $15, **67, 127**

Casa Larga Vineyards 1995 Fiore delle Stelle Vidal Icewine, NY, $25, **276**

$Castle Vineyards 1995 Pinot Noir, CA, $14, **151**

$Castoro Cellars 1994 Zinfandel, CA, $9.95, **84, 183**

$Castoro Cellars 1995 Guibbini Vineyard Estate Zinfandel, CA, $14, **183**

$Castoro Cellars 1995 Reserve Chardonnay, CA, $12.95, **201**

$Castoro Cellars 1995 Zinfandel, CA, $9.95, **83, 183**

$ ⏛Cathedral Cellar 1994 Cabernet Sauvignon, SAFR, $12, **60, 94**

Caymus 1993 Cabernet Sauvignon, CA, $25, **95**

Cecchetti-Sebastiani Cellar 1993 Cabernet Sauvignon, CA, $28, **95**

$Cedar Brook 1994 Cabernet Sauvignon, CA, $8.99, **61, 95**

$Cedar Brook 1995 Merlot, CA, $8.99, **68, 127**

⏛Cedar Creek 1994 Riesling Icewine, CAN, (Can $) 49.95, **276**

$ ⏛Cedar Creek 1995 American Vidal, CAN, $7, **234**

⏛Cedar Creek 1995 Ice Wine, CAN, (Can $) 49.95, **276**

$ ⏛Cedar Creek 1996 Waterfall Mist Dry White Riesling, CAN, $8, **75, 240**

Cedar Mountain 1995 Cabernet Royale Cabernet Port, CA, $21.50, **286**

Chalk Hill 1993 Cabernet Sauvignon, CA, $23, **95**

Chalk Hill 1994 Botrytised Semillon, CA, $35, **279**

Chalone 1992 Estate Pinot Noir, CA, $26, **151**

Chalone 1994 Estate Reserve Chardonnay, CA, $45, **201**

Chalone 1994 Reserve Chenin Blanc, CA, $16, **224**

$Chameleon Cellars 1995 Sangiovese, CA, $15, **67, 121**

$Chandelle of Sonoma 1995 Spirit of Flight Chardonnay, CA, $12, **201**

$Chandon NV Cuvée 391 Blanc de Noirs, CA, $12, **79, 267**

Chandon NV Reserve Cuvée 490, CA, $18, **268**

⏛Chapel Hill 1994 The Vicar Cabernet Shiraz, AUS, $17, **165**

Chappellet 1994 Moelleux Chenin Blanc, CA, $40, **279**

$Chappellet 1995 Old Vine Cuvée Dry Chenin Blanc, CA, $12, **224**

Charles B. Mitchell Vineyards 1995 Grand Reserve (Bordeaux-style red blend), CA, $28, **165**

Charles Krug 1992 Generations (Bordeaux-style red blend), CA, $30, **165**

$Charles Krug 1993 Cabernet Sauvignon, CA, $14, **61, 95**

Charles Krug 1993 Reserve Merlot, CA, $21.50, **127**

Charles Krug 1993 Vintage Selection Cabernet Sauvignon, CA, $35, **95**

$Charles Krug 1995 Merlot, CA, $15, **67,127**

🄿Charles Melton 1995 Shiraz, AUS, $35, **176**

Chateau Benoit 1994 Estate Reserve Pinot Noir, OR, $25, **151**

🄿Chateau des Charmes 1994 St. David's Bench Chardonnay, CAN, (Can $) 19.75, **201**

Chateau Grand Traverse 1995 Johannisberg Riesling Icewine, MI, $65, **276**

$Chateau Julien 1995 Private Reserve Chardonnay, CA, $15, **201**

$🄿Chateau La Joya 1996 Cabernet Sauvignon, CHI, $10.99, **61, 95**

$🄿Chateau La Joya 1996 Merlot, CHI, $9.99, **68, 127**

Chateau Lorane 1993 Durif, OR, $18, **139**

Chateau Montelena 1992 The Montelena Estate Cabernet Sauvignon, CA, $36, **95**

🄿Chateau Reynella 1994 Basket Pressed Cabernet Sauvignon, AUS, $22.50, **95**

🄿Chateau Reynella 1994 Shiraz, AUS, $22.50, **176**

🄿Chateau Reynella 1995 Chardonnay, AUS, $21.25, **201**

Chateau St. Jean 1991 Reserve Cabernet Sauvignon, CA, $38, **36, 96**

Chateau St. Jean 1992 Reserve Merlot, CA, $35, **127**

Chateau St. Jean 1992 Special Select Late Harvest Johannisberg Riesling, CA, $25, **279**

Chateau St. Jean 1993 Cinq Cepages Cabernet Sauvignon, CA, $18, **96**

$Chateau St. Jean 1993 Robert Young Vineyards Pinot Blanc, CA, $12, **70, 237**

Chateau St. Jean 1993 Robert Young Vineyards Reserve Chardonnay, CA, $57.50/1.5L, **201**

Chateau St. Jean 1994 Merlot, CA, $18, **127**

Chateau St. Jean 1994 Pinot Noir, CA, $18, **153**

$Chateau St. Jean 1995 Johannisberg Riesling, CA, $8.99, **240**

$Chateau St. Jean 1995 La Petite Etoile Fumé Blanc, CA, $13, **246**

Chateau Ste. Michelle 1993 Cabernet Sauvignon, WA, $15.99, **96**

Chateau Ste. Michelle 1993 Cold Creek Merlot, WA, $29.99, **127**

Chateau Ste. Michelle 1993 Cold Creek Vineyard Cabernet Sauvignon, WA, $26, **96**

Chateau Ste. Michelle 1993 Meritage (Bordeaux-style red blend), WA, $30, **165**

Chateau Ste. Michelle 1994 Canoe Ridge Estate Vineyard Chardonnay, WA, $28, **202**

$Chateau Ste. Michelle 1994 Chardonnay, WA, $13.99, **201**

Chateau Ste. Michelle 1994 Chateau Reserve Merlot, WA, $40, **127**

Chateau Ste. Michelle 1994 Cold Creek Vineyard Merlot, WA, $28, **36, 128**

Chateau Ste. Michelle 1994 Indian Wells Vineyard Merlot, WA, $30, **37, 128**

David Bruce 1994 Chalone Pinot Noir, CA, $30, **38, 153**

David Bruce 1994 Pinot Noir, CA, $25, **39, 153**

David Bruce 1994 Reserve Cabernet Sauvignon, CA, $18, **98**

$David Bruce 1995 Petite Syrah, CA, $14, **39, 70, 146**

David Bruce 1995 Shell Creek Vineyard Reserve Petite Syrah, CA, $18, **39, 146**

Davis Bynum 1995 Limited Edition Chardonnay, CA, $17, **204**

Davis Bynum 1995 Pinot Noir, CA, $16, **153**

$Davis Bynum 1996 Shone Farm Sauvignon Blanc, CA, $10.50, **246**

De Loach 1993 Estate Bottled O.F.S. Cabernet Sauvignon, CA, $25, **99**

De Loach 1994 O.F.S. Estate Bottled Cabernet Sauvignon, CA, $16, **40, 99**

De Loach 1995 Chardonnay, CA, $16, **205**

$De Loach 1995 Cuvée Chardonnay, CA, $12, **205**

De Loach 1995 O.F.S. Estate Bottled Zinfandel, CA, $25, **40, 183**

De Loach 1995 O.F.S. Estate Bottled Chardonnay, CA, $27.50, **40, 205**

De Loach 1995 Papera Ranch Zinfandel, CA, $18, **186**

De Loach 1995 Pelletti Ranch Zinfandel, CA, $18, **186**

De Loach 1996 Estate Bottled Late Harvest Gewurztraminer, CA, $16, **280**

$De Loach Vineyards 1996 White Zinfandel, CA, $8, **261**

De Lorimier 1994 Mosaic Meritage (Bordeaux-style red blend), CA, $20, **166**

$De Lorimier 1995 Estate Bottled Spectrum (Bordeaux-style white blend), CA, $12, **82, 257**

$De Lorimier 1996 Sauvignon Blanc, CA, $10, **246**

De Rose 1993 Cedolini Vineyard Dry Farm Hillside Reserve Zinfandel, CA, $20, **184**

Delaney Vineyards 1995 Barrel Fermented Sur Lie Chardonnay, TX, $18.95, **204**

Dickerson 1994 Limited Reserve Zinfandel, CA, $24.99, **184**

Dolce 1993, CA, $50, **280**

Domain Hill & Mayes 1994 Bighorn Ranch Reserve Chardonnay, CA, $18, **205**

Domaine Carneros 1992 Taittinger Brut, CA, $21, **268**

Domaine Drouhin 1994 Lauréne Pinot Noir, OR, $42, **153**

$Domaine Michel 1994 Cabernet Sauvignon, CA, $12, **61, 99**

Domaine Serene 1994 Evenstad Reserve Pinot Noir, OR, $30, **153**

Domaine Serene 1994 Reserve Pinot Noir, OR, $20, **153**

$Domaine St. George 1994 STG Premier Cuvée Merlot, CA, $11.99, **69, 129**

Dos Cabezas Wine Works 1996 Sauvignon Blanc, AZ, $16, **247**

Dr. Konstantin Frank 1995 Cabernet Sauvignon, NY, $22, **99**

Dr. Konstantin Frank 1995 Riesling Icewine, NY, $29.95, **41, 276**

$Dr. Konstantin Frank 1996 Semi Dry Johannisberg Riesling, NY, $10, **240**

$Dr. Konstantin Frank NV Salmon Run Johannisberg Riesling, NY, $8.95, **240**

Dry Creek Vineyard 1994 Red Meritage (Bordeaux-style blend), CA, $25, **166**

Dry Creek Vineyard 1994 Reserve Cabernet Sauvignon, CA, $25, **41, 99**

Dry Creek Vineyard 1994 Reserve Chardonnay, CA, $17, **205**

Dry Creek Vineyard 1994 Reserve Merlot, CA, $30, **129**

Dry Creek Vineyard 1994 Zinfandel, CA, $20, **184**

Dry Creek Vineyard 1995 Merlot, CA, $18.75, **129**

Dry Creek Vineyard 1995 Reserve Fumé Blanc, CA, $15.75, **41, 247**

$Dry Creek Vineyard 1996 Fumé Blanc, CA, $11.50, **247**

Duck Pond 1994 Fries Family Reserve Pinot Noir, OR, $25, **154**

$Duck Pond 1995 Pinot Gris, OR, $12, **231**

$Duck Pond 1996 Barrel Fermented Chardonnay, OR, $8, **65, 205**

$Duck Pond 1996 Estate Grown Pinot Gris, OR, $12, **231**

$Duck Walk Vineyards 1995 Late Harvest Gewurztraminer, NY, $14.95, **280**

Duckhorn 1994 Merlot, CA, $26, **129**

–E–

$E. & J. Gallo NV Sheffield Cellars Cream Sherry, CA, $3.99, **289**

Eberle 1991 Estate Bottled Reserve Cabernet Sauvignon, CA, $35, **99**

$Eberle 1995 Côtes-du-Robles (Rhône-style red blend), CA, $13, **41, 73, 166**

$Eberle 1996 Estate Muscat Canelli, CA, $10, **284**

Eberle 1996 Fralich Vineyard Viognier, CA, $20, **255**

Edgewood Estate 1993 Cabernet Franc, CA, $16, **89**

Edgewood Estate 1993 Cabernet Sauvignon, CA, $18, **99**

Edgewood Estate 1993 Malbec, CA, $18, **139**

Edmeades 1994 Zinfandel, CA, $16, **42, 184**

Edmeades 1995 Eaglepoint Vineyard Zinfandel, CA, $19, **184**

Edmeades 1995 Zinfandel, CA, $19, **184**

Edna Valley Vineyard 1999 Brut, CA, $25, **268**

Edna Valley Vineyard 1995 Paragon Chardonnay, CA, $16.50, **205**

Ehlers Grove 1995 Merlot Reserve, CA, $25, **129**

Eikendal 1992 Classique (Bordeaux-style red blend), SAFR, $16, **167**

$ Eikendal 1996 Chardonnay, SAFR, $12.99, **205**

$ Eikendal 1996 Classique (Bordeaux-style red blend), SAFR, $13.99, **73, 167**

$ Eikendal 1996 Merlot, SAFR, $13.99, **69, 129**

Eileen Hardy 1994 Shiraz, AUS, $45, **176**

Elk Cove 1994 La Boheme Vineyard Pinot Noir, OR, $35, **154**

$Elk Cove 1996 Pinot Gris, OR, $12, **231**
Elk Run 1995 Vin de Jus Glacé Riesling, MD, $16, **280**
Elkhorn Peak Cellars 1995 Fagan Creek Pinot Noir, CA, $24, **154**
Eola Hills 1996 Vin d'Epice Gewurztraminer, OR, $20, **228**
Equinox 1991 Blanc de Blanc Reserve, CA, $40, **265**
Equinox NV Blanc de Blanc, CA, $23, **265**
Erath 1994 Weber Vineyard Reserve Pinot Noir, OR, $25, **154**
$Erath 1996 Pinot Gris, OR, $12, **231**
Estancia 1994 Reserve Chardonnay, CA, $20, **205**
$Estancia 1995 Pinot Noir, CA, $10.50, **154**
Estate Baccala 1995 Zinfandel, CA, $16, **184**
$ ⌂ Etchart 1995 Cabernet Sauvignon, ARG, $6.99, **61, 99**
$ ⌂ Etchart 1996 Torrontés, ARG, $5.99, **231**
Étude 1994 Pinot Noir, CA, $28, **154**
Evesham Wood 1994 Temperance Hill Vineyard Pinot Noir, OR, $24, **154**

–F–

$ ⌂ Fairview 1993 Shiraz Reserve, SAFR, $14.99, **80, 177**
$ ⌂ Fairview 1994 Merlot, SAFR, $14.99, **69, 129**
$Fallbrook 1995 Chardonnay, CA, $6.99, **65, 205**
$Famille Bonverre 1995 Cabernet Sauvignon, CA, $9, **61, 99**
Fanucchi 1995 Wood Road Old Vines Zinfandel, CA, $26, **184**
$Fanucchi 1996 Fanucchi Wood Road Vineyard Trousseau Gris, CA, $12, **231**
Farella-Park 1993 Estate Bottled Cabernet Sauvignon, CA, $28, **100**
$Ferrante Wine Farm 1996 Barrel Fermented Chardonnay, OH, $9.99, **66, 206**
$Ferrante Wine Farm NV Niagara Bianco, OH, $5.99, **234**
$Ferrante Wine Farm NV Pink Catawba, OH, $5.99, **261**
Ferrari-Carano 1991 Reserve Red (Bordeaux-style blend), CA, $47, **167**
Ferrari-Carano 1995 Reserve Fumé Blanc, CA, $18, **247**
Ferrari-Carano 1993 Reserve Chardonnay, CA, $30, **206**
Ferrari-Carano 1994 Chardonnay, CA, $20, **206**
Ferrari-Carano 1994 Tre Terre Chardonnay, CA, $26, **206**
Fess Parker 1994 American Tradition Reserve Syrah, CA, $28, **177**
Fess Parker 1994 Reserve Chardonnay, CA, $22, **206**
Fess Parker 1994 Syrah, CA, $18, **177**
Fess Parker 1995 American Tradition Reserve Pinot Noir, CA, $28, **154**
Fess Parker 1995 Chardonnay, CA, $16, **206**
$Fetzer 1993 Barrel Select Cabernet Sauvignon, CA, $12.99, **62, 100**
$Fetzer 1994 Barrel Select Zinfandel, CA, $8.99, **84, 185**
$Fetzer 1994 Bien Nacido Vineyard Reserve Pinot Noir, CA, $14.99, **155**

Fetzer 1994 Sangiacomo Vineyard Chardonnay, CA, $16.99, **206**

$Fetzer 1995 Barrel Select Chardonnay, CA, $10.99, **206**

$Fetzer 1995 Barrel Select Pinot Noir, CA, $12.99, **155**

$Fetzer 1995 Gamay Beaujolais, CA, $6.99, **139**

$Fetzer 1996 Gamay Beaujolais, CA, $12.99, **42, 139**

$Fetzer 1996 Gewurztraminer, CA, $6, **42, 66, 228**

$Fetzer 1996 Johannisberg Riesling, CA, $6.99, **75, 241**

$Fetzer 1996 Sundial Chardonnay, CA, $6.99, **64, 206**

Ficklin NV Aged 10 Years Estate Bottled Tawny Port, CA, $22, **43, 286**

$Ficklin NV Tinta Port, CA, $12, **286**

Fife 1994 Max Cuvée (Rhône-style red blend), CA, $18.50, **167**

$Firelands Winery NV Sparkling Riesling, OH, $9.95, **79, 271**

$Firesteed 1996 Pinot Noir, OR, $9.99, **71, 155**

Firestone 1993 Red Reserve (Bordeaux-style red blend), CA, $30, **43, 167**

$Fisher 1994 Coach Insignia Chardonnay, CA, $12.99, **206**

Fisher 1994 Whitney's Vnyrd Chardonnay, CA, $24.99, **207**

Flora Springs 1993 Rutherford Reserve Cabernet Sauvignon, CA, $40, **100**

Flora Springs 1993 Trilogy (Bordeaux-style red blend), CA, $30, **167**

Flora Springs 1994 Chardonnay, CA, $24, **207**

Flora Springs 1994 Trilogy (Bordeaux-style red blend), CA, $35, **167**

Flora Springs 1995 Carneros Chardonnay, CA, $24, **207**

Folie à Deux 1995 Reserve Cabernet Sauvignon, CA, $24, **100**

$Folie à Deux 1995 Sangiovese, CA, $15, **67, 121**

$Folie à Deux NV Menage à Trois (Muscat, Chardonnay, Chenin Blanc), CA, $8, **82, 257**

Foppiano 1993 Centennial Selection, La Grande Anniversaire Petite Sirah, CA, $24, **147**

$Forest Glen 1993 Cabernet Sauvignon, CA, $12, **62, 100**

$Forest Glen 1994 Cabernet Sauvignon, CA, $9.99, **62, 100**

$Forest Glen 1995 Merlot, CA, $9.99, **68, 129**

$Foris 1995 Pinot Noir, OR, $11, **71, 155**

$Foris Vineyards 1996 Pinot Gris, OR, $11, **231**

$Fox Hollow 1996 Merlot, CA, $8.99, **68, 130**

Fox Run 1995 Cabernet Port, NY, $19.99, **286**

Foxen 1994 Merlot, CA, $22, **130**

Franciscan 1993 Magnificat (Bordeaux-style red blend), CA, $22.50, **167**

Franciscan 1994 Cuvée Sauvage Chardonnay, CA, $30, **207**

Freemark Abbey 1992 Cabernet Sauvignon, CA, $19, **100**

Freemark Abbey 1993 Cabernet Sauvignon, CA, $18, **100**

French Lick Winery 1995 Gewurztraminer, IN, $18.95, **228**

–G–

$Gainey Vineyards 1996 Johannisberg Riesling, CA, $10, **241**

$Galleano 1996 Carignane, CA, $8, **43, 139**

$Geyser Peak 1995 Shiraz, CA, $15, **45, 80, 177**

Geyser Peak 1995 Winemaker's Selection Cabernet Franc, CA, $20, **46, 89**

Geyser Peak 1995 Winemaker's Selection Petite Verdot, CA, $20, **46, 140**

$Geyser Peak 1995 Zinfandel, CA, $14, **185**

$Geyser Peak 1996 Chardonnay, CA, $14, **207**

$Geyser Peak 1996 Gewurztraminer, CA, $7.50, **66, 228**

Geyser Peak 1996 Late Harvest Riesling, CA, $16, **280**

$Geyser Peak 1996 Sauvignon Blanc, CA, $8.50, **46, 247**

$Geyser Peak 1996 Trione Cellars Johannisberg Riesling, CA, $7.50, **75, 241**

$ ⌂ Giesen 1995 Botrytised Riesling, NZEAL, $14.99, **280**

⌂ Giesen 1995 Burnham School Road Reserve Chardonnay, NZEAL, $24, **207**

$Glen Ellen 1996 Proprietor's Reserve Gamay Beaujolais, CA, $4.99, **140**

$Glen Ellen Expressions 1994 Cabernet Sauvignon, CA, $11, **62, 102**

Glen Fiona 1995 Syrah, WA, $30, **177**

$Glenora 1992 Brut, NY, $12.99, **78, 268**

$Gloria Ferrer 1988 Royal Cuvée Brut, CA, $14, **46, 79, 268**

Gloria Ferrer 1989 Royal Cuvée Brut, CA, $19, **269**

$Gloria Ferrer Champagne Caves NV Blanc de Noirs, CA, $15, **47,** 79, **267**

$Gloria Ferrer NV Brut, CA, $15, **79, 268**

Godwin 1995 Chardonnay, CA, $20, **208**

$Gold Hill 1994 Estate Bottled Merlot, CA, $15, **69, 130**

Gold Hill Vineyard 1994 Cabernet Franc, CA, $16, **89**

$Good Harbor Vineyards 1995 Pinot Gris, MI, $15, **231**

$Gordon Brothers 1992 Cabernet Sauvignon, WA, $14.49, **62, 102**

$Grand Cru 1996 Merlot, CA, $7.99, **69, 130**

$Grand Cru Vineyards 1996 Premium Selection White Zinfandel, CA, $7.99, **262**

$Granite Springs 1994 Carousel Series (Bordeaux-style red blend), CA, $12, **73, 168**

$Granite Springs 1995 Petite Sirah, CA, $13, **70, 147**

$ ⌂ Gray Monk 1995 Broderson Vineyard Gewurztraminer, CAN, (Can $) 11.95, **228**

$Greenwood Ridge 1996 Sauvignon Blanc, CA, $9.50, **247**

Greenwood Ridge Scherrer Vineyard 1995 Zinfandel, CA, $16, **47, 185**

$Grey Wolf Cellars 1995 Zinfandel, CA, $13, **185**

Grgich Hills 1993 Cabernet Sauvignon, CA, $28, **47, 102**

Grgich Hills 1994 Chardonnay, CA, $28, **208**

Grgich Hills 1994 Violetta (Late Harvest Chardonnay/Riesling), CA, $50, **281**

Grgich Hills 1994 Zinfandel, CA, $18, **185**

$Grgich Hills 1995 Fumé Blanc, CA, $14, **247**

⌂ Grove Mill 1996 Sauvignon Blanc, NZEAL, $17, **247**

$Grove Street 1995 Malbec, CA & ARG, $7.50, **140**

Gruet 1992 Blanc de Blanc, NM, $20, **265**

$Gruet NV Brut, NM, $13, **79, 269**

Guenoc 1992 Beckstoffer Vineyard Cabernet Sauvignon, CA, $40, **102**

Guenoc 1993 Beckstoffer Reserve Cabernet Sauvignon, CA, $40.50, **102**

Guenoc 1993 Bella Vista Cabernet Sauvignon, CA, $25.50, **102**

Guenoc 1993 Petit Verdot, CA, $18, **140**

Guenoc 1994 Beckstoffer Reserve Cabernet Sauvignon, CA, $40.50, **102**

Guenoc 1994 Bella Vista Reserve Cabernet Sauvignon, CA, $25.50, **102**

Guenoc 1994 Genevieve Magoon Reserve Chardonnay, CA, $25, **208**

Guenoc 1994 Genevieve Magoon Unfiltered Reserve Chardonnay, CA, $30, **208**

$Guenoc 1994 Petite Sirah, CA, $14.50, **70, 147**

$Guenoc 1994 Red Meritage (Bordeaux-style blend), CA, $15, **48, 73, 168**

Guenoc 1994 Vintage Port, CA, $25, **48, 287**

$Guenoc 1995 Estate Sauvignon Blanc, CA, $12.50, **248**

Guenoc 1995 Genevieve Magoon Reserve Chardonnay, CA, $25, **48, 208**

$Guenoc 1995 Estate Bottled Chardonnay, CA, $14.50, **208**

Guenoc 1995 Reserve Chardonnay, CA, $22.50, **208**

$Guenoc 1995 Zinfandel, CA, $11, **84, 186**

$Gundlach-Bundschu 1994 Rhinefarm Vineyard Cabernet Franc, CA, $14, **89**

$Gundlach-Bundschu 1995 Morse Vineyard Zinfandel, CA, $14, **186**

–H–

$Habersham 1994 Estate Chardonnay, GA, $10, **208**

$Hagafen 1996 Johannisberg Riesling, CA, $10, **241**

$Hahn 1995 Chardonnay, CA, $10, **66, 208**

🏷Hamilton 1996 Ewell Reserve Merlot, AUS, $22.25, **130**

🏷Hamilton Ewell 1995 Cabernet/Merlot, AUS, $20, **168**

Handley Cellars 1992 Méthode Champenoise Brut, CA, $19, **269**

Handley Cellars 1993 Cellar Select Chardonnay, CA, $20, **209**

Handley Cellars 1994 Reserve Pinot Noir, CA, $22, **155**

Handley Cellars 1995 Chardonnay, CA, $16, **209**

Handley Cellars 1995 Pinot Mystere, CA, $18, **140**

$Handley Cellars 1996 Sauvignon Blanc, CA, $12, **248**

Hanzell 1994 Chardonnay, CA, $29, **209**

$🏷Hardy's 1995 Chardonnay, AUS, $7, **64, 209**

$🏷Hardys 1992 Thomas Hardy Cabernet Sauvignon, AUS, $45, **102**

🏷Hardys 1994 Cabernet Sauvignon, AUS, $17, **103**

$🏷Hardys Nottage Hill 1996 Chardonnay, AUS, $7, **66, 209**

$ ⌂ Hardys NV Whiskers Blake Tawny Port, AUS, $14, **287**

$Hart 1995 Mourvèdre, CA, $12, **140**

$Hart 1996 Grenache Rosé, CA, $7.50, **49, 262**

Hartford Court 1994 Arrendell Vineyard Pinot Noir, CA, $40, **156**

Hartford Court 1994 Dutton Ranch Sanchietti Vineyard Pinot Noir, CA, $35, **156**

Hartford Court 1995 Hartford Vineyard Zinfandel, CA, $40, **49, 186**

Havens 1994 Bourriquot (Bordeaux-style red blend), CA, $25, **168**

$ ⌂ Hawthorne Mountain Vineyard Merlot, CAN, $13.49, **69, 130**

Haywood 1994 Los Chamizal Vineyards Zinfandel, CA, $16, **186**

Haywood 1994 Rocky Terrace Zinfandel, CA, $22, **186**

$Haywood 1995 Vintner's Select Cabernet Sauvignon, CA, $8, **62, 103**

$ ⌂ Hector Stagnari 1992 Tannat Viejo, Uruguay, $12, **140**

Hedges 1992 Red Mountain Reserve Red (Bordeaux-style blend), WA, $25, **168**

Hedges 1994 Cabernet Sauvignon, WA, $20, **103**

Heitz 1991 Martha's Vineyard Cabernet Sauvignon, CA, $65, **103**

Heitz 1991 Trailside Vineyard Cabernet Sauvignon, CA, $45, **103**

Heitz 1992 Martha's Vineyard Cabernet Sauvignon, CA, $68, **103**

Heitz 1992 Trailside Vineyard Cabernet Sauvignon, CA, $48, **103**

$Heitz 1993 Grignolino Port, CA, $12.75, **287**

Helena View 1993 Cabernet Franc, CA, $22, **89**

Helena View 1993 Cabernet Sauvignon, CA, $20, **89**

Henry Estate 1993 Barrel Select Pinot Noir, OR, $18, **156**

$Henry Estate 1994 Chardonnay, OR, $15, **209**

⌂ Henschke 1993 Cyril Henschke Cabernet Sauvignon, AUS, $66, **103**

⌂ Henschke 1993 Keyneton Estate (Red blend), AUS, $30, **168**

⌂ Henschke 1994 Cyril Henschke Cabernet Sauvignon, AUS, $66, **104**

⌂ Henschke 1994 Mount Edelstone Shiraz, AUS, $49, **177**

Hermannhof 1992 Norton, MO, $19.99, **144**

$Hermannhof 1995 Seyval Blanc, MO, $13.19, **234**

$Hermannhof 1995 Vignoles, MO, $13.75, **234**

$Hinman 1994 Pinot Gris, OR, $11, **232**

$Hogue Cellars 1995 Chardonnay, WA, $10, **65, 209**

$Hogue Cellars 1995 Johannisberg Riesling, WA, $6, **75, 241**

$Hogue Cellars 1996 Chenin Blanc, WA, $6.99, **224**

$Hogue Cellars 1996 Johannisberg Riesling, WA, $10, **74, 241**

$Hogue Cellars 1996 Late Harvest Johannisberg Riesling, WA, $6.45, **281**

$Hogue Cellars 1996 Semillon, WA, $8.99, **253**

$Hoodsport 1995 Puget Sound Island Belle, WA, $9, **144**

$Hoodsport 1995 Riesling, WA, $7.99, **75, 241**

$Horton 1993 Montdomaine Heritage (Bordeaux-style red blend), VA, $15, **73, 168**

$Horton 1994 Vidal Blanc, VA, $8, **234**

Horton 1995 Viognier, VA, $20, **255**

⌘ Hunter's 1996 Sauvignon Blanc, NZEAL, $18, **248**

Husch 1994 Estate Bottled Reserve Chardonnay, CA, $18, **209**

$Husch 1995 Estate Bottled Chardonnay, CA, $12.50, **209**

$Husch 1995 Estate Bottled Sauvignon Blanc, CA, $9.50, **248**

$Husch 1995 Gewurztraminer, CA, $10, **228**

$Husch 1996 Estate Bottled Late Harvest Gewurztaminer, CA, $14, **281**

Hyatt 1992 Reserve Cabernet Sauvignon, WA, $24.99, **104**

Hyatt 1993 Reserve Merlot, WA, $32, **130**

Hyatt 1994 Reserve Cabernet Sauvignon Reserve, WA, $30, **104**

Hyatt 1994 Reserve Merlot, WA, $29.99, **130**

–I–

$Indian Creek Winery 1994 Pinot Noir, ID, $14.95, **71, 156**

Indian Springs 1995 Sangiovese, CA, $16, **121**

$Indian Springs 1995 Syrah, CA, $15, **80, 178**

$Indigo Hills 1995 Chardonnay, CA, $10, **66, 210**

⌘ Inniskillin Wines 1995 Petronio Vineyards Chenin Blanc Ice Wine, CAN, $36, **276**

Iron Horse 1999 Brut LD, CA, $45, **269**

Iron Horse 1990 Blanc de Blancs, CA, $24.50, **265**

Iron Horse 1990 Vrais Amis (Sparkling Brut), CA, $23.50, **269**

Iron Horse 1993 Wedding Cuvée, CA, $23,50, **266**

$Ivan Tamas 1995 Pinot Grigio, CA, $8.95, 232

–J–

$J. Lohr 1994 South Ridge Syrah, CA, $14, **81, 178**

$J. Lohr 1995 Riverstone Chardonnay, CA, $14, **210**

$J. Lohr 1996 Wildflower Valdiguie, CA, $8.50, **140**

$J. Lohr Winery 1994 Seven Oaks Cabernet Sauvignon, CA, $14, **62, 104**

$J.Lohr 1996 Bay Mist Riesling, CA, $7.50, **75, 241**

$ ⌘ Jacob's Creek 1994 Cabernet Sauvignon, AUS, $7.99, **62, 104**

$ ⌘ Jacob's Creek 1995 Semillon-Chardonnay, AUS, $7, **82, 257**

$ ⌘ Jacob's Creek 1995 Shiraz Cabernet, AUS, $6.99, **72, 169**

$ ⌘ Jacob's Creek 1996 Semillon-Chardonnay, AUS, $6.99, **82, 257**

Jade Mountain 1993 Syrah, CA, $18, **178**

Jarvis 1993 Estate Grown Cave Fermented Cabernet Sauvignon, CA, $55, **104**

Jarvis 1994 Estate Grown Cave Fermented Chardonnay, CA, $36, **210**

Jarvis 1994 Estate Grown Merlot, CA, $45, **131**

⌐Lindemans 1992 Limestone Ridge Vineyard Cabernet-Shiraz-Merlot, AUS, $22, **170**

⌐Lindemans 1993 Coonawarra Pyrus Meritage (Bordeaux-style red blend), AUS, $22, **170**

⌐Lindemans 1993 Limestone Ridge Vineyard Shiraz Cabernet, AUS, $27.99, **170**

$⌐Lindemans 1994 Padthaway Cabernet-Merlot, AUS, $14.99, **73, 170**

$⌐Lindemans 1995 Chardonnay, AUS, $12.99, **212**

$⌐Lindemans 1996 Bin 65 Chardonnay, AUS, $7.50, **66, 212**

Liparita 1993 Cabernet Sauvignon, CA, $32, **106**

Lockwood 1994 Estate Grown Estate Bottled Cabernet Sauvignon, CA, $16, **106**

$Lockwood 1994 Pinot Blanc, CA, $9, **70, 237**

Lolonis 1994 Private Reserve Zinfandel, CA, $19, **187**

Longoria 1994 Huber Vineyard Chardonnay, CA, $22.99, **212**

$Lorval Wines 1995 Merlot, TX, $8.99, **69, 131**

Louis M. Martini 1994 Monte Rosso Vineyard Cabernet Sauvignon, CA, $30, **106**

Louis M. Martini 1994 Reserve Merlot, CA, $18, **131**

$Louis M. Martini 1995 Chardonnay, CA, $10.50, **66, 212**

–M–

$M.G. Vallejo 1995 Gewurztraminer, CA, $7, **66, 229**

$M.G. Vallejo 1995 Merlot, CA, $6.99, **68, 132**

$Maddalena 1995 Johannisberg Riesling, CA, $7, **51, 75, 242**

$Madrona 1995 Estate Bottled Shiraz/Cabernet, CA, $10, **74, 170**

$Madrona 1995 Estate Bottled Zinfandel, CA, $10, **84, 187**

⌐Magnotta 1991 Limited Edition Cabernet Sauvignon, CAN, $18, **106**

⌐Magnotta 1991 Limited Edition Merlot, CAN, $18, **51, 131**

⌐Magnotta 1994 Gran Riserva White, CAN, (Can $) 11.95, **212**

⌐Magnotta 1995 Limited Edition Vidal Icewine, CAN, $45, **277**

⌐Magnotta 1995 Sauvignon Blanc Reserve, (Can $) 7.35, **249**

⌐Magnotta 1996 Vidal Icewine Limited Edition, CAN, $45, **277**

⌐Magnotta NV Rossana Rosé (Sparkling brut rosé), CAN, (Can $) 11.95, **271**

Maison Deutz 1992 Brut Reserve, CA, $20, **269**

$Maison Deutz NV Brut Cuvée, CA, $12.75, **79, 269**

Maison Deutz NV Brut Rosé, CA, $20, **271**

$⌐Manso de Velasco 1995 Cabernet Sauvignon, CHI, $14, **62, 106**

Marcelina 1995 Chardonnay, CA, $18, **212**

⌐Marienberg 1994 Shiraz, AUS, $38, **178**

$Markham 1995 Barrel Fermented Chardonnay, CA, $12.49, **212**

Marquam Hill 1994 Chardonnay, OR, $16, **212**

Martin Brothers 1994 Vecchio Nebbiolo, CA, $20, **121**

$Martin Brothers 1996 Allegro Moscato, CA, $10, **284**

$Page Mill 1994 O'Shaughnessy Vineyard Merlot, CA, $15, **69, 132**

Pahlmeyer 1994 Merlot, CA, $28, **132**

Palmer 1992 Méthode Champenoise Special Reserve Brut, NY, $20, **270**

$Palmer 1994 Select Harvest Gewurztraminer, NY, $15, **282**

Palmer 1994 Select Reserve Red (Bordeaux-style blend), NY, $19.99, **171**

Panther Creek 1994 Bednarik Vineyard Pinot Noir, OR, $35, **158**

Paradigm 1993 Cabernet Sauvignon, CA, $30, **108**

Paradise Ridge NV Private Reserve Blanc de Blanc, CA, $17, **265**

Paraiso Springs 1994 Pinot Noir, CA, $17, **158**

$Paraiso Springs 1995 Baby Blush, CA, $12.50, **262**

$Paraiso Springs 1995 Chardonnay, CA, $13, **215**

$Paraiso Springs 1995 Johannisberg Riesling, CA, $9, **242**

Paraiso Springs 1995 Late Harvest Johannisberg Riesling, CA, $25, **282**

Paraiso Springs 1996 Santa Lucia Highlands Reserve Barrel Fermented Pinot Blanc, CA $22.50, **238**

$Parducci 1994 Petite Sirah, CA, $9.99, **70, 147**

⌂ Parker 1994 Terra Rossa Cabernet Sauvignon, AUS, $24, **108**

$Patrick M. Paul 1993 Conner Lee Vineyards Merlot, WA, $12, **69, 132**

Patz & Hall 1994 Chardonnay, CA, $28.99, **215**

Patz & Hall 1995 Chardonnay, CA, $28.99, **215**

$Paul Thomas 1995 Cabernet-Merlot, WA, $11, **74, 172**

$Pedroncelli 1994 Mother Clone Zinfandel, CA, $11.50, **84, 188**

$Pedroncelli 1994 Pedroni-Bushnell Vineyard Zinfandel, CA, $11.50, **83, 188**

$Pedroncelli 1994 Three Vineyard Cabernet Sauvignon, CA, $12.50, **63, 108**

$Pedroncelli 1995 Vintage Selection Cabernet Sauvignon, CA, $10, **63, 108**

$Pedroncelli 1996 Vintage Selection Rosé of Zinfandel, CA $7, **262**

Peju 1993 HB Vineyard Cabernet Sauvignon, CA, $40, **108**

Peju Province 1994 Cabernet Franc, CA, $25, **90**

Peju Province 1995 Chardonnay, CA, $16, **215**

⌂ Penfolds 1993 Bin 389 Cabernet/Shiraz, AUS, $19, **172**

⌂ Penfolds 1993 Bin 407 Cabernet Sauvignon, AUS, $17, **109**

⌂ Penfolds 1993 Bin 707 Cabernet Sauvignon, AUS, $45, **109**

⌂ Penfolds 1994 Bin 28 Kalimira Shiraz, AUS, $16.99, **179**

$ ⌂ Penfolds Club Port Reserve, AUS, $15, **287**

⌂ Penfolds Grandfather Fine Old Liqueur Port, AUS, $58.99, **287**

⌂ Penley 1993 Shiraz-Cabernet, AUS, $25, **172**

⌂ Penley 1994 Cabernet Sauvignon, AUS, $40, **109**

⌑Penley 1994 Shiraz-Cabernet, AUS, $25, **172**

Pepperwood Springs 1995 Pinot Noir, CA, $20, **158**

$Perry Creek 1995 Wenzell Vineyards Mourvèdre, CA, $12.50, **52, 141**

$Perry Creek 1996 Muscat Canelli, CA, $9.50, **285**

⌑Petaluma 1993 Cabernet Sauvignon, AUS, $24.99, **109**

⌑Petaluma 1994 Piccadilly Valley Chardonnay, AUS, $28, **215**

⌑Peter Lehmann 1991 Mentor, AUS, $28, **172**

⌑Peter Lehmann 1992 Stonewell Shiraz, AUS, $40, **179**

Peter Michael 1994 Cuvée Indigéne Chardonnay, CA, $39.99, **216**

Peter Michael 1994 Mon Plasir Chardonnay, CA, $34.99, **216**

Pezzi King 1995 Zinfandel, CA, $22, **188**

Piedmont 1995 Native Yeast Unfiltered Chardonnay, VA, $24, **216**

Piedmont 1995 Special Reserve Chardonnay, VA, $16, **216**

⌑Pillitteri Estates 1994 Icewine, CAN, (Can $) 29.95, **277**

$Pindar 1994 Port, NY, $12.99, **287**

Pindar 1995 Sunflower Chardonnay, NY, $16.99, **216**

Pine Ridge 1995 Chardonnay, CA, $30, **216**

Plam 1993 Cabernet Sauvignon, CA, $35, **52, 109**

Plam 1994 Merlot, CA, $25, **133**

⌑Plantagenet 1994 Mount Barker Shiraz, AUS, $24, **179**

$Plum Creek Cellars 1994 Merlot, CO, $12.99, **69, 133**

Ponzi 1993 Reserve Pinot Noir, OR, $26.99, **158**

$Ponzi 1994 Chardonnay, OR, $15, **216**

Ponzi 1994 Reserve Pinot Noir, OR, $35, **158**

Portteus 1993 Reserve Cabernet Sauvignon, WA, $25, **109**

Portteus 1995 Zinfandel, WA, $18, **188**

$Post Familie 1996 White Muscadine, ARK, $5.50, **234**

Powers 1994 Mercer Ranch Vineyard Cabernet Sauvignon, WA, $18, **109**

Prager 1993 Aria White Port, CA $32.50, **287**

$Prejean Winery 1995 Late Harvest Vignoles, NY, $12, **282**

$Prejean Winery 1995 Semi Dry Gewurztraminer, NY, $12, **229**

Preston 1993 Cabernet Sauvignon Reserve, WA, $21, **109**

$Preston 1996 Gamay Beaujolais, CA, $10.99, **141**

Pride Mountain Vineyards 1994 Cabernet Franc, CA, $20, **90**

Prince Michel 1990 Le Ducq (Bordeaux-style red blend), CA, $50, **172**

Prince Michel 1991 Le Ducq (Bordeaux-style red blend), CA, $65, **172**

Prince Michel 1995 Barrel Select Chardonnay, VA, $17, **216**

–Q–

Quady 1986 Frank's Vineyard Vintage Port, CA, $15.50, **288**

Quady 1989 Vintage Starboard (Port), CA, $19, **288**

$Quady 1990 Vintage Starboard (Port), CA, $14, **53, 288**

$Quady 1993 Late Bottled Vintage Port, CA, $12, **288**

$Quady 1995 Elysium, CA, $14, **285**

$Quady 1995 Essensia, CA, $14, **53, 285**

$Quady 1996 Electra, CA, $7.50, **53, 285**
$Quady 1996 Elysium, CA, $14, **53, 285**
$Quady NV Batch 88 Starboard Port, CA, $14, **288**
⌐ Quail's Gate 1994 Late Harvest Botrytis Affected, CAN, (Can $) 24.95, **283**
Quail Ridge 1991 Cabernet Sauvignon Reserve, CA, $40, **110**
$Quivera 1995 Dry Creek Cuvée (Rhône-style red blend), CA, $13, **74, 172**

–R–

$R.H. Phillips 1995 EXP Syrah, CA $12, **81, 179**
$R.H. Phillips 1996 EXP Viognier, CA, $12, **255**
Rabbit Ridge 1994 Avventura Reserve Migliore di Vigneto (Bordeaux-Italian red blend), CA, $25, **172**
Rabbit Ridge 1994 Nebbiolo, CA, $18, **122**
Rabbit Ridge 1995 Frank Johnson Vineyard Pinot Noir, CA, $16, **158**
$Rabbit Ridge 1995 Sceales Family Vineyard Grenache, CA, $12, **141**
Rabbit Ridge 1995 Winemaker's Grand Reserve Chardonnay, CA, $28, **216**
$Rabbit Ridge 1995 Zinfandel, CA, $13, **189**
Ramsay 1995 Aglianico, CA, $21, **122**
Ramsay 1995 Mourvèdre, CA, $17, **141**
Ravenswood 1994 Merlot, CA, $26.50, **133**
Ravenswood 1995 Cooke Vineyard Zinfandel, CA, $21.50, **189**
Ravenswood 1995 Dickerson Vineyard Zinfandel, CA, $21.50, **189**
Ravenswood 1995 Monte Rosso Vineyard Zinfandel, CA, $21.50, **189**
Ravenswood 1995 Wood Road Zinfandel, CA, $21.50, **189**
Raymond 1994 Reserve Cabernet Sauvignon, CA, $19, **110**
$Raymond 1995 Reserve Chardonnay, CA, $14, **216**
Redhawk 1994 Estate Reserve Pinot Noir, OR, $25, **158**
$ ⌐ Reif Estate 1996 Select Late Harvest Vidal, CAN, $12.50, **283**
Renaissance 1994 Estate Cabernet Sauvignon, CA, $16, **110**
Renaissance 1994 Late Harvest, CA, $18, **283**
$Renaissance 1996 Estate Bottled Sauvignon Blanc, CA, $11, **250**
Renwood 1995 Grandpère Zinfandel, CA, $24, **189**
Renwood 1995 Jack Rabbit Flat Zinfandel, CA, $24, **189**
Renwood 1995 Linsteadt Vineyard Barbera, CA, $24, **122**
Rey Sol 1996 Le Mediterrané Estate Marsanne, CA, $16, **232**
Richardson 1994 Horne Vineyard Cabernet Sauvignon, CA, $18, **110**
Richardson 1995 Horne Vineyard Cabernet Sauvignon, CA, $18, **54, 110**
Richardson 1995 Merlot, CA, $18, **133**
Ridge 1991 Monte Bello Cabernet Sauvignon, CA, $120, **110**
Ridge 1992 Geyserville Zinfandel, CA, $27.50, **189**
Ridge 1992 Monte Bello Cabernet Sauvignon, CA, $80, **110**
Ridge 1993 Cabernet Sauvignon, CA, $19, **110**

Ridge 1995 Lytton Springs Zinfandel, CA, $22.50, **189**
Ridge 1995 Sonoma Station Zinfandel, CA, $16, **190**
Ridge 1995 Zinfandel, CA, $20, **190**
$River Run 1995 Cote d'Aromas (Rhône-style red blend), CA, $15, **74, 173**
$River Run 1996 Wirz Vineyard Carignane, CA, $13, **141**
Robert Biale 1995 Old Vineyards Late Picked Zinfandel, CA, $22.99, **190**
Robert Hunter 1992 Brut de Noirs Sparkling Wine, CA, $25, **266**
Robert Hunter 1992 Brut, CA, $25, **270**
Robert Keenan 1994 Merlot, CA, $28, **133**
Robert Mondavi 1992 Napa Reserve Pinot Noir, CA, $45, **159**
Robert Mondavi 1993 Cabernet Sauvignon, CA, $20, **110**
Robert Mondavi 1993 Reserve Cabernet Sauvignon, CA, $50, **111**
Robert Mondavi 1994 Chardonnay, CA, $24, **217**
$Robert Mondavi 1994 Coastal Winery Cabernet Sauvignon, CA, $11, **63, 111**
Robert Mondavi 1994 Reserve Pinot Noir, CA, $35, **159**
Robert Mondavi 1994 Unfiltered Merlot, CA, $22, **133**
$Robert Mondavi 1995 Coastal Zinfandel, CA, $10, **83, 190**
Robert Pecota 1994 Steven Andre Vineyard Merlot, CA, $25, **133**
Robert Pepi 1994 Two-Heart Canopy Sangiovese, CA, $18, **122**
Rochioli 1993 Pinot Noir, CA, $18, **159**
Rochioli 1994 Estate Pinot Noir, CA, $22, **159**
$Rochioli 1996 Sauvignon Blanc, CA, $14.99, **250**
Rodney Strong 1993 Reserve Cabernet Sauvignon, CA, $30, **111**
Rodney Strong 1994 Merlot, CA, $16, **133**
Rodney Strong 1994 Old Vines Zinfandel, CA, $16, **190**
Rodney Strong 1994 River East Vineyard Pinot Noir, CA, $16, **159**
$Rodney Strong 1995 Chardonnay, CA, $11, **217**
Roederer Estate 1991 L'Ermitage Brut, CA, $35, **270**
Rombauer 1995 Chardonnay, CA, $20.99, **217**
℞ Rosemount 1993 Balmoral Syrah, AUS, $35, **179**
℞ Rosemount 1993 Roxburgh Chardonnay, AUS, $30, **217**
℞ Rosemount 1993 Show Reserve Cabernet Sauvignon, AUS, $18.50, **111**
℞ Rosemount 1994 Balmoral Syrah, AUS, $35, **179**
℞ Rosemount 1994 G.S.M. (Rhône-style red blend), AUS, $16, 173
℞ Rosemount 1994 Mountain Blue No. 1 (Bordeaux-style blend), AUS, $16, **173**
℞ Rosemount 1994 Mountain Blue Shiraz Cabernet Sauvignon, AUS, $25, **54, 173**
℞ Rosemount 1994 Show Reserve Syrah, AUS, $18.50, **179**

🗓Rosemount 1995 Show Reserve Chardonnay, AUS, $18.50, **217**

$ 🗓Rosemount 1996 Grenache Shiraz, AUS, $8.95, 74, **173**

$ 🗓Rosemount 1996 Semillon Chardonnay, AUS, $7.95, **82, 257**

$ 🗓Rosemount 1996 Traminer Riesling (Gewurztraminer/ Riesling blend), AUS, $7.95, **82, 258**

Rosenblum 1994 Holbrook Mitchell Trio Meritage (Bordeaux-style red blend), CA, $38, **173**

Rosenblum 1994 Yountville Vineyards Cabernet Sauvignon, CA, $20, **111**

Rosenblum 1995 Brandlin Ranch Zinfandel, CA, $23, **190**

Rosenblum 1995 Cabernet Sauvignon, CA, $33, **111**

Rosenblum 1995 Continente Vineyard Old Vine Zinfandel, CA, $18, **190**

Rosenblum 1995 Harris Kratka Vineyard Old Vine Zinfandel, CA, $20, **190**

$Rosenblum 1995 Kenefick Ranch Carignane, CA, $15, **141**

Rosenblum 1995 Kenefick Ranch Petite Sirah, CA, $17, **147**

Rosenblum 1995 Old Vines Zinfandel, CA, $17.50, **190**

Rosenblum 1995 Pato Vineyard Reserve Zinfandel, CA, $18, **190**

Rosenblum 1995 Reserve Zinfandel, CA, $25, **191**

$Rosenblum 1996 Semillon, CA, $14, **253**

🗓Rothbury Estate 1994 Reserve Bottling Shiraz, AUS, $18, **179**

Round Hill 1990 Van Asperen Signature Reserve Cabernet Sauvignon, CA, $30, **111**

Round Hill 1991 Van Asperen Signature Reserve Cabernet Sauvignon, CA, $24, **111**

$Round Hill 1995 Chardonnay, CA, $12, **217**

🗓Rust en Verde 1992 Estate Red (Cabernet/Shiraz), SAFR, $25, **173**

$Rutherford Hill 1993 Chardonnay, CA, $12, **217**

$Rutherford Ranch 1995 Merlot, CA $11, 69, **133**

$Rutherford Vintners 1995 Barrel Select Cabernet Sauvignon, CA, $8.99, **112**

$Rutherford Vintners 1996 Chardonnay, CA, $8.99, 66, **217**

–S–

S. Anderson 1992 Blanc de Noirs, CA, $22, **268**

S. Anderson 1992 Brut, CA, $24, **270**

S. Anderson 1994 Reserve Merlot, CA, $28, **133**

St. Clement 1993 Cabernet Sauvignon, CA, $23.50, **112**

St. Clement 1993 Howell Mountain Cabernet Sauvignon, CA, $40, **112**

St. Clement 1994 Oroppas (Bordeaux-style red blend), CA, $30, **173**

St. Clement Vineyards 1994 Merlot, CA, $24, **134**

St. Francis 1992 Reserve Cabernet Sauvignon, CA, $21.99, **112**

St. Francis 1993 Reserve Cabernet Sauvignon, CA, $29, **112**

St. Francis 1995 Old Vines Zinfandel, CA, $22, **191**

St. Francis 1995 Pagani Vineyard Reserve Zinfandel, CA, $29, **191**

St. Francis 1995 Reserve Chardonnay, CA, $20, **217**

Ⓓ St. Hallett 1993 Old Block Shiraz, AUS, $22, **180**

Ⓓ St. Hugo 1993 Coonawarra Cabernet Sauvignon, AUS, $17.99, **112**

St. Innocent 1994 Seven Springs Vineyard Pinot Noir, OR, $28.50, **159**

St. Innocent 1994 Temperance Hill Vineyard Pinot Noir, OR, $32.50, **159**

$St. James 1993 Ozark Highlands Norton, MO, $13.99, **144**

$St. James 1995 Late Harvest Seyval Blanc, MO, $12.99, **283**

$St. James 1995 Vintner's Reserve Seyval, MO, $9.99, **234**

$St. James 1996 School House White (Native varieties blend), MO, $7.89, **235**

$St. James NV Concord Velvet Red, MO, $6, **144**

$St. Julian 1994 Chambourcin, MI, $9.50, **144**

$St. Julian 1995 Cabernet Franc, MI, $14.95, **90**

St. Julian 1995 Merlot, MI, $20, **134**

$St. Julian NV Solera Cream Sherry, MI, $12, **289**

$St. Supéry 1995 Sauvignon Blanc, CA, $9.90, **250**

$St. Supéry 1996 Dollarhide Ranch Sauvignon Blanc, CA, $9.90, **250**

$Ste. Genevieve NV Sauvignon Blanc, CA, $7.99, **76, 250**

Saintsbury 1993 Reserve Chardonnay, CA, $21.99, **217**

Ⓓ Sandalford 1995 Chardonnay, AUS, $18.99, **218**

Sanford 1994 Pinot Noir, CA, $19, **159**

Sanford 1995 Pinot Noir, CA, $25, **159**

$Sanford 1995 Sauvignon Blanc, CA, $10, **250**

$ Ⓓ Santa Ana 1996 Chardonnay-Chenin Blanc, ARG, $3.99, **82, 258**

Santa Barbara 1994 Reserve Chardonnay, CA, $22, **218**

Santa Barbara 1995 Reserve Pinot Noir, CA, $40, **160**

Santa Barbara 1995 Syrah, CA, $16, **54, 180**

$ Ⓓ Santa Carolina 1995 Reserve Merlot, CHI, $8.99, **69, 134**

$ Ⓓ Santa Digna 1995 Cabernet Sauvignon, CHI, $6.99, **63, 112**

$ Ⓓ Santa Julia 1994 Oak Reserve Malbec, ARG, $6, **141**

Ⓓ Santa Rita 1994 Casa Réal, Old Vines Cabernet Sauvignon, CHI, $23, **112**

Scharffenberger 1991 Prestige Cuvée Allure Brut, CA, $18, **270**

Schramsberg 1990 Blanc de Noirs, CA, $23.75, **268**

Schramsberg 1990 Blanc de Noirs, CA, $24.50, **268**

Schramsberg 1990 J. Schram, CA, $50, **270**

Schramsberg 1992 Brut Rosé, CA, $22.75, **272**

Schramsberg 1992 Champagne, CA, $22.75, **272**

Schuetz Oles 1994 Korte Ranch Zinfandel, CA, $16, **191**

Schug 1994 Heritage Reserve Pinot Noir, CA, $30, **160**

$ Ⓓ Seaview 1994 Chardonnay, AUS, $8.99, **65, 218**

Ⓓ Seaview 1994 Edwards & Chaffey Cabernet Sauvignon, AUS, $27, **112**

Sebastiani 1992 Cherryblock Old Vines Estate Bottled Cabernet Sauvignon, CA, $40, **113**

$Sebastiani 1994 Cabernet Sauvignon, CA, $12.99, **63, 113**

Sebastiani 1994 Sonoma Cask Barbera, CA, $20, **55, 122**

$Sebastiani 1994 Sonoma Cask Merlot, CA, $14.99, **69, 134**

$Sebastiani 1995 Chardonnay, CA, $11.99, **218**

Sebastiani 1995 Dutton Ranch Chardonnay, CA, $25, **218**

Sebastiani 1994 Town Merlot, CA, $25, **134**

$Sebastiani 1994 Old Vines Mourvèdre, CA, $12.99, **142**

Sebastiani 1995 Domenici Vineyard Old Vines Zinfandel, CA, $16, **191**

Secret House 1995 Pinot Noir, OR, $18, **160**

$Secret House 1996 White Riesling, OR, $8, **75, 243**

$ ☐ Selaks 1995 Sauvignon Blanc, NZEAL, $12.99, **258**

Selby 1994 Merlot, CA, $25, **134**

Selby 1995 Chardonnay, CA, $20, **218**

Seven Hills 1993 Merlot, WA, $20, **134**

Seven Hills 1994 Seven Hills Vineyard Merlot, WA, $24, **134**

Seven Hills 1995 Klipson Vineyard Merlot, WA, $24, **134**

Seven Hills 1995 Seven Hills Vineyard Merlot, WA, $24, **134**

Shafer 1994 Merlot, CA, $26, **135**

Shafer 1994 Red Shoulder Ranch Chardonnay, CA, $23, **218**

$Shale Ridge 1996 Estate Grown and Bottled Chardonnay, CA, $10.50, **218**

Siduri 1995 Pinot Noir, OR, $30, **160**

Sierra Vista 1994 Red Rock Ridge Syrah, CA, $16.50, **180**

$Sierra Vista 1995 Estate Bottled Vintner's Select Zinfandel, CA, $8, **84, 191**

Sierra Vista 1996 Estate Bottled Chardonnay, CA, $16, **218**

$Sierra Vista 1996 Estate Bottled Fumé Blanc, CA, $8.50, **250**

$Sierra Vista 1996 Fleur de Montagne (Rhône-style red blend), CA, $13.50, **55, 74, 173**

Signorello 1994 Las Amigas Vineyard Pinot Noir, CA, $35, **160**

Signorello 1995 Chardonnay, CA, $27.50, **218**

Signorello 1995 Founder's Reserve Chardonnay, CA, $40, **218**

Signorello 1995 Hope's Cuvée Chardonnay, CA, $60, **219**

$Silvan Ridge 1994 Chardonnay, OR, $15, **219**

$Silvan Ridge 1994 Pinot Gris, OR, $15, **232**

Silvan Ridge 1994 Pinot Noir, OR, $22, **160**

$Silvan Ridge 1995 Semi-Sparkling Early Muscat, OR, $12, **55, 79, 272**

$Silvan Ridge 1995 Unfiltered Pinot Gris, OR, $15, **232**

Silver Lake Winery 1993 Merlot Reserve, WA, $25, **135**

Silver Lake Winery 1993 Red Wine Reserve (Bordeaux-style red blend), WA, $15.99, **174**

Silver Oak 1991 Bonny's Vinyard Cabernet Sauvignon, CA, $50, **113**

$Silver Ridge 1993 Cabernet Sauvignon, CA, $9.99, **63, 113**

Silverado 1993 Limited Reserve Cabernet Sauvignon, CA, $48, **113**

$Stone Hill NV Hermannsberger Red Table Wine, MO, $8.49, **144**

$Stone Hill NV Pink Catawba, MO, $6.79, **262**

🏠 Stonechurch 1994 Vidal Icewine, CAN, $32, **278**

Stonestreet 1992 Legacy (Bordeaux-style red blend), CA, $40, **174**

Stonestreet 1993 Legacy (Bordeaux-style red blend), CA, $40, **174**

Stonestreet 1994 Estate Merlot, CA, $30, **135**

Stonestreet 1994 Pinot Noir, CA, $30, **56, 160**

Stonestreet 1995 Chardonnay, CA, $25, **220**

🏠 Stoney Ridge 1996 Late Harvest Riesling Traminer, CAN, (Can $) 19.95, **283**

🏠 Stoney Ridge 1996 Riesling Traminer Ice Wine, CAN, (Can $) 49.95, **278**

Storrs 1994 Aron Michael Cuvée Merlot, CA, $28, **135**

Storrs 1994 Beauregard Ranch Ben Lomond Zinfandel, CA, $18, **192**

Storrs 1995 Lion Oaks Vineyard Zinfandel, CA, $25, **192**

Storybook Mountain Vineyards 1993 Reserve Zinfandel, CA, $25, **192**

$ 🏠 Sumac Ridge 1995 Private Reserve Pinot Blanc, CAN, $10.95, **71, 238**

$Sutter Home 1990 Amador County Reserve Zinfandel, CA, $9.95, **84, 192**

$Sutter Home 1992 Reserve Cabernet Sauvignon, CA, $11.95, **63, 114**

$Sutter Home 1996 Gewurztraminer, CA, $5.95, **66, 229**

$Sutter Home 1996 Moscato (Muscat Alexandria), CA, $5.95, **285**

$Sutter Home 1996 White Soleo, CA, $4.45, **83, 258**

Swanson 1993 Chardonnay, CA, $20, **220**

Swanson 1993 Estate Cabernet Sauvignon, CA, $22, **114**

Swanson 1994 Estate Alexis (Red blend), CA, $33, **174**

Swanson 1994 Estate Bottled Sangiovese, CA, $22, **122**

Swanson 1995 Estate Bottled Chardonnay, CA, $24, **220**

Swanson 1995 Estate Bottled Sangiovese, CA, $24, **122**

Swanson 1995 Estate Merlot, CA, $24, **135**

$ 🏠 Swartland 1994 Cabernet Sauvignon, SAFR, $9.99, **63, 114**

$Swedish Hill 1995 Late Harvest Vignoles, NY, $11.99, **56, 283**

$Swedish Hill NV Spumante, NY, $8.99, **79, 272**

–T–

$Taft Street 1994 Merlot, CA, $14, **69, 135**

$Taft Street 1995 Cabernet Sauvignon, CA, $12, **63, 114**

$Taft Street 1995 Chardonnay, CA, $10, **66, 220**

Talbott 1994 Sleepy Hollow Vineyard Chardonnay, CA, $28, **220**

$ 🏠 Taltarni 1996 Estate Grown Sauvignon Blanc, AUS, $12, **251**

$Talus 1995 Pinot Noir, CA, $7.99, **72, 161**

$Talus 1995 Zinfandel, CA, $7.99, **84, 192**

$Tartan Hill Winery 1995 Tartan Mist, MI, $5, **235**

⌘ Te Kairanga 1995 Reserve Chardonnay, NZEAL, $49.99, 220

Tefft Cellars 1994 Winemaker's Reserve Merlot, WA, $25, **135**

$Temecula Crest 1995 Nebbiolo, CA, $15, **67, 122**

$Tessera 1995 Cabernet Sauvignon, CA, $9.99, **63, 114**

$Tessera 1995 Chardonnay, CA, $9.99, **66, 220**

Thackrey 1994 Orion Rossi Vineyard Syrah, CA, $30, **180**

Thomas Fogarty 1995 Chardonnay, CA, $16.50, **220**

Thomas Fogarty 1995 Estate Reserve Chardonnay, CA, $22, **220**

Thornton 1995 Aleatico, CA, $18, **283**

Thornton 1995 Limited Bottling Carignane, CA, $16, **142**

Thornton NV Artist Series Cuvée de Frontignan, CA, $20, **272**

Thornton NV Cuvée Rouge, CA, $18, **272**

$Three Islands Lonz Winery NV Madeira, OH, $5.95, **289**

⌘ Tim Adams 1994 Aberfeldy Shiraz, AUS, $17.90, **180**

$Titus 1995 Zinfandel, CA, $15, **192**

Tobin James 1995 James Gang Reserve Zinfandel, CA, $20, **192**

Topolos 1995 Pagani Ranch Zinfandel, CA, $40, **193**

Topolos 1995 Rossi Ranch Zinfandel, CA, $24.50, **193**

Topolos at Russian River 1995 Old Vines Alicante Bouschet, CA, $18, **142**

Torii Mor 1994 Reserve Pinot Noir, OR, $28, **161**

Trefethen Vineyards 1994 Estate Cabernet Sauvignon, CA, $24, **114**

$Trellis Vineyards 1995 Cabernet Sauvignon, CA, $13.99, **63, 115**

$Trentadue 1993 Carignane, CA, $10, **142**

Trentadue 1994 Estate Bottled Cabernet Sauvignon, CA, $19, **115**

Trentadue Winery 1994 Petite Sirah Port, CA, $20, **288**

$Troon Vineyards 1995 Cabernet Sauvignon, CA, $13.50, **63, 115**

Trout Gulch 1995 Trout Gulch Vineyards Chardonnay, CA, $16, **220**

Tualatin 1994 Estate Reserve Pinot Noir, OR, $20, **161**

$Tualatin 1995 Pinot Noir, OR, $12.50, **71, 161**

$Tualatin 1996 Muller Thurgau, OR, $7, **232**

$Tulocay 1995 Oak Creek Vineyards Chardonnay, CA, $15, **221**

$Turning Leaf 1993 Sonoma Reserve Winemaker's Choice Zinfandel, CA, $10, **84, 193**

$Turning Leaf 1993 Sonoma Reserve Winemaker's Choice Barrel Aged Cabernet Sauvignon, CA, $10, **63, 115**

$Twin Brook 1995 Pinot Gris, PA, $13.89, **232**

$Twin Hills 1992 Cabernet Sauvignon, CA, $15, **63, 115**

$Twin Hills 1993 Zinfandel, CA, $13.50, **193**

Tyee Wine Cellars 1994 Pinot Noir, CA, $17.95, **161**

⌘ Tyrrell's 1990 Vat 9 Shiraz, AUS, $29.99, **180**

⌂ Tyrrell's 1992 Aged Release Vat 1 Semillon, AUS, $39.95, **253**

⌂ Tyrrell's 1996 Moon Mountain Chardonnay, AUS, $19.95, **221**

–V–

V. Sattui 1992 Reserve Cabernet Sauvignon, CA, $60, **115**

V. Sattui 1994 Morisoli Vineyard Cabernet Sauvignon, CA, $25, **115**

V. Sattui 1994 Preston Vineyard Cabernet Sauvignon, CA, $30, **115**

V. Sattui 1994 Suzanne's Vineyard Cabernet Sauvignon, CA, $20, **116**

$V. Sattui 1996 Gamay Rouge, CA, $12.25, **142**

$V. Sattui 1996 Johannisberg Dry Riesling, CA, $11.25, **243**

$V. Sattui 1996 Muscat, CA, $12.25, **285**

$V. Sattui 1996 Sauvignon Blanc, CA, $15, **251**

V. Sattui 1995 Carsi Vineyard Chardonnay, CA, $22, **221**

Van der Kamp 1993 English Cuvée Méthode Champenoise Brut, CA, $20, **270**

Van Duzer 1994 Reserve Chardonnay, OR, $18, **221**

$Van Roekel Vineyards 1996 Rosé of Syrah, CA, $12.95, **262**

⌂ Vasse Felix 1995 Semillon, AUS, $21, **253**

⌂ Vasse Felix 1995 Shiraz, AUS, $21, **180**

Venezia 1994 Meola Vineyards Cabernet Sauvignon, CA, $20, **56, 116**

Venezia 1995 Beaterra Chardonnay, CA, $20, **221**

Venezia 1995 Bianca Nuovo Mondo, CA, $20, **56, 258**

Venezia 1995 Eagle Point Ranch Sangiovese, CA, $24, **123**

Venezia 1995 Nuovo Mondo Sangiovese, CA, $24, **57, 123**

Venezia 1995 Regusci Chardonnay, CA, $20, **221**

Venezia 1995 Stella Bianca White Table Wine, CA, $20, **57, 258**

Venezia 1995 Trione Vineyard Sangiovese, CA, $24, **123**

$Venezio Vineyard 1994 Cabernet Sauvignon, CA, $10.50, **63, 116**

$Ventana 1996 Barrel Fermented Estate Chenin Blanc, CA, $8, **225**

$Ventana 1996 Gold Stripe Estate Bottled Chardonnay, CA, $12, **221**

$Vichon 1995 Sauvignon Blanc, CA, $7.99, 76, **251**

Vigil 1995 Terra Vin Cabernet Franc, CA, $20, **90**

$Vigil 1995 Terra Vin (Rhône-style red blend), CA, $12, 74, **174**

⌂ Vignoble Le Cep D'Argent 1995 Archer, CAN, (Can $) 18.95, **288**

$ ⌂ Villa Maria 1996 Private Bin Chardonnay, NZEAL, $13, **221**

Villa Mt. Eden 1993 Grand Reserve Cabernet Sauvignon, CA, $16, **116**

Villa Mt. Eden 1993 Signature Series Cabernet Sauvignon, CA, $45, **116**

$Villa Mt. Eden 1994 Chardonnay, CA, $9.50, 66, **221**

Villa Mt. Eden 1994 Grand Reserve Cabernet Sauvignon, CA, $18, **116**

Villa Mt.Eden 1994 Grand Reserve Merlot, CA, $16, **135**

Villa Mt. Eden 1994 Grand Reserve Monte Rosso Vineyard Zinfandel, CA, $16, **193**

Villa Mt. Eden 1995 Bien Nacido Vineyard Grand Reserve Pinot Blanc, CA, $16, **238**

$Villa Mt. Eden 1994 Zinfandel, CA, $9.50, **84, 193**

$Villa Mt. Eden 1995 Cellar Select, CA, $9.50, **161**

Villa Mt. Eden 1995 Grand Reserve Pinot Noir, CA, $16, **161**

$ ℗Vina Gracia 1994 Premium Cabernet Sauvignon, CHI, $12.99, **60, 116**

$ ℗Vina Tarapaca 1992 Gran Reserva Cabernet, CHI, $15, **63, 116**

$ ℗Vina Tarapaca 1995 Reserve Merlot, CHI, $9, **68, 135**

Vino Noceto 1995 Sangiovese, CA, $12, **67, 123**

$ ℗Viu Manent 1996 Malbec, CHI, $8, **142**

$Voss 1996 Sauvignon Blanc, CA, $12, **251**

–W–

$W.B. Bridgman 1993 Cabernet Sauvignon, WA, $11.99, **64, 116**

$Wagner Vineyards 1995 Ice Wine, NY, $9.99, **278**

Waterbrook 1994 Cabernet Franc, WA, $19.99, **90**

Waterbrook 1994 Cabernet Sauvignon, WA, $19.99, **117**

Waterbrook 1994 Merlot, WA, $19.99, **136**

$Weinstock 1995 Cabernet Sauvignon, CA, $10.99, **64, 117**

$Wellington 1993 Mohrardt Ridge Vineyard Cabernet Sauvignon, CA, $14, **64, 117**

$Wellington 1993 Random Ridge Cabernet Sauvignon, CA, $15, **64, 117**

$Wellington 1994 Alegria Vineyard Syrah, CA, $15, **81, 180**

Wellington 1995 100 Year Old Vines Zinfandel, CA, $18, **193**

$Wellington 1995 Alegria Vineyard Syrah, CA, $15, **181**

Wellington 1995 Casa Santinamaria Zinfandel, CA, $16, **193**

$Wente Bros. 1994 Riva Ranch Reserve Arroyo Seco Chardonnay, CA, $14.99, **222**

$Wente NV Reserve Brut, CA, $12, **78, 270**

Westport Rivers 1991 Blanc de Blancs, MA, $34.95, **265**

Westport Rivers 1992 RJR Cuvée Brut, MA, $20.95, **270**

Westport Rivers 1993 Gold Label Chardonnay, MA, $18.95, **222**

Westport Rivers 1993 Imperial Sec Sparkling Riesling, MA, $24.95, **272**

Westport Rivers 1994 Estate Grown Chardonnay, MA, $18.95, **222**

$Whidbey 1990 Port, WA, $12.99, **288**

White Hall Vineyards 1995 Cabernet Franc, VA, $17.99, **90**

Whitehall Lane 1994 Cabernet Sauvignon, CA, $19, **117**

Whitehall Lane 1994 Leonardini Vineyard Reserve Merlot, CA, 32, **136**

York Mountain 1991 Cabernet Sauvignon, CA, $16, **118**
$York Mountain 1994 Merlot, CA, $14, **69, 136**
$York Mountain 1994 Zinfandel, CA, $12, **84, 193**
Yorkville Cellars 1995 Eleanor of Aquitaine (Bordeaux-style white blend), Randle Hill Vineyard, CA, $16, **258**
$Yorkville Cellars 1995 Organically Grown Merlot, CA, $15, **69, 136**

–Z–

$Zabaco 1993 Cabernet Sauvignon, CA, $9, **64, 118**
Zaca Mesa 1995 Chapel Vineyard Chardonnay, CA, $18, **222**
Zaca Mesa 1995 Syrah, CA, $18, **181**
Zaca Mesa 1995 Zaca Vineyard Rousanne, CA, $17, **232**
Zaca Mesa 1996 Misty Ridge Vineyard Viognier, CA, $18, **255**
ZD 1993 Library Selection Chardonnay, CA, $30, **222**
ZD Wines 1994 Cabernet Sauvignon, CA, $30, **118**
ZD Wines 1994 Pinot Noir, CA, $25, **162**
ZD Wines 1995 Pinot Noir, CA, $25, **162**

ABOUT THE AUTHOR

Gail Bradney has edited numerous books, among them many well-known cookbooks and five books by leading wine authority Robert Parker. This is her second edition of BEST WINES! She lives in Woodstock, New York, with her five-year-old son.

The Print Project has an outstanding reputation for assembling and presenting consumer information in a way that's useful and appealing. They're best known for THE WHOLESALE-BY-MAIL CATALOG, the leading consumer guide to discount mail-order shopping. This annual celebrates its twentieth anniversary in 1998, and has sold more than 2 million copies.

FEEDBACK

We welcome your feedback. To contact The Print Project with questions or comments, or for information on bulk purchases of BEST WINES!, please write:

The Print Project
P.O. Box 703
Bearsville, NY 12409